Henry Richard Fox Bourne

The Other Side of the Emin Pasha Relief Expedition

Henry Richard Fox Bourne

The Other Side of the Emin Pasha Relief Expedition

ISBN/EAN: 9783337323936

Printed in Europe, USA, Canada, Australia, Japan

Cover: Foto ©Andreas Hilbeck / pixelio.de

More available books at **www.hansebooks.com**

The Other Side

OF THE

EMIN PASHA RELIEF EXPEDITION

BY

H. R. FOX BOURNE

London
CHATTO & WINDUS, PICCADILLY
1891

PREFACE

This little book would not have been written had not Mr. H. M. Stanley lately amplified and supplemented by letters and speeches some of the misleading statements in his volumes entitled 'In Darkest Africa.' It appeared to me necessary that the blame should be laid where it is due; and I have taken the task upon myself, believing that, though it might have been more fully executed by a writer personally acquainted with some or all of the men assailed, there are advantages in its being attempted by an outsider who has none but public ends to serve.

Whatever is here said in defence or justification of Emin Pasha, Major Barttelot, Mr. Jameson, and others, and in condemnation of Mr. Stanley, is merely incidental to the main design of this book. The design is twofold: in the first place, to explain how and why the Emin Pasha Relief Expedition failed to achieve the purpose for which it was avowedly planned, and, in so far as it succeeded, was successful only in directions which, whether good or bad in themselves, were no part of its intention as notified to the public; in the second place, to draw from this lamentable business a lesson which it forcibly teaches, and which, in these days of wholesale European encroachment in Africa, ought to be taken to heart. The two objects coincide, but the second is far more important than the first. The chief reason for finding fault with this Expedition is that, by exposing its blunders and ill effects, something may perhaps be done to deter civilised Englishmen from ever again sanctioning or applauding such proceedings as make up its history.

The narratives of those actually engaged in the Expedition, and especially Mr. Stanley's, have been freely quoted from. Lest printer or transcriber should be charged with inaccuracy, it is proper to state that Mr. Stanley's idiosyncrasies in punctuation and construction of sentences have been carefully reproduced.

BROADWAY CHAMBERS, WESTMINSTER, S.W.:
February 14, 1891.

CONTENTS

CHAPTER I

ANTECEDENTS

1. *Emin Pasha and the Equatorial Province.*

	PAGE
Emin's earlier occupations	1
The Equatorial Province	2
Emin's government of it and his difficulties	3
His appeals for help	5
Proposals for relieving him	8
The conditions on which he was willing to be relieved . .	11

2. *Mr. H. M. Stanley and the Congo Free State.*

Mr. Stanley's earlier occupations	12
His exploits at Bumbiré	14
His Congo expeditions	20
The Congo Free State	21
Tippoo-Tib's rise and progress	23
The loss of Stanley Falls	24

CHAPTER II

THE PURPOSES OF THE EXPEDITION

The origin of the Emin Relief Expedition	26
The question of routes	28
King Leopold's requirements	30
The adoption of the Congo route	32
Sir William Mackinnon's requirements	34

	PAGE
Arrangements with the Sultan of Zanzibar	35
A bargain with Tippoo-Tib	37
Another bargain with Tippoo-Tib	41
The Egyptian Government's offer to Emin	44
Mr. Stanley and his comrades	46

CHAPTER III

ON THE WAY TO YAMBUYA

Mr. Stanley's soldiers and carriers	48
A 'shindy' at starting	49
Troubles at the Congo mouth	51
The march to Leopoldville	51
How Mr. Stanley 'enforced discipline'	53
Difficulties at Leopoldville	60
The voyage to Yambuya	62
Black sufferers and white offenders	63
Major Barttelot and Tippoo-Tib	67
The capture of Yambuya	69
Provision for the rear-column	70

CHAPTER IV

SOME OF MR. STANLEY'S WANDERINGS

The advance column and its duties	73
The first day in the Great Forest	74
Dealings with the natives	76
Mr. Stanley on his carriers	78
A court-martial in the forest	79
With Tippoo-Tib's slave-raiders	81
On the way to the Albert Nyanza	82
'Foraging' in a land of plenty	83
A modern Joshua	88
Punishing Mazamboni	89
In search of Emin Pasha	93
More fighting	97
At Fort Bodo	98
To the Albert Nyanza again	99
In search of Major Barttelot	102

CHAPTER V

THE REAR-COLUMN

	PAGE
Mr. Stanley's instructions to Major Barttelot	103
Tippoo-Tib's grievance	105
Mr. Stanley and Major Barttelot	105
The rear-column as left by Mr. Stanley	108
Early troubles at Yambuya	109
Woman-stealing for food	110
Difficulties with the Arabs	112
Difficulties with the natives	113
Major Barttelot's defects	116
Bartholomew and Msa	117
Burgari Mahommed	118
John Henry	120
Appeals to Tippoo-Tib	121
Mr. Stanley on the Manyuema	122
Increasing troubles	123
Major Barttelot's prostration	126
The forward movement	127
Its collapse	129
The death of Major Barttelot	131
Mr. Jameson's last efforts	133
Mr. Stanley's complaints	134
Mr. Stanley's responsibility	136

CHAPTER VI

THE 'RELIEF' OF EMIN

Blunders and hindrances	141
Mr. Stanley's offers and promises	142
His first meeting with Emin	146
His first proposal to Emin	147
Other proposals	148
The first instalment of 'relief'	153
Mr. Jephson's mission	155
Mr. Stanley's proclamation to Emin's people	158
Its reception in the Equatorial Province	159

	PAGE
The mutiny at Laboré	161
The deposition of Emin	163
Emin's appeals to Mr. Stanley	165
Mr. Stanley's answer	168
The second instalment of 'relief'	169
The withdrawal of Emin	171
Mr. Stanley in danger	172
The arrest of Emin's followers	173
The march towards Zanzibar	176

CHAPTER VII

MR. STANLEY'S LATER WANDERINGS

Explorations in the Congo State	179
Explorations in British East Africa	181
Troubles and triumphs on the march	182
The return to the Zanzibar coast	186
The list of casualties	187

CHAPTER VIII

RESULTS

The relief asked for by Emin Pasha	189
The promises and achievements of the Relief Expedition	190
The wrecking of Emin's province and his own ruin	192
Gains for the British East Africa Company	195
Intended services to the Congo State	197
The aggrandisement of Tippoo-Tib	199
Encouragement of slave-raiding	200
A promise-breaking Expedition	201

THE OTHER SIDE

OF THE

EMIN PASHA RELIEF EXPEDITION

CHAPTER I

ANTECEDENTS

1. *Emin Pasha and the Equatorial Province*

EMIN PASHA had been Governor of the Equatorial Province for ten years before he was 'relieved' by Mr. H. M. Stanley. In order to understand the facts reviewed in the following pages, the reader must bear in mind some of earlier date.

Emin, whose European name is Eduard Schnitzer, who was born at Oppeln in Silesia in 1840, and who graduated as a doctor of medicine at Berlin in 1864, had travelled much in Turkey, practising as a physician and studying natural history, before he entered the Egyptian service in 1876. He was then sent as principal medical officer to the Equatorial Province of which General Gordon was at that time Governor. Gordon employed him on much besides scientific work, and in

March 1878, after his chief had been made Governor-General of the Soudan, he succeeded to the office which he held, amid difficulties that would have overwhelmed most men, through the next ten years. His change of name was part of his policy. 'From the very first,' says his biographer, 'this determined man threw himself heart and soul into his work, and, as he sought a sphere of labour amongst people of foreign customs and mode of thought, he was perfectly willing to give up every external indication which might stand in the way of his obtaining an unhampered entrance into the Mohammedan world. The German humanitarian believed it only possible to fulfil his office satisfactorily by permitting no external evidence of his Frankish origin to appear. The name he chose for this purpose was Emin, "the faithful one," and certainly no one has ever proved himself more worthy of bearing such a name as the description of his character.'[1]

At the time of Emin's appointment as Governor of the Equatorial Province the ambitious scheme of the Khedive Ismail for establishing a great Egyptian empire over the Soudan was at its height. This scheme was in part the result of Sir Samuel Baker's philanthropic project for suppressing one great branch of the African slave-trade by securing orderly rule in the Eastern Soudan; and Sir Samuel Baker's conquests and vigorous administration between 1869 and 1872 were supplemented by General Gordon's work, which continued till 1879. Baker brought into subjection nearly

---

[1] *Emin Pasha in Central Africa*, edited by Professor G. Schweinfurth, Professor F. Ratzel, Dr. R. W. Felkin, and Dr. G. Hartlaub, p. xii.

all the country south of Egypt proper and down to Lake Albert Nyanza, and he had friendly relations with Mtesa, the king of Uganda, and other potentates further south. The vast area, comprising more than a million square miles, was divided into several provinces, all superintended from Khartoum, and it was the most southern of these that was entrusted to Emin Bey, as he was then called. But in the troubles consequent on Ismail's deposition, and on the progress of the Mahdist movement, the dream of Egyptian sovereignty in the Eastern Soudan was wrecked. After the failure of the English expeditions of 1881, 1883, and 1884, the whole country beyond Wady Halfa was virtually abandoned, with the exception of Suakin on the coast and so much of the Equatorial Province as Emin could retain.

Emin's position, anomalous and perilous from the first, was greatly embarrassed by the collapse of the Egyptian empire. The province of which he took charge in March 1878 had no clearly defined limits. It was merely an aggregate of the territories occupied by native tribes that resented the inroads of Arab slave-hunters and looked to the representative of the Khedive for protection. Emin was supplied with a large number of Egyptian subordinates, but these were no better, if not worse, than the average of self-seeking and dishonest men in the service of the Cairo Government; and he received no other support or assistance from the Cairo authorities. He had to rely upon his own resources in maintaining all the power he exercised, even before the Mahdist rising separated him completely from Egypt, and after 1885 he stood entirely alone. His success was marvellous. With a firm hand he held in check and rendered useful the corrupt Egyptian officials and the untrustworthy Egyptian soldiers who were his instruments of government. He befriended the natives and advanced them in civilisation. He kept the Arab slave-raiders at bay, and, while Mahdism was triumphant in the north, one melancholy episode being the overthrow of Lupton Bey in the adjacent province of Bahr-el-Ghazal, he actually, by amicable dealings, increased for a time the extent of his dominions. It was only after the Mahdists had been emboldened by the utter discomfiture of the English and Egyptians in the Khartoum and Senaar districts that his position was seriously endangered, and that he began to despair of indefinitely maintaining it without outside help.

His situation was concisely and pathetically explained in two letters that he wrote in December 1885 from Wadelai, whither he had been forced to retire from Lado, his previous head-quarters. To Mr. C. H. Allen, Secretary of the British and Foreign Anti-Slavery Society, he said:—

'Ever since the month of May 1883 we have been cut off from all communication with the world. Forgotten and abandoned by the Government, we have been compelled to make a virtue of necessity. Since the occupation of the Bahr-el-Ghazal we have been vigorously attacked, and I do not know how to describe to you the admirable devotion of my black troops throughout a long war, which, for them at least, has no advantage. Deprived of the most necessary things for a long time, without any pay, my men fought valiantly, and when at last hunger weakened them, when, after nineteen days of incredible privation and sufferings, their strength was exhausted, and when the last torn leather of the last boot had been eaten, then they cut a way through their enemies, and succeeded in saving themselves.'

To Dr. R. W. Felkin he wrote :—

'You will probably know through the daily papers that poor Lupton, after having bravely held the Bahr-el-Ghazal Province, was compelled, through the treachery of his own people, to surrender to the emissaries of the late Mahdi, and was carried by them to Kordofan. My province, and also myself, I only saved from a like fate by a stratagem ; but at last I was attacked, and many losses, both in men and ammunition, were the result, until I delivered such a heavy blow to the rebels at Rimo, in Makraka, that I compelled them to leave me alone. Before this took place they informed us that Khartoum fell, in January 1885, and that Gordon was killed. Naturally, on account of these occurrences, I have been compelled to evacuate our more distant stations and withdraw our soldiers and their families, still hoping that our Government will send us help. . . . Even if it were the intention of the Government to deliver us over to our fate, the least they could have done was to release us from our duties. We should then have known that we were considered to have become valueless. . . . Any way, it was necessary for us to seek some way of escape, and, in the first place, it was urgent to send news of our existence to Egypt. With this object in view, I went south, after having made the necessary arrangements at Lado, and came to Wadelai. . . . As to my future plans, I intend to hold this country as long as possible. I hope that when our letters arrive in Egypt, in seven or eight months, a reply will be sent to me, *viâ* Khartoum or Zanzibar. If the Egyptian Government still exists in the Soudan, we naturally expect them to send us help. If, however, the Soudan has been evacuated, I shall take the whole of the people towards the south. I shall then send the whole of the Egyptian and Khartoum officials, *viâ* Uganda or Karagwé, to Zanzibar, but shall remain myself with my black troops at Kabba-Rega's until the Government inform me as to their wishes.'

Kabba-Rega, it should be noted, is the king of Unyoro, the district south of the Albert Nyanza, and separating the Equatorial Province from Uganda, which is north of the Victoria Nyanza, Karagwé stretching to the west. Kabba-Rega claimed suzerainty over all this country, and Signor Casati, the Italian traveller of long experience, who had latterly become a colleague or officer of Emin, was at this time remaining in Unyoro. In Uganda Mr. A. M. Mackay, the heroic missionary, had been allowed by Mtesa, the former king, to teach Christianity, with the aid of several English and native colleagues. But under Mtesa's son, Mwanga, a policy of persecution was in force, Bishop Hannington being one of its victims; and the treacherous and bloodthirsty disposition of Mwanga and his councillors added greatly to the difficulties of Emin in his efforts to obtain relief from Egypt or England by the route from Zanzibar to Wadelai through Uganda. To Mr. Mackay's friendship the neglected Governor owed much. Mr. Mackay's letters about him, and the reports of Dr. Junker, the Russian traveller, who visited Emin in 1884, chiefly aroused the European sympathy which was intended to save the Equatorial Province and its guardian from destruction.

On July 6, 1886, six months after the letters just quoted, Emin wrote thus to Mr. Mackay:—

'I am in no hurry to break away from here, or to leave those countries in which I have now laboured for ten years. . . . All my people, but especially the negro troops, entertain a strong objection against a march to the south and thence to Egypt, and mean to remain here until they can be taken north. Meantime, if no danger overtakes us, and our ammunition holds out for some time longer, I mean to follow your advice and remain here till help comes to us from some quarter. . . . I shall determine on a march to the coast only in a case of dire necessity. . . . My people have become impatient through long delay, and are anxiously looking for help at last. It would also be most desirable that some commissioner came here from Europe, in order that my people may actually see that there is some interest taken in them. I would defray with ivory all expenses of such a commission. As I once more repeat, I am ready to stay and hold these countries as long as I can until help comes, and I beseech you to do what you can to hasten the arrival of such assistance.'[1]

'Poor Emin Bey!' wrote Mr. Mackay from Uganda on July 11, 1886—

'What could he do? He withdrew all his garrisons from Nyam-Nyam, Makraka, Kalika, and other provinces, and concentrated his forces on the Nile, at Lado and other stations. . . . The Makraka people and others implore him to reoccupy his former stations among them, as, now the government is gone, absolute internecine war prevails among the blacks themselves, while all dread another invasion by the Mahdi's people, the Arabs. Emin has several hundreds of Egyptian soldiers yet in Lado, Dufilé, Wadelai, and Fatiko, and has to support them and their families and others, some 4,000 people in all. He has several thousand tusks of ivory, but can get nothing to buy with it, and his people are relapsing into savagery for want of clothing. We have tried here, in company with Dr. Junker, to purchase cloth to send him. After buying over 2,000

---

[1] This and the preceding letters were published in the *Times*, and are quoted in Mr. Stanley's *In Darkest Africa*, vol. i. pp. 26-28.

dollars' worth, and getting a caravan ready to start for Wadelai, and Mwanga's permission, a hitch has occurred, and the goods are lying still in our house. Mwanga had to be bribed heavily to give the permission, and now he refuses, for some reason or other. But we believe the things will yet be allowed to go. Emin first proposed to bring away all his people, passing this way to Zanzibar, and abandoning entirely the last stronghold of civilisation and pledges of future peaceful government in the whole Equatorial Province. We wrote earnestly begging him not to do so, but to hold on, as help will surely come in time. Before he received our communication he had to change his purpose, as he found that his people would not leave that fine country. Emin cannot abandon them to anarchy. What is to be done to help him to re-establish a proper government on the Equator?'[1]

That letter was written by Mr. Mackay to his father, and has only recently been published. Others that he sent in 1886 to Sir John Kirk, the British Consul at Zanzibar, were official communications. They were, in fact, urgent appeals to our Government for assistance to Emin, and plainly indicated the nature of the assistance desired. 'From Dr. Junker's letter,' wrote Mr. Mackay, on May 14, 'you will have seen that Emin Bey has had the good fortune to have secured the loyalty of the people he governs. Emin seems to have learnt Gordon's secret of securing the affection of his subjects, and has bravely stuck to them. There can be no doubt at all but that, had he been anxious to leave, he could have easily made a dash for the coast, either through the Masai-land or this way. But what would be the fate of the thousands of people who have remained loyal on the

[1] *Mackay of Uganda*, pp. 291, 292.

Upper Nile? They do not want to be taken out of their own fertile country, and taken to the deserts of Upper Egypt. Dr. Emin is on all hands allowed to be a wise and able Governor. But he cannot remain for ever where he is, nor can he succeed by himself, even should the Mahdi's troops leave him undisturbed in the future. His peculiar position should be taken advantage of by our country, which undertook to rescue the garrisons of the Soudan.' Again, on June 28 Mr. Mackay reported concerning Emin: 'He finds that his people, officers and men, refuse to leave the Soudan. Hence he is prepared to remain some years with them, provided only he gets supplies of cloth, &c.'

The representations of Mr. Mackay, Dr. Junker, and others, had weight with the British representatives at Zanzibar, especially as the position of Mr. Mackay himself and of his colleagues and converts in Uganda was seriously imperilled by the persecution of Christians in which King Mwanga indulged in July and afterwards. In September, Acting-Consul-General Holmwood wrote to Lord Iddesleigh and Sir Evelyn Baring, suggesting the necessity of promptly relieving both Emin and the Uganda missionaries, the relief he recommended being, not their withdrawal from the scenes of their self-sacrificing and beneficent labours, but their protection in continuing them. Mr. Holmwood urged the sending of an adequate supply of ammunition and other stores to Emin, and the despatch of 'five hundred native troops, armed with modern rifles and under experienced leaders,' to oppose Mwanga. 'Were Uganda free from this tyrant,' he said, 'the Equatorial Province, even should the present elementary system of communication remain unmodified, would be within eight weeks' post of Zanzibar, and a safe depôt on the Albert Nyanza would provide a base from which any further operations that might be decided upon for the retention of the Upper Nile could be undertaken effectively and without anxiety.'[1]

Mr. Holmwood's risky project for a military invasion of Uganda appears to have been at once scouted by the authorities in London; but those in Cairo favoured both it and the plan for sending assistance to Emin. On November 23, Sir Evelyn Baring telegraphed to Lord Iddesleigh, reporting that Dr. Junker, whose scheme Dr. Schweinfurth endorsed, was prepared to conduct an expedition for the relief of Emin, to which 'the Egyptian Government would not be unwilling to contribute 10,000*l.*,' and that 'his plan would include dethroning the present king of Uganda by giving help to the party hostile to him;' and asking 'whether Her Majesty's Government has any objection to the Egyptian Government taking this proposed action.' 'Dr. Schweinfurth,' wrote Sir Evelyn Baring in his despatch, 'attaches great importance to Dr. Junker being made the leader of the expedition.'[2]

Dr. Schweinfurth's and Dr. Junker's scheme was forestalled under circumstances to be presently referred to; but the 10,000*l.* offered by the Egyptian Government, in order that it might be carried out, was claimed and diverted to another purpose by the British Government.

In April 1887, Emin, whom the Egyptian Government had in the interval promoted to the rank of Pasha,

---

[1] *Parliamentary Papers*, C. 5601, pp. 2–4.
[2] *Ibid.* pp. 8, 9.

heard through Mr. Mackay that an Expedition from England was on its way to him. Part of a letter to Dr. Felkin, in which he expressed the joy and thankfulness with which he received the news, but clearly stated the only conditions on which he was prepared to accept the proffered help, must here be quoted :—

'I could never have believed that I, a stranger, and my poor people, could have received such generous thoughts, and that anyone would be ready to make such sacrifices for us. If, however, the people in Great Britain think that as soon as Stanley or Thomson comes I shall return with them, they greatly err. I have passed twelve years of my life here, and would it be right of me to desert my post as soon as the opportunity for escape presented itself? I shall remain with my people until I see perfectly clearly that both their future and the future of our country is safe.

'The work that Gordon paid for with his blood I will strive to carry on, if not with his energy and genius, still according to his intentions and in his spirit. When my lamented chief placed the government of this country in my hands he wrote to me, "I appoint you for civilisation and progress's sake." I have done my best to justify the trust he had in me, and that I have to some extent been successful, and have won the confidence of the natives, is proved by the fact that I and my handful of people have held our own up to the present day. I remain here the last and only representative of Gordon's staff. It therefore falls to me, and is my bounden duty, to follow up the road he showed us. Sooner or later a bright future must dawn for these countries; sooner or later these people will be drawn into the circle of the ever-advancing civilised world. For twelve long years I have striven and toiled, and sown the seeds for future harvest—laid the foundation stones for future buildings. Shall I now give up the work, because a way may soon open to the coast? Never!

'If England wishes really to help us, she must try, in the first place, to conclude some treaty with Uganda and Unyoro, by which the condition of those countries may be improved both morally and politically. A safe road to the coast must be opened up, and one which shall not be at the mercy of the moods of childish kings or disreputable Arabs. This is all we want, and it is the only thing necessary to permit of the steady development of these countries. If we possessed it we could look the future hopefully in the face. . . .

'I should like here again to mention that, if a relief expedition comes to us, I will on no account leave my people. We have passed through troublous times together, and I consider it would be a shameful act on my part were I to desert them. They are, notwithstanding all their hardships, brave and good, with the exception of the Egyptians. We have known each other many years, and I do not think it would be easy at present for a stranger to take up my work and to win at once the confidence of the people. It is, therefore, out of the question for me to leave; so I shall remain. All we would ask England to do is to bring about a better understanding with Uganda, and to provide us with a free and safe way to the coast. This is all we want. Evacuate our territory? Certainly not!'[1]

2. *Mr. H. M. Stanley and the Congo Free State.*

The career of Mr. Stanley, to whom the duty of relieving Emin Pasha was assigned in 1886, is well known. But about him also a few pertinent facts must be recalled.

A year younger than Emin, Mr. Stanley began to

---

[1] *Emin Pasha in Central Africa*, pp. 509, 510.

make acquaintance with Africa in 1868, when, as special correspondent of the *New York Herald*, he accompanied the British military expedition to Abyssinia. In 1871 he made his famous journey in search of Dr. Livingstone, whom he found at Ujiji, on Lake Tanganyika, and with whom he explored a portion of the lake. In 1874, having spent part of the interval—again as a war correspondent—in following the British campaign in Ashanti, he started on a more important enterprise. Leaving Zanzibar with a party of over three hundred native carriers, he proceeded to Lake Victoria Nyanza, part of which he explored. After visiting Uganda and Unyoro, near the Equatorial Province of which Emin was three years later appointed Governor, he travelled southward to Lake Tanganyika, and, reaching the southern branch of the Congo, known as the Lualaba, tracked the river along its whole course to the Atlantic.

This journey, which occupied two years and nine months, solved many geographical problems, and communicated much valuable information about regions hitherto but little known. Mr. Stanley's zeal and success won for him a prominent place among modern travellers, and none can question the boldness of his exploit. But there were ugly sides to it. If the barbarous tribes whom Mr. Stanley startled by his intrusion among them showed him friendship, he generally dealt kindly with them in return. 'Whenever I find myself in Stanley's track,' wrote Mr. Mackay, who was on the shore of Lake Victoria Nyanza three years later, and whose words are weighty, 'I find his treatment of the natives has invariably been such as to win from them the highest respect for the face of a white man.[1] But Mr. Mackay only followed Mr. Stanley over districts in which Mr. Stanley saw no occasion to be angry. When his anger was roused the result was, on his own showing, deplorable.

Of this there was conspicuous evidence in his conduct to the natives of Bumbiré, a small island on the western side of the Victoria Nyanza, with an estimated population of about four thousand. During an exploring tour in one of his boats, Mr. Stanley, driven thereto by lack of food, visited this island in April 1875; but the people on the shore resented his approach, and, when he was near enough, rushed into the water and hauled up his boat. Some quarrelling and scuffling ensued, in the course of which the boat's oars and a drum were seized by the natives; but after a few hours parleying with the chief, Shekka, and his men, Mr. Stanley contrived, without bloodshed, to re-enter and float his boat. According to his report:—

'As soon as I saw the savages had arrived in the presence

[1] *Mackay of Uganda*, p. 97. In justice to Mr. Stanley the following should also be quoted from a letter of Mr. Mackay's written in June 1880: 'Let the enemies of this enterprising traveller scoff as they will, it is a fact indisputable that with his visit there commenced the dawn of a new era in the court of Uganda. The people themselves date from Mr. Stanley's day the commencement of leniency and law in place of bloodshed and terror. "Since Stanley came," they say, "the king no more slaughters innocent people as he did before; he no more disowns and disinherits in a moment an old and powerful chief, and sets up a puppet of his own who was before only a slave"' (p. 217). Yet Mr. Stanley's influence was only transitory. He made friends with Mtesa in 1875, and prepared for Mr. Mackay's mission; but in 1886 Mr. Mackay himself had bitter experience of the fickleness and cruelty of Mtesa's son.

of Shekka with our drum, I shouted to my men to push the boat into the water. With one desperate effort my crew of eleven hands lifted and shot it forth into the lake, the impetus they had given it causing it to drag them all into deep water. In the meantime, the savages, uttering a furious howl of disappointment and baffled rage, came rushing like a whirlwind towards their canoes at the water's edge. I discharged my elephant rifle, with its two large conical balls, into their midst; and then, assisting one of the crew into the boat, told him to help his fellows in while I continued to fight. My double-barrelled shot-gun, loaded with buckshot, was next discharged with terrible effect; for, without drawing a single bow or launching a single spear, they fell back up the slope of the hill, leaving us to exert our wits to get ourselves out of the cove before the enemy should decide to man their canoes. My crew was composed of picked men, and in this dire emergency they did ample justice to my choice. Though we were without oars, they were at no loss for a substitute. As soon as they found themselves in the boat they tore up the seats and footboards and began to paddle, while I was left to single out with my rifles the most prominent and boldest of the enemy. Twice in succession I succeeded in dropping men determined on launching the canoes; and, seeing the sub-chief who had commanded the party that took the drum, I took deliberate aim with my elephant rifle at him. That bullet, as I have since been told, killed the chief and two others who happened to be standing a few paces behind him; and the extraordinary result had more effect, I think, on the superstitious minds of the natives than all previous or subsequent shots. On getting out of the cove we saw two canoes loaded with men coming out in pursuit from another small inlet. I permitted them to approach within a hundred yards of us, and this time I used the elephant rifle with explosive balls. Four shots killed five men and sank the canoes. This decisive affair disheartened the enemy, and we were left to pursue our way unmolested—not, however, without hearing a ringing voice shouting out to us, "Go and die in the Nyanza!" When the savages counted their losses, they found fourteen dead and wounded with ball and buckshot; which, although I should consider to be very dear payment for the robbery of eight ash oars and a drum, was barely equivalent, in fair estimation, to the intended massacre of ourselves.'[1]

That punishment of the natives for objecting to Mr. Stanley's visit, refusing to sell him food, and in the course of the scramble seizing some of his boat's gear, and even for what he supposed to be an 'intention' to kill him and his crew, might have been considered sufficiently severe. But Mr. Stanley was not satisfied with it. In July, after some other excursions, he resolved to wreak full vengeance on Shekka. He first sent a message to the people of Bumbiré that, if they would hand over to him Shekka and two of his head men, they would be forgiven. This proposal not being acceded to, he seized the king and three chiefs of Iroba, which he was then visiting, on the mainland, and kept them in chains as hostages until the Iroba people had captured Shekka for him. That was soon done, and Shekka was 'at once chained heavily,' as an initial step. Then, in August, Mr. Stanley organised a party of his own men and of forced auxiliaries, comprising fifty musketeers and two hundred and thirty spearmen, and embarking them in eighteen canoes returned to Bumbiré. He felt it all the more incumbent upon him

[1] *Daily Telegraph*, August 7, 1876. Mr. Stanley gives a different and more picturesque account of this performance in his *Through the Dark Continent* (pp. 146–152); but his description written shortly after the event is presumably more accurate.

to show firmness, he says, because several of his followers had shortly before gone to the island to steal bananas, and had then been so roughly handled that six of them died of their wounds. Mr. Stanley considered that 'duty, respect, and gratitude' to his allies, 'apart from the justice which, according to all laws, human and divine, savage and civilised, especially when committed with malice prepense, and the memory of our narrow escape from their almost fatal wiles, and the days of agony we had suffered,' together with 'the vital, absolute, and imperative necessity of meeting the savages lest they should meet us,' sanctioned and compelled the proceedings thus described :—

'The enemy, perceiving my intention to disembark, rose from their coverts and ran along the hills to meet us, which was precisely what I wished they would do, and accordingly I ordered my force to paddle slowly so as to give them time. In half an hour the savages were all assembled in knots and groups, and after approaching within a hundred yards of the beach I formed my line of battle, the American and English flags waving as our ensigns. Having anchored each canoe, so as to turn its broadside to the shore, I ordered a volley to be fired at one group which numbered about fifty, and the result was several killed and many wounded. The savages, perceiving our aim and the danger of standing together, separated themselves and advanced to the water's edge, slinging stones and shooting arrows. I then ordered the canoes to advance within fifty yards of the shore, and to fire at close quarters. After an hour the savages saw that they could not defend themselves, and retreated up the slope, where they continued still exposed to our bullets. I then caused the canoes to come together, and told them to advance in a body to the beach, as if about to disembark. This caused the enemy to make an effort to repulse our landing, and accordingly hundreds came down with their spears ready on the launch. When they were close enough the bugles sounded a halt, and another volley was fired into the spearmen, which had such a disastrous effect that they retired far away, and our work of chastisement was consummated. Not many cartridges were fired, but as the savages were so exposed, on a slope covered with only short grass, and as the sun in the afternoon was directly behind us and in their faces, their loss was great. Forty-two were counted on the field, lying dead, and over a hundred were seen to retire wounded, while on our side only two men suffered contusions from stones slung at us.'[1]

These proceedings, when made known in England a year after their occurrence, elicited an indignant protest from the Aborigines Protection Society, which pointed out to Lord Derby, then Foreign Minister, that 'the destruction of the forty-two human beings who were struck dead by Mr. Stanley's bullets, together with the probable death of many of the hundred or more who received agonising wounds from explosive bullets, was an act of blind and ruthless vengeance, which calls for severe animadversion, if not for stronger measures, on the part of Her Majesty's Government,' especially as Mr. Stanley had hoisted the British flag while engaged on his filibustering diversion. Lord Derby, in his reply, averred that Mr. Stanley, being an American citizen, employed on an unofficial expedition, was not amenable to English law, but that he would be informed that he had 'no authority to hoist the British flag;' and that 'his lordship cannot but

[1] *Daily Telegraph*, August 10, 1876. I have again preferred to quote Mr. Stanley's first report instead of that rewritten for his book; but compare *Through the Dark Continent*, pp. 175–186.

hope that Mr. Stanley may eventually be able to afford some explanation or justification of his proceedings.' The matter was also freely discussed in the English newspapers, and brought before the attention of Parliament; but Mr. Stanley's only attempt at 'explanation or justification' appears to have been made at a banquet given to him at Cape Town, where he called in October 1877 on his way back from S. Paul de Loanda to Zanzibar. In the course of his speech, as reported by a correspondent of the *Times*, he said:—

'He only wished he could get every member of Exeter Hall to explore by the same route he had gone from the Atlantic to longitude 23°. He would undertake to provide them with seven tons of Bibles, four tons of Prayer Books, any number of surplices, and a church organ into the bargain, and if they reached as far as longitude 23° without chucking some of these Bibles at some of the negroes' heads, he would——' The conclusion of the sentence was lost in the burst of laughter which followed. As he sat down he said:—'I tell you that if ever I should find myself where I have to exercise command over men and restrain them from molesting others unnecessarily, I will always remember the spirit which guides Exeter Hall, which is simply a charitable, forbearing spirit, Christian-like and forgiving, I admit; but if I have command over such people as these Arabs who are here with me, if I invite their confidence and take them among a lot of savages, and those savages raise a hand needlessly against any of my people, I swear to you that I will also forget the views of Exeter Hall, and call upon what little bit of manliness is in me to assert itself.'

No other atrocities as heinous as those committed at Bumbiré are recorded of Mr. Stanley's travelling across Africa in 1875–77; but his policy and conduct throughout the Expedition, as avowed and boasted of in his book, 'Through the Dark Continent,' showed no such regard of the laws of humanity as is claimed for the earlier journeyings chronicled in 'How I found Livingstone.'

There was not so much to complain of and perhaps more to admire in his next great African enterprise. The report of his explorations in the Congo region reached Europe at a time when His Majesty Leopold II., the King of the Belgians, was interesting himself in Central Africa, and helped to forward the work that King Leopold had taken in hand. The African International Association, of which His Majesty was the founder, and which, on the amicable retirement of the other European Powers from partnership in it, virtually became a Belgian organisation, had been started in 1876. In 1878 Mr. Stanley accepted service under King Leopold, and took charge of an Expedition which left Banana Point, at the mouth of the Congo, in August 1879, and gradually worked its way up to Stanley Pool, where, in November 1881, Leopoldville was founded.

The intervening two years and more were spent by Mr. Stanley in investigating the river and its margins, arranging treaties with the native chiefs, establishing local centres for trade and administration, opening up roads, and in other ways preparing for what was intended to be the beneficent commercial and political development of this part of Africa. His supreme duty was to make friends of the natives, which could only be done by proceeding leisurely and cautiously, and he accomplished his task with considerable success.

After retracing his course and making useful excur

sions on the way into new districts, Mr. Stanley paid a visit to Europe in 1882; but he promptly returned to Stanley Pool, whence he started on a fresh journey, following the Upper Congo as far as Stanley Falls, the farthest point as yet reached by the Belgian pioneers of civilisation. He also entered the Aruwimi, a branch of the Congo, going as far as Yambuya, since famous as the site chosen for the long halt of the Emin Relief Expedition. The stations and the trade openings that he started have not in all, if in any cases, been as prosperous as he expected them to be; but when he again reached Europe, in July 1884, he was able to present to King Leopold a brilliant report of the work done during his five years service. The International African Association was, as he says, and mainly through his efforts, 'in possession of treaties made with over four hundred and fifty independent African chiefs, whose rights would be conceded by all to have been indisputable, since they held their lands by undisturbed occupation, by long ages of succession, by real right divine.'[1]

The International Association—so called, but actually only a Belgian corporation—having acquired such large and despotic rights, it was proper that it should be reconstituted, and this was done with the sanction of the European Conference assembled at Berlin in November 1884. The Berlin Treaty of 1885, the outcome of the Conference, provided for the future management of the entire district styled the Conventional Basin of the Congo, of which portions, on the Atlantic side, are held or claimed by France and

[1] *The Congo and the Founding of its Free State*, vol. ii. p. 379.

Portugal, but of which the chief part, comprising an area estimated at more than a million square miles, was placed under the sovereignty of King Leopold, and was henceforth to be known as the Congo Free State. To Mr. Stanley's enterprise this notable change in African affairs is largely due; and it is important to remember that he still holds dignified, though not clearly defined, office under King Leopold and the Congo Free State.

Even before Mr. Stanley returned to Europe in 1884, however, there were signs that the vast territory he had nominally acquired for his Belgian employers was not all held on sure or lasting conditions. Many of the native chiefs who were supposed to have signed treaties surrendering their independence repudiated those treaties as soon as rough attempts were made to act upon them. Mr. Stanley, moreover, had forgotten, or was not aware, that suzerainty over the whole of Central Africa was claimed by the Sultan of Zanzibar. Though this potentate made no effort himself to exercise authority over any part of the country, he was keen in obtaining as much tribute as he could from the recognised chiefs in the nearer districts, and from any adventurers who went inland in search of slaves and ivory. As soon as it was known that Europeans were seeking to establish themselves in the Congo Basin, the adventurers lost no time in asserting their alleged rights or those of the Sultan of Zanzibar. One of these adventurers, the boldest and the most successful, had so much influence, though only indirectly, on the movements of the Emin Relief Expedition, that something must here be said about him.

This adventurer was Tippoo-Tib, with whom Mr. Stanley had made acquaintance in 1876 when he was tracking his way from Lake Tanganyika to the Lualaba branch of the Congo. Famous and dreaded even then, although he only ruled and roamed over the comparatively small stretch of ground near the Lualaba, this great slave-raider had guided Mr. Stanley along a part of his road in return for heavy payment or promise of payment. Livingstone had had relations with him several years before that, and had found that he justified the title he assumed, the meaning of 'Tipo-Tipo' being in English 'gatherer of great wealth.' Not content with being a mere slave-hunter, Tippoo, from the first, aspired to empire. More than twenty years ago, as Livingstone reported, he set up a despotism in Itawa, exacting as tribute all the ivory found there, and desolating the country by his raids. He afterwards moved farther west, and, shortly before Mr. Stanley's meeting with him, he had been visited at Nyangwe by Commander Lovett Cameron, who testifies to his hospitality. He soon established a wide-spread dominion over the Manyuema, peopling most of the district watered by the Lualaba; and when Mr. Stanley paid his second visit to Stanley Falls in 1883, and there planted a station for the International African Association, he found Tippoo's people in possession of the country, though it is not certain that Tippoo himself was ever in this locality before 1884. The Manyuema chiefs and others, who are in the position of vassals to Tippoo, it should be mentioned, though generally spoken of as Arabs, have in them very little Arab blood, if any.

Leaving Stanley Falls in December, 1883, Mr.

Stanley entrusted the station to the temporary care of Mr. Binnie, who a few months later was replaced by Lieutenant Wester. In October 1884, Lieutenant Wester made a treaty with the Arabs, a son of Tippoo-Tib being one of the signatories, by which they undertook to abstain from raiding for slaves or ivory to the west of Stanley Falls, and to remain at peace with the whites in the district. The natives at the same time placed themselves under the protection of the International Association, presently merged in the Congo Free State. Before the year was out, however, Tippoo arrived at the head of a large force, and, in the name of the Sultan of Zanzibar, repudiated the treaty with Lieutenant Wester, to which his son had been a party. Hence arose an angry controversy, soon resulting in open quarrel.

Mr. Walter Deane was sent up from Leopoldville with a company of men to take the command at Stanley Falls, and to defend it and the native allies from Arab attacks. 'The spirit of his orders,' as Mr. J. R. Werner says, 'was that he was to afford protection to the natives, to do all in his power to prevent raids and put down the slave trade, and to keep on good terms with the Arabs'[1]—conditions incompatible with one another. Mr. Deane, wounded and invalided for a time, contrived to hold his position till August 1886; but in the previous May or June an event occurred which had serious consequences. A female slave, who had been tied up by her Arab master for two or three

---

[1] *A Visit to Stanley's Rear-Guard*, p. 94. The whole story of 'the loss of Stanley Falls' is told by Mr. Werner from personal knowledge, pp. 87–127.

days and cruelly flogged, having escaped and sought Mr. Deane's protection, Mr. Deane refused to restore her. 'As an Englishman I will not, and, as an officer of the State, I cannot give her up,' he said to Bwana Nzigé, Tippoo-Tib's brother and deputy, who came to expostulate with and threaten him. There was not much more than threatening till September. In the interval the Arabs had seized one of the women belonging to the station, and had fired on some of Mr. Deane's soldiers; but they had affected to make peace after the arrival of the Congo State steamer, the 'Stanley.' On the departure of the 'Stanley,' however, serious trouble arose. The station was attacked, and after three days fighting, when all the ammunition had been spent, the place was captured by the Arabs, Mr. Deane and a few followers who had not deserted him having to take refuge in the bush after setting fire to the station. Mr. Deane was picked up after nearly a month's wandering and privation; but what remained of King Leopold's Stanley Falls Station had been converted into a centre of government for Tippoo-Tib's slave-raiding host.

The practical effect of this catastrophe, small in itself, was that the over-zealous and premature effort of the Congo State authorities to plant civilisation in Central Africa was to a large extent wrecked.

CHAPTER II

THE PURPOSES OF THE EXPEDITION

To Dr. R. W. Felkin, of Edinburgh, belongs the chief credit of directing public attention in England to the duty of responding to Emin Pasha's appeal for help in continuing his humane work in Central Africa. Dr. Felkin had visited Emin in 1882, and by publishing some of the letters received from him in 1886 he aroused wide-spread interest in his perilous condition. At Dr. Felkin's instigation, moreover, the Royal Scottish Geographical Society petitioned the Government for assistance in equipping an Expedition on the lines recommended by two other friends of Emin, who had personal knowledge of his requirements and of the Equatorial Province—Dr. Schweinfurth and Dr. Junker. But preference was given by the Government to a scheme proposed to it by Mr. (now Sir William) Mackinnon, the chairman of the British India Steam Navigation Company.

'Early in October, 1886,' says Mr. Stanley, ' Sir William Mackinnon and Mr. J. F. Hutton, ex-president of the Manchester Chamber of Commerce, had spoken with me respecting the possibilities of conveying relief to Emin, with a view to enabling him to hold his own. To them it seemed that he only required ammunition, and I shared their opinion, and they were very earnest in their intention to collect funds for the support he required.'[1]

Mr. Joseph Thomson, of great experience in African travel, and especially familiar with the country described in his 'Through Masai-land,' Mr. H. H. Johnston, now British Consul at Mozambique, and others, were talked of as leaders of the proposed Expedition. But Sir William Mackinnon favoured Mr. Stanley, who wrote to him on November 15 : ' Let me say that, if there is any real intention and purpose to carry the proposal into effect, you may fully command my services. To that object I would devote them freely and gratuitously, without hope of fee or reward.'[2]

On the same day Sir William Mackinnon wrote to the Foreign Office, calling attention to the 'general feeling in the country that some effort should be made to open up communication with Emin Bey, and that the Government should, in some way or other, take immediate action in the matter ;' also suggesting that ' it might be worthy of consideration whether the services of the well-known, eminent explorer, Mr. H. M. Stanley, should not be secured.'[3]

The receipt of that letter at the Foreign Office was followed by other communications between it and Sir William Mackinnon, as well as communications by telegraph with Sir Evelyn Baring. The result was that Lord Iddesleigh, while declaring that the relief of Emin was ' a responsibility which Her Majesty's Government could not undertake,' sanctioned ' a peaceful

[1] *In Darkest Africa*, vol. i. p. 31.
[2] *Parliamentary Papers*, C. 5601, p. 7.   [3] *Ibid.* p. 4.

Relief Expedition,' to be organised and conducted by Mr. Stanley, and directed Sir Evelyn Baring to obtain for this purpose the 10,000*l.* offered by the Egyptian Government for Dr. Junker's proposed Expedition—Sir William Mackinnon having promised that if this 10,000*l.* was secured, he would 'at once set to work to get together' another 10,000*l.* to make up the 20,000*l.* which Mr. Stanley had stated to be necessary. As, however, 'Emin Bey was believed to have considerable quantities of ivory, which might be utilised for repayment of outlays connected with any scheme of relief,' Sir William Mackinnon stipulated, on behalf of the Emin Pasha Relief Committee which he was forming, that 'if this expectation should be realised, a just proportion [of the ivory] should be made over to them in repayment of their outlay.'[1]

The business was so far arranged that Mr. Stanley, who had in the meanwhile gone to America, was recalled by telegram; and, reaching London on December 25, he lost no time in preparing for the work he had undertaken.

But to understand the nature of that work we must go back to an earlier date.

When Mr. Stanley was asked in October to conduct the Expedition, he tells us, he reported that, 'as for routes, there were four almost equally feasible.' He declared, however, that 'the first, *viâ* Masai-land, was decidedly objectionable,' as it passes through an ill-watered and grainless country, and any Zanzibaris recruited as carriers to traverse it would be certain to desert in great numbers. 'The second, *viâ* Victoria

[1] *Parliamentary Papers,* C. 5601, pp. 5–8.

Nyanza and Uganda, which was naturally the best, was rendered impossible for a small Expedition because of the hostility of Uganda.' 'The third was *viâ* Msalala, Karagwé and Ankori, and Unyoro and Lake Albert,' open to the same objections as the second, and, like that and the first, to the facilities afforded for desertion. 'Desertion of late from East Coast Expeditions had assumed alarming proportions, owing to the impunity with which the Zanzibaris could decamp with rifles and loads, and the number of opportunities presented to them. Fifty per cent. loss was unavoidable, and no precautions would avail to prevent desertion.' 'With money enough,' added Mr. Stanley, 'every route is possible; but, as I understand it, you propose to subscribe a moderate amount, and, therefore, there is only one route which is safely open for the money, and that is the Congo.'[1]

. From the first, Mr. Stanley recommended this roundabout journey, which would involve a long sea-voyage from Zanzibar to the West Coast of Africa, and thence more than two thousand miles of river and inland travelling to Wadelai, which is less than a thousand miles distant from the East Coast. 'By this route,' he wrote to Sir William Mackinnon, on November 15, 'Emin Bey can be reached safely by the middle of June 1887, and Emin Bey, as well as the Relief Expedition, could reach the sea by the middle of December, 1887.'[2]

But the Emin Relief Committee, listening for a time to the counsels of other experienced travellers,

[1] *In Darkest Africa*, vol. i. pp. 32, 33.
[2] *Parliamentary Papers*, C. 5601, p. 7.

and perhaps then anxious to comply with Emin's request and the wishes of his friends, preferred that a selection should be made from one of the East Coast routes; and Mr. Stanley professed himself complaisant. 'Very good,' he reports that he said, 'it is perfectly immaterial to me. Let us decide on the East Coast route *viâ* Msalala, Karagwé, Ankori, and Unyoro. If you hear of some hard fighting, I look to you that you will defend the absent. . . . It is decided that the means of defence must be put into Emin's hands, and you have entrusted me with the escort of it. So be it.'[1]

Mr. Stanley went so far, after he had received on December 31 formal authority to commence his preparations, as to telegraph orders to Zanzibar for porters to be engaged at Bagamoyo to convey goods to Mpwapwa. But he quickly reverted to his original proposals, and he persuaded his new employers to sanction the change. As to any previous communications that may have passed between him and his older employer, King Leopold, the sovereign of the Congo Free State, we are not informed; but on January 4, 1887, Sir William Mackinnon wrote to tell him of a letter from the King, 'showing how anxious he is the Congo route should be taken, and how unwilling to allow a break in the continuity of your connection with the Congo State, as he considers you a pillar of the State.' Consequently, on January 5, Mr. Stanley went to the Foreign Office, and, as he says, 'revealed the King's desire that the Expedition should proceed *viâ* Congo;' and on the 8th he received an official letter from the King's secretary, saying: 'According to your

[1] *In Darkest Africa*, vol. i. p. 35.

own estimate, the Expedition proceeding by the eastern coast would occupy about eighteen months. His Majesty considers that he would be failing in his duty towards the State were he to deprive it of your services, especially as the latter will be certainly needed before the expiration of this lapse of time.' Mr. Stanley's note in his diary for this day is more concise and more explicit: 'Received letters from the King. He lays claim to my services.'[1]

Fortunately for those who chose the Congo route, the French Government, hearing of an Expedition by way of the Albert Nyanza, pointed out to Lord Iddesleigh that this might cause danger to the French missionaries in Uganda. 'It also,' Mr. Stanley assures us, 'became evident that the Germans of the East Africa Company suspected that, though ostensibly a humanitarian Expedition, our professions only cloaked designs sinister to their interests; that, in fact, Mr. Stanley was only bent upon large annexation schemes.'[2] Moreover, King Leopold, as an inducement to adoption of the Congo route, offered, should that be taken, 'to show the Expedition all goodwill,' and 'to gratuitously place at its disposal the whole of the State's naval stock, inasmuch as will allow the working arrangements of its own administration.'[3]

These, however flimsy and meaningless, were cogent arguments for willing ears; but it must be clearly understood that, whatever Mr. Stanley's intentions may all along have been, the promoters of the Expedition

[1] *In Darkest Africa*, vol. i. pp. 43-45
[2] *Parliamentary Papers*, C. 5906, p. 3.
[3] *In Darkest Africa*, vol. i. p. 44.

were induced to sanction the Congo route, which they had at first condemned, because they found that King Leopold objected to any other route being taken by Mr. Stanley while he remained in the service of the Congo State, and that, unless this route was taken, either Mr. Stanley must break with King Leopold, or some other leader must be found for the Expedition. They chose what seemed to be the lesser evil. As Mr. Stanley says, 'The Committee was informed once more of the objections to my route from East Africa, and, other reasons just as forcible being presented to them, they permitted me to accept the King of the Belgians' generous offer of the Congo route, and the assistance of the steam flotilla of the Upper Congo.'[1]

This change of plan necessitated other changes, and the overcoming of fresh difficulties consequent upon it. On January 12 the Emin Relief Committee had to write to Lord Salisbury, who had assumed the duties of Foreign Minister after Lord Iddesleigh's untimely death, stating that their funds were 'not sufficient to enable them to carry out the whole object of the Expedition *via* the Congo route, in consequence of the cost of transport from Zanzibar to Banana Point,' and asking the Government 'to place a steam vessel at the disposition of the Expedition to carry out the service of transport of five hundred Zanzibaris, and the material belonging to the Expedition from Zanzibar to Banana.' With this request the Government was unable to comply, but it undertook to supply coal, 'free of charge,' to the 'Madura,' which was lent by the British India Steam Navigation Company for conveyance of the party. It

[1] *Parliamentary Papers*, C. 5906, p. 4.

also ordered the Egyptian Government to pay, 'at once, to the account of the Relief Committee,' for use by Mr. Stanley on the Congo route, the 10,000*l.* which had been promised for use by Dr. Junker on the Uganda route; and, further, to make itself responsible for any expenses incurred by Mr. Stanley or the Congo State in conveying 'the women and children and any Egyptians desirous of returning to their country,' who might be sent home by way of the Congo and the Atlantic and Indian Oceans.[1]

The general scheme of the Expedition having been finally decided upon, Mr. Stanley lost no time in completing the detailed arrangements he had already commenced, and he showed all his usual ardour and talent in making the preparations. Notwithstanding inevitable hindrances from banquets and interviews at home, and visits to King Leopold at Brussels and the Prince of Wales at Sandringham, he was ready to start for Suez on January 21. For the completeness of these arrangements great credit is due not only to him but also to Sir William Mackinnon, the chairman, Sir Francis de Winton, the secretary, and the other members of the Emin Relief Committee.

There can be no doubt, moreover, that several of the members of the Emin Relief Committee and subscribers to the Emin Relief Fund entered in perfect good faith on the work they undertook, and honestly persevered in it according to their knowledge and opportunities. Among the principal subscribers were the Royal Geographical Society of London and two members of the Scottish Geographical Society, who may be presumed to

[1] *Parliamentary Papers,* C. 5601, pp. 11-13, 16.

D

have had the interest of science especially at heart. Some others were genuine philanthropists. At the same time, it must be noted that by far the largest contributor—with the exception of the Egyptian Government, which was not a free agent in the business—was Sir William Mackinnon, the founder and president of the Imperial British East Africa Company, to which a Royal Charter was granted in September 1888. Besides Sir William Mackinnon, five other members of the Emin Relief Committee and three other subscribers to the Emin Relief Fund were among the original directors of the British East Africa Company.

The connection between the Expedition and the Company needs explaining. As far back as 1878 Sir William Mackinnon entered into negotiations with the late Sultan of Zanzibar, Barghash, in the hope of obtaining from him a lease of his supposed territories on the African mainland, estimated at 590,000 square miles, and stretching on to Lakes Nyassa, Tanganyika and Victoria Nyanza and the borders of Uganda. Had that proposed concession been obtained in 1878, Sultan Barghash would have become the pensioner of Sir William Mackinnon and his friends, and these latter would have been masters, not only of the empire now owned by them, but also of a large part of the country which has been since declared to be within the German 'sphere of influence.' But Sultan Barghash was dilatory, and the British Government did not encourage the project. In spite of zealous and repeated efforts, Sir William Mackinnon had to wait ten years for adoption of the project in a modified form. Perhaps he is not to be blamed for desiring to utilise Mr. Stanley's services in achieving his long delayed purpose. The method he pursued, however, can hardly be commended. No one may suppose that he gave 3,000*l*. himself and persuaded others to contribute more than thrice that amount merely for the sake of relieving Emin Pasha. The relief of Emin was evidently only a pretext and an opportunity for facilitating the establishment of the British East Africa Company; and from that point of view, if from no other, it was a success.

Mr. Stanley took with him from England a letter of Sir William Mackinnon's to his old friend Sultan Barghash. 'I pray you,' wrote Sir William, 'to communicate freely with Mr. Stanley on all points, as freely as if I had the honour of being there to receive the communications myself.' That letter was delivered as soon as possible after Mr. Stanley's arrival at Zanzibar on February 22. 'We entered heartily into our business,' says Mr. Stanley: 'how absolutely necessary it was that he should promptly enter into an agreement with the English within the limits assigned by the Anglo-German Treaty. It would take too long to describe the details of the conversation, but I obtained from him the answer needed.' A few days later Mr. Stanley wrote to a friend: 'I have settled several little commissions at Zanzibar very satisfactorily. One was to get the Sultan to sign the concessions which Mackinnon tried to obtain a long time ago. . . . For eight years to my knowledge the matter had been placed before His Highness, but the Sultan's signature was difficult to obtain.'[1] The Sultan was the more easily persuaded to accede to Mr. Stanley's demands because his health

[1] *In Darkest Africa*, pp. 62, 68, 69.

was failing and he knew that he could not live much longer. The concession asked for was promised, and, the necessary formalities being concluded after Mr. Stanley's departure from Zanzibar, the document was signed on May 24, 1887. The incorporation of the Imperial British East Africa Company followed in due course.

In Sir William Mackinnon's letter to the Sultan there was a notable sentence. After thanking the Sultan for his assistance in procuring carriers for the Emin Relief Expedition, and informing him that the Expedition would take the Congo route, Sir William added: 'It is probable Mr. Stanley will return by the East Coast land route, and, as I know him to be deeply interested in your Highness's prosperity and welfare, I am sure if he can render any service to your Highness during his progress back to the coast, he will do so most heartily.'[1] What service Mr. Stanley could render to the Sultan by travelling over territory that was about to be virtually ceded to Sir William Mackinnon is not apparent, but we have here an intimation that Mr. Stanley, who had condemned the short land route as ' decidedly objectionable ' for reaching Emin Pasha, and who had proposed to deport as well as to approach Emin by way of the Congo, was already thinking of returning to Zanzibar by the ' decidedly objectionable ' path. As a large part of the country between Wadelai and the Zanzibar coast was about to be handed over to the section of the Emin Relief Committee which issued in the British East Africa Company, there were good

---

[1] *In Darkest Africa*, vol. i. p. 61.

reasons why the acquisition of this country should not be retarded and hampered by a hostile march through it while the negotiations were in progress. But there were equally good reasons—as later events proved— why Mr. Stanley should traverse it at the head of a triumphant force as soon as it had become the property of the British East Africa Company. It is evident that Sir William Mackinnon and his friends lost nothing by allowing Mr. Stanley to proceed by way of the Congo in his search for Emin, and that they had much to gain from his returning by the Eastern route.

But, as has been noted, the chief and in itself sufficient motive for Mr. Stanley's selecting the Congo route is to be found in the requirements of his principal employer, King Leopold; and of the 'little commissions at Zanzibar' which he 'settled' in February 1887 the one for King Leopold was, as far as the Emin Relief Expedition was concerned, much more important than the one he 'settled' for Sir William Mackinnon.

While Mr. Stanley was at Zanzibar Tippoo-Tib was there also. The great Arab slave-raider was paying one of his periodical visits to the East Coast for the purpose of disposing of the slaves and the ivory he had procured in the interior. On this occasion he had brought along with the marketable goods and chattels three Krupp shells which Mr. Deane had used in his luckless attempt to protect Stanley Falls in September 1886. The shells, says Mr. Stanley, were used by Tippoo-Tib 'to exhibit to his friends as the kind of missiles which the Belgians pelted his settlements with, and he was exceedingly wroth, and nourished a deep scheme of retaliation; it took me some time to quiet his spasms of resentment.'¹

Mr. Stanley's visit to King Leopold in January, before he started for Zanzibar, has been mentioned. 'While at Brussels,' he says, 'I was consulted by H.M. the King of the Belgians respecting Tippoo-Tib and his designs on the Congo State. I advised that he should be employed as an agent of the Congo State, it being a far cheaper and more humane method to disarm his hostility than the costly method of force, and I was entrusted with the mission to negotiate with him. With the help of Mr. F. Holmwood [the Acting Consul-General at Zanzibar], Tippoo-Tib was enlisted as the salaried governor of the Stanley Falls region, whose duty it would be to arrest the advance of the Arabs down the Congo, and to save its rich and populous banks from the devastation which I saw in 1883 had already commenced below the Falls.'²

There may be shrewdness, warranted by experience, in the proverbial policy of setting a thief to catch a thief; but when the thief to be caught is the thief appointed to office under the thief-catcher-in-chief, the experiment is more novel and more hazardous. Mr. Stanley, however, had no hesitation in making a compact with the great slave-raider and empire-maker whom he met at Zanzibar on February 25. The following is the text of the agreement signed by the two contracting parties and certified by Mr. Holmwood:—

'Mr. Henry Morton Stanley, on behalf of His Majesty the King of the Belgians and Sovereign of the Congo State,

---

[1] *In Darkest Africa*, vol. i. p. 69.
[2] *Parliamentary Papers*, C. 5906, p. 4.

appoints Hamed-bin Mohammed al Marjebi, Tippoo-Tib, to be Wali of the Independent State of the Congo at Stanley Falls district at a salary of 30*l.* per month, payable to his agent at Zanzibar, on the following conditions :—

'1. Tippoo-Tib is to hoist the flag of the Congo State at its station near Stanley Falls, and to maintain the authority of the State on the Congo and all its affluents at the said station downwards to the Bujine or Aruwimi River, and to prevent the tribes thereon, as well Arabs as others, from engaging in the slave trade.

'2. Tippoo-Tib is to receive a resident officer of the Congo State, who will act as his secretary in all his communications with the Administrator-General.

'3. Tippoo-Tib is to be at full liberty to carry on his legitimate private trade in any direction, and to send his caravans to and from any places he may desire.

'4. Tippoo-Tib shall nominate a *locum tenens*, to whom, in case of his temporary absence, his powers shall be delegated, and who, in the event of his death, shall become his successor in the Waliship; but His Majesty the King of the Belgians shall have the power of veto should there be any serious objection to Tippoo-Tib's nominee.

'5. This arrangement shall only be binding so long as Tippoo-Tib or his representative fulfils the conditions embodied in this agreement.'[1]

The significance of this second of the 'little commissions' settled by Mr. Stanley during his three days halt at Zanzibar must be clearly apprehended, as it affords a key to at least one of the stupendous blunders or perversions of the Emin Relief Expedition, and helps to explain others. Mr. Stanley says in the transcript from his diary :—

[1] *Parliamentary Papers,* C. 5601, p. 23.

'Tippoo-Tib is a much greater man to-day than he was in 1877, when he escorted my caravan preliminary to our descent down the Congo. He has invested his hard-earned fortune in guns and powder. Adventurous Arabs have flocked to his standard, until he is now an uncrowned king of the region between Stanley Falls and Tanganyika Lake, commanding many thousands of men inured to fighting and wild equatorial life. If I discovered hostile intentions, my idea was to give him a wide berth; for the ammunition I had to convey to Emin Pasha, if captured and employed by him, would endanger the existence of the infant State of the Congo and imperil all our hopes. Between Tippoo-Tib and Mwanga, king of Uganda, there was only a choice of the frying-pan and the fire. Tippoo-Tib was the Zubehr of the Congo Basin—just as formidable if made an enemy as the latter would have been at the head of his slaves. . . . Therefore, with due caution, I sounded Tippoo-Tib on the first day and found him fully prepared for any eventuality—to fight me or be employed by me. I chose the latter, and we proceeded to business.'[1]

It seems, then, that though Mr. Stanley had rejected the East Coast route to the Equatorial Province on the alleged ground that he could not face the resistance of Mwanga, the king of the little district of Uganda, he had equal cause in taking the Congo route to dread the opposition of Tippoo-Tib, the all-powerful despot in Central Africa and the usurper at Stanley Falls. But Mr. Stanley thought he could conciliate Tippoo-Tib by bribing him and recognising his usurpation, and he was the more, if not solely, inclined to take this course, because by doing so the signal failure of the Congo Free State to exercise any authority over the Stanley Falls district or anywhere to the east of Leopoldville would

[1] *In Darkest Africa*, vol. i. p. 63.

be ostensibly repaired. If Tippoo-Tib, who had not only taken possession of the larger half of the Congo State but also threatened nearly all the rest, could be bought over to nominal subjection, and induced to carry on his slave raiding and ivory stealing under a pretence of forbidding and preventing 'Arabs and others from engaging in the slave trade,' the *amour propre* of the Belgian Sovereign and officers of the Congo State might be humoured, and the Congo State might again pose before the world as a civilising and successful organisation. Moreover, the immediate business that Mr. Stanley had on hand, an expedition along and beyond the Congo in search of Emin Pasha, might be rendered possible. But if Mr. Stanley expected Tippoo-Tib to keep faith with him, he lacked on this occasion his usual shrewdness.

Nor was that the only bargain which with a light heart Mr. Stanley made with Tippoo-Tib. Before he left England the Emin Relief Committee had heard of the stores of ivory that had been collected in the Equatorial Province, and it had claimed that a fair proportion of this ivory, if it could be got hold of, should be used towards defraying the expenses of the Expedition, perhaps of yielding a profit on it. The Egyptian Government also claimed a share of the ivory; and, with somewhat more reason, as Emin had collected it in his capacity of Egyptian Governor. The joint claims had been recognised, and one of Mr. Stanley's 'little commissions' was to see to this business. Dr. Junker, he reports, had informed him when they met at Cairo that Emin had seventy-five tons of ivory, which, Mr. Stanley reckoned, at 8s. a pound would be worth 60,000l. He proceeds : ' Why not attempt the carriage of this ivory to the Congo? Accordingly, I wished to engage Tippoo-Tib and his people to assist me in conveying the ammunition to Emin Pasha, and on return to carry this ivory. After a good deal of bargaining I entered into a contract with him, by which he agreed to supply six hundred carriers at 6*l.* per loaded head—each round trip from Stanley Falls to Lake Albert and back. Thus, if each carrier carries seventy pounds weight of ivory, one round trip will bring to the fund 13,200*l.* net at Stanley Falls.'[1]

'This contract,' Mr. Stanley says, ' was entered into in presence of the British Consul-General ;' but, unfortunately, if it was put in writing at all, the text is not on record. But in order to clench it, as he thought, he agreed to give Tippoo-Tib and ninety-six of his wives and followers a free passage by sea from Zanzibar to the Congo, ' with board included,' and after that to convey them safely to Stanley Falls.[2]

By February 25 all was ready for the starting of what was still called the Emin Relief Expedition, though it is manifest that the relief of Emin Pasha was only one of its purposes, and that even this purpose had been considerably altered from its original shape.

The Emin Relief Committee was constituted, as Sir William Mackinnon informed Lord Iddesleigh on November 27, 1886, ' to organise and send out a private Expedition to open communications with and carry relief to Emin Bey.'[3] On that understanding the 10,000*l.* which the Egyptian Government had consented

---

[1] *In Darkest Africa*, vol. i. p. 64.   [2] *Ibid.* vol. i. p. 71.
[3] *Parliamentary Papers*, C. 5601, p. 9.

to spend on Dr. Junker's proposed Expedition was diverted to Mr. Stanley's Expedition. On that understanding some, at any rate, of the English admirers of Emin contributed to the fund raised by Sir William Mackinnon. There was at first no thought, or at any rate no mention, of forcibly withdrawing Emin from the scene of his heroic labours throughout more than ten years. But before long it was suggested that Emin should be encouraged, if he would, to avail himself of Mr. Stanley's help in transferring to safe quarters the non-combatant portion of his followers, and of even himself retiring to a more accessible place than Wadelai. On January 12, 1887, Sir Francis de Winton, the secretary of the Emin Relief Committee, adduced to Lord Salisbury as one of the advantages of the Congo route, 'that it offers far greater facilities for the withdrawal of the women and children at present with Emin Bey; it would also open up a sure and certain route for any further relief to Emin, and for his own ultimate retreat.'[1] Emin's withdrawal seemed only a remote contingency; and in an interview he had with Dr. Schweinfurth and Dr. Junker at Cairo on January 28, Mr. Stanley says, he told them that 'the relief of Emin Pasha is the object of the Expedition, the said relief consisting of ammunition in sufficient quantity to enable him to withdraw from his dangerous position in Central Africa in safety, or to hold his own, if he decides to do so, for such length of time as he may see fit.'[2]

But it is clear that by this time, or only a day or two later, it was resolved that Mr. Stanley should

---

[1] *Parliamentary Papers*, C. 5601, p. 11.
[2] *In Darkest Africa*, vol. i. p. 52.

endeavour to deport Emin, and that, if Emin chose to remain in the Equatorial Province, he should do so at his own risk, and without hope of further pay or succour from Egypt. On February 2, Nubar Pasha, writing to inform Emin of Mr. Stanley's approach, said :—

'The Expedition commanded by Mr. Stanley has been formed and organised in order to go to you with the provisions and stores, of which you must certainly be in want. Its object is to bring you, your officers, and soldiers, back to Egypt by the way which Mr. Stanley shall think most suitable. I have nothing to add to what I have just said of the objects of the Expedition. Only His Highness leaves you, your officers, your soldiers and others entirely free to stay where you are, or to make use of the help he sends for your return. But, of course, and this must be made clear to your officers, soldiers, or others, if some do not wish to return they are free to remain, but at their own risk and by their own desire, and that they cannot expect any other help from the Government. That is what I wish you to make clear to those who may wish to remain.'[1]

A similar letter was signed by the Khedive himself, and Mr. Stanley's entry in his diary on the same day may probably be regarded as an accurate summary of the situation :—

'We stand thus, then : Junker does not think Emin will abandon the province ; the English subscribers to the fund hope he will not, but express nothing—they leave it to Emin to decide ; the English Government would prefer that he would retire, as his province under present circumstances is almost inaccessible, and certainly he, so far removed, is a cause of anxiety. The Khedive sends the above order for Emin to accept of our escort, but says, "You may

---

[1] *Parliamentary Papers*, C. 5601, p. 15.

do as you please. If you decline our proffered aid you are not to expect further assistance from the Government." Nubar Pasha's letter conveys the wishes of the Egyptian Government, which are in accordance with those of the English Government as expressed by Sir Evelyn Baring.'[1]

Thus we can see to what extent the original purpose of the Emin Relief Expedition had been departed from before it left Zanzibar. The intention was no longer 'to open communications with and carry relief to Emin,' but to frighten him into retiring from the Equatorial Province and returning to Egypt, by a threat of complete abandonment if he refused to be 'relieved' in Mr. Stanley's way.

It is only reasonable to assume, however, that the 'relief' of Emin, of whatever sort, was but a subordinate purpose of the Emin Relief Expedition in the development it had reached in February 1887. Two other and weightier purposes have been revealed in some of the foregoing quotations.

One was the acquisition from the Sultan of Zanzibar, by the promoters of the Imperial British East Africa Company, of the great stretch of territory between the eastern coast and Lake Victoria Nyanza, an arrangement negotiated by Mr. Stanley while he was at Zanzibar, and to be strengthened by his expected victorious march across the country after he had 'rescued' Emin Pasha.

The other, yet weightier, was the conversion of Tippoo-Tib from a dangerous assailant into a salaried officer of the Congo Free State.

Yet another purpose of the Emin Relief Expedition,

[1] *In Darkest Africa*, vol. i. p. 58.

perhaps the weightiest of all with its leader, was the providing of a fresh opportunity to Mr. Stanley for exercising and exhibiting to all the world his talents as an explorer in Africa. Besides minor exploits, he had already, as he boasted, 'found Livingstone' in one Expedition, 'completed the work left unfinished by Livingstone' in another, and 'established the Congo Free State' in a third. He is scarcely to be blamed when the conduct of a fourth was offered to him, for so enlarging and altering the comparatively simple task of 'relieving Emin Pasha' as to make the business more ambitious and more imposing than anything he had yet accomplished.

Nor can we find fault with the comrades whom he selected, as he tells us, 'out of the hundreds of eager applicants for membership of his staff,' if, with or without very keen desire to be of service to Emin, they were actuated by other and various motives.

So eager were two of these volunteers, Mr. J. S. Jameson and Mr. Mounteney Jephson, to take part in the Expedition, that they paid 1,000*l.* apiece for the privilege.[1] Both went, as modern knights-errant, in search of adventures; but Mr. Jameson, besides being actuated, as he said, by a desire to 'do some good in this world, and make a name which was more than an idle one,'[2] had a laudable enthusiasm for natural history. He had already travelled in South Africa and elsewhere in search of birds, butterflies, and beetles, and he hoped to collect many new specimens in the Equatorial regions.

---

[1] To be strictly accurate, Mr. Jephson's 1,000*l.* was contributed by his friend the Countess de Noailles.

[2] *Story of the Rear-Column*, edited by Mrs. J. S. Jameson, p. 31

Three other members of the staff, Lieutenant W. G. Stairs, of the Royal Engineers, Captain R. H. Nelson, of Methuen's Horse, and Major E. M. Barttelot, of the 7th Fusiliers, were also in search of adventures. Among the rest, Mr. Rose Troup and Mr. Herbert Ward, who was attached to it at a later date, had previously been in the service of the Congo State, and were well acquainted with part of the country to be traversed. Surgeon Parke, engaged in Egypt, replaced Dr. Leslie, who had been invited to act as medical attendant on the Expedition, but had resigned on hearing the terms of the contract Mr. Stanley expected him to sign.[1] Mr. William Bonny, formerly of the Army Medical Department, was also engaged in a subordinate capacity.

[1] Dr. Leslie wrote: 'I could not sign the contract, which I thought unfair. I wished to insert after the agreement to publish nothing until six months after Mr. Stanley's official report was written, the words, "except in the case of my reputation being attacked." The committee would not hear of this; but the attacks made on all the members of the rear-guard show that the proviso was not an unnecessary one. I also objected to pledge myself to treat the sick according to his directions, which I thought the contract, as worded, implied.'—*Major Barttelot's Diaries and Letters*, p. 51.

CHAPTER III

ON THE WAY TO YAMBUYA

LEAVING Zanzibar on February 25, 1887, Mr. Stanley had with him on board the 'Madura,' besides Tippoo-Tib and his party, 605 Zanzibar carriers, 62 Soudanese soldiers, and 13 Somalis—these latter being, according to Mr. Jameson, ' picked men procured at Aden, armed with Winchester rifles, for Stanley's special guard—splendid fellows.'[1]

Mr. Stanley tells us that his object in obtaining the Soudanese was 'to enable them to speak for him to the Soudanese of Equatoria,' and ' to be pushed forward as living witnesses of his commission ' in the event of the Egyptians with Emin Pasha ' affecting to disbelieve firmans and the writings of Nubar.'[2] These Soudanese soldiers had been obtained for Mr. Stanley by Colonel Chermside. They were placed under the control of Major Barttelot, who wrote of them at starting: 'The men are recruited from what is known as the Black Battalion, from the remnant of Gordon's men who came down the Nile with us, and from the Mudir of Dongola's bashi-bazouks. They are at present a most lawless and undisciplined lot, but by the time we get to the Congo

---

[1] *Story of the Rear-Column*, p. 4.
[2] *In Darkest Africa*, vol. i. p. 68.

I hope to have them well in hand. . . . These Soudanese soldiers have been giving trouble. I think Chermside must have picked out the biggest scoundrels he could find.'[1]

The Zanzibaris had been selected for Mr. Stanley in anticipation of his arrival at Zanzibar, but were approved by him. Most, if not all, were slaves working out their freedom.[2] So large a number of actually free men were doubtless not procurable, and Mr. Stanley only did as he and others had done before in employing slave-labour. But had some of the subscribers to the Emin Relief Fund been aware that it was Mr. Stanley's intention to place himself, during the course of the Expedition, in the position of a slave-owner, they would probably have withheld their support or required that the project should be carried out in some way more consistent with English opposition to the system of slavery.

The great majority of the men taken by Mr. Stanley to the Congo were not only slaves hired by him from their owners, to whom all payment for their services was made, but, as very soon appeared, a very unmanageable gang of slaves. Some of the disgraceful conditions under which the Expedition started from Zanzibar, and which were continued and aggravated throughout, are here revealed by Mr. Stanley :—

'Two hours from Zanzibar, what is called a "shindy" took place between the Zanzibaris and Soudanese. For a

---

[1] *Diaries and Letters*, pp. 55, 56.

[2] Two months afterwards, when inspecting the men at Leopoldville, Mr. Stanley was, he says, 'of the opinion that only about 150 were free men, and that all the remainder were either slaves or convicts.'—*In Darkest Africa*, vol. i. p. 93.

short time it appeared as though we should have to return to Zanzibar with many dead and wounded. It rose from a struggle for room. The Soudanese had been located directly in the way of the Zanzibaris, who, being ten times more numerous, required breathing space. They were all professed Moslems, but no one thought of their religion as they seized upon firewood and pieces of planking to batter and bruise each other. The battle had raged some time before I heard of it. As I looked down the hatchway the sight was fearful—blood freely flowed down a score of faces, and ugly pieces of firewood flew about very lively. A command could not be heard in that uproar, and some of us joined in with shillelaghs, directing our attacks upon the noisiest. It required a mixture of persuasiveness and sharp knocks to reduce the fractious factions to order, especially with the Soudanese minority, who are huge fellows. . . . After we had wiped the blood and perspiration away I complimented the officers, especially Jephson, Nelson, and Bonny, for their share in the fray. They had behaved most gallantly. The result of the scrimmage is ten broken arms, fifteen serious gashes with spears on the face and head, and contusions on shoulders and backs not worth remark, and several abrasions of the lower limbs.'

Mr. Stanley adds approvingly :—

'There is a great deal in Mounteney Jephson, though he is supposed to be effeminate. He is actually fierce when roused, and his face becomes dangerously set and fixed. I noted him during the late battle aboard, and I came near crying out "Bravo, Jephson!" though I had my own stick, "big as a mast," as the Zanzibaris say, to wield. It was most gallant and plucky. He will be either made or marred if he is with this Expedition long enough.' [1]

The 'Madura,' with its strange cargo, reached Banana Point, at the mouth of the Congo, on March 18. There

[1] *In Darkest Africa*, vol. i. pp. 72, 73.

Mr. Stanley had expected to obtain the assistance of the Congo State which King Leopold had promised to his party in conveying it to the neighbourhood of Stanley Falls. As this was not forthcoming, he had to avail himself, for part of the way, of help offered by some Dutch and English traders, and, after that, to proceed by land to Leopoldville, which was reached on April 21.

The incidents of the five weeks' journey sufficiently demonstrated—though not perhaps to Mr. Stanley—the folly of selecting the Congo route to the Equatorial Province, and of trusting to the promise of assistance from the Congo State in traversing it. For some of the disasters that befell his unwieldy caravan of about eight hundred human beings Mr. Stanley is to be commiserated rather than blamed; but as, on the score of his large experience of travel in Central Africa, all the detailed arrangements of the Expedition had been assigned to and readily undertaken by him, he cannot be relieved from responsibility. It is clear, moreover, that if the difficulties which arose, even at this early stage of the work, were in part inevitable, they were greatly aggravated by Mr. Stanley's misconduct.

When the march began, the six hundred Zanzibaris were divided into companies, each committed to the care of one of the English officers, Mr. Stanley himself being in front at the head of a small party of picked Zanzibaris and his dozen Somalis. Major Barttelot was in charge of the Soudanese soldiers. Each officer was required to keep his division together, to see that none of the men deserted and that none of their loads were lost, and to account at night-time for the day's proceedings. 'The work we are doing is not fit for any white man,' Mr. Jameson wrote in his diary on March 29, 'but ought to be given to slave-drivers. It is all very nice for Mr. Stanley, who rides ahead straight on to the next camp, where we arrive hours afterwards, having done nothing all day but kick lazy carriers and put the loads on to the heads of those who choose to fling them down.' And on April 3: 'The work was truly sickening, as every twenty yards one had to stop to put a load on a man's head who had flung it down, and very likely give him a good dose of stick before he would go on. The work must greatly resemble slave-driving.'[1] 'I felt like a brute, flogging the men to get them on,' Major Barttelot wrote on the same April 3; and on a later date he said in a letter to his sister: 'I did not hit anybody (on the march) for a long time, but I found that Stanley did, right and left, and that it really was the only plan to get these Zanzibaris on. Stanley expected us to hit the men, though he always took their part when they complained. We have been nothing but slave-drivers since we started, and the trouble I have had to get the Soudanese along was something dreadful.'[2]

After he had been a fortnight on the road, Mr. Stanley deemed it necessary to adopt sterner measures for the management of his slave-caravan, and, instead of marching in advance with his selected party, and leaving his subordinates to do the required amount of flogging and kicking, to give them practical lessons in their duty. He says:—

[1] *Story of the Rear-Column*, pp. 14, 17.
[2] *Diaries and Letters*, pp. 79, 121.

'On reaching Mwembé, April 6, I was particularly struck with the increase of demoralisation in the caravan. So far, in order not to press the people, I had been very quiet, entrusting the labour of bringing the stragglers to the younger men, that they might be experienced in the troubles which beset Expeditions in Africa; but the necessity of enforcing discipline was particularly demonstrated on this march. The Zanzibaris had no sooner pitched the tents of their respective officers than they rushed like madmen among the neighbouring villages, and commenced to loot native property, in doing which one named Khamis bin Athman was shot dead by a plucky native. This fatal incident is one of those signal proofs that discipline is better than constant forbearance, and how soon even an army of licentious, insubordinate, and refractory men would be destroyed.'[1]

How Mr. Stanley 'enforced discipline,' when he took the work in hand, we learn from two of the young men whom he was making accustomed to 'the troubles which beset Expeditions in Africa.' Here are extracts from Mr. Jameson's and Major Barttelot's diaries for April 7 :—

'Marched to Vombo, quite the quickest march we have done, owing to a good level road, and Mr. Stanley doing rearguard with some of his Somalis himself. How he did lay his stick about the lazy ones, and the Somalis whacked away too! It was a sight for sore eyes to see the lame, the sick, the halt and the blind running with their loads as if they were feathers; and I was delighted to see some of my men catch it hot, after I had been told by Mr. Stanley himself not to strike them.'[2]

---

[1] *In Darkest Africa*, vol. i. p. 84.
[2] *Story of the Rear-Column*, p. 18.

'Stanley, as rearguard, got on A 1. He flogged loafers and they all kicked amazingly.'[1]

Mr. Stanley himself moralises, in two very comprehensive sentences, on the pleasures and advantages of his severity as shown in the quick march he made on April 7 :—

'There is nothing more agreeable than the feeling one possesses after a good journey briefly accomplished. We are assured of a good day's rest ; the remainder of the day is our own to read, to eat, to sleep, and be luxuriously inactive, and to think calmly of the morrow ; and there can scarcely be anything more disagreeable than to know that, though the journey is but a short one, yet relaxation of severity permits that cruel dawdling on the road in the suffocating high grass, or scorched by a blistering sun—the long line of carriers is crumpled up into perspiring fragments—water far when most needed ; not a shady tree near the road ; the loads robbed and scattered about over ten miles of road ; the carriers skulking among the reeds or cooling themselves in groves at a distance from the road; the officers in despair at the day's near close, and hungry and vexed, and a near prospect of some such troubles to recur again to-morrow and the day after. An unreflecting spectator hovering near our line of march might think we were unnecessarily cruel ; but the application of a few cuts to the confirmed stragglers secure eighteen hours' rest to about 800 people and their officers, save the goods from being robbed—for frequently these dawdlers lag purposely behind for such intentions—and the day ends happily for all, and the morrow's journey has no horrors for us.'[2]

Some 'unreflecting spectators' may find it difficult to regard with as much complacency as Mr. Stanley the

[1] *Diaries and Letters*, p. 80.
[2] *In Darkest Africa*, vol. i. p. 84.

picture he draws of his march to Stanley Pool. With
stick in hand, he drove forward his motley throng of
soldiers and carriers, securing a 'happy ending' for
each day by the ordinary slave-driver's devices, with
some startling additions thereto, and seeing 'no horror'
in the repetition of these devices during each 'morrow's
journey.'

On April 8 the Soudanese soldiers, who had eaten
in thirteen days all the rations supplied to them for
twenty, threatened to mutiny. The following is Major
Barttelot's account of the scene, written on the same
day :—

'One man stepped forward as spokesman, and said that,
unless they had rations given them, they would not go a
step further; that they had been brought there under false
pretences, and if they had known how he would treat them
they would never have come. This was interpreted by
Assad Farran. Stanley replied, "Don't come a step further;
go back ! But if you do, I will tell all the country round
to shoot you down, and I will chase you from hill to hill
with the Zanzibaris." Then, turning to Assad Farran, he
said, " And you will go with them, your lot is with them,"
implying more or less he held him responsible. Of course
Assad Farran demurred, and Stanley said, "I will drive you
out with the bayonet myself !" Then Assad spoke to
Stanley very fairly, and said he had nothing to do with the
Soudanese; that he had come to Mr. Stanley as interpreter
or servant, and as such he had been hired at Shepherd's
Hotel at Cairo. But Stanley only gave him the same
replies.

'Later on I told Stanley I was sorry the Soudanese had
caused him so much trouble. He said he blamed me for it.
I told him I was often away from them, working with the
rearguard. He said, "I never asked you to go on rear-

guard," and such like. He then said that my reputation would be blasted as a military officer if the Soudanese revolted and had to be shot down. I said, "As how?" He said it would be in every paper, and General Brackenbury would hear of it, and he had the ear of Wolseley. I replied, "Thank God, my reputation with Lord Wolseley does not rest with what General Brackenbury thought or said."'

In a letter to a friend about this incident Major Barttelot wrote:—

'Afterwards, turning to me, Stanley said it was in his power to ruin me in the service. I said to him that that was an empty threat, for it would take a great deal more than he could say to do that. He punished me afterwards by making me march by myself to Leopoldville with seventy men, who were noted for their laziness and incapacity for carrying loads, and my Soudanese; warning me, if I lost a single load, to look out.'[1]

There was perhaps some excuse for thus separating the Soudanese from the Zanzibaris, as there had all along been quarrelling and fighting between them; but there seems to have been none for punishing Major Barttelot by ordering him to take charge of the unruly gang and keep a day's march ahead of the others. As Mr. Jameson said of Barttelot, 'It looks strange on Mr. Stanley's part to send him by himself with the very worst and most rebellious lot in camp, who will not move a yard so long as they know that all the food is behind them.'[2]

On the following day Mr. Jameson also had experience, not for the first time, of Mr. Stanley's injustice. We read in his diary for April 10:—

[1] *Letters and Diaries*, pp. 81, 82.
[2] *Story of the Rear-Column*, p. 19.

'This morning Mr. Stanley placed me in a very false position with my men. Just as we were starting, I told him that one of my chiefs was very ill indeed, and that I did not think he could go on. He told me not to bring him any reports of the kind, that he would not listen to them, and that his orders were for all the sick to go on, and that I was to see that they did so. I only said "Very well, sir." I behaved very cruelly in making the man get up, amidst the murmurs of all the chiefs, and then driving him on. In a few yards he fell down and could not get up. Mr. Stanley, on passing, recognised him, and went up to see how he was. He called to Dr. Parke to come to him, and told him that as he was a good man we must not lose him ; gave him medicine then and left more with him, at the same time telling one of the officers of the State to look after him, get him into a hut, and do everything he could for him. Of course all the men now look upon me as a brute, and Mr. Stanley as a sort of guardian angel, although I was only carrying out his own orders.' [1]

There was a worse instance a week later. On April 18 Mr. Jameson wrote :—

'I found out that one of the ammunition-boxes carried by my company had been lost to-day, so I reported the matter to Mr. Stanley after sending back two chiefs all along the road to look for it. Mr. Stanley ordered the whole company to fall in, and then made each man take a load from the heap of loads brought in. He asked the chief who had received the loads in camp to recognise those of the men who had brought in theirs. He did not remember seeing one unfortunate man, so Mr. Stanley fixed upon him as the man who had lost the box, although he is really one of my best carriers, and swore he brought in his box, and showed Mr. Stanley the tree he cut down to keep the boxes

[1] *Story of the Rear-Column*, p. 20.

off the ground. Mr. Stanley then called the Somalis, and gave all my chiefs, with the exception of the one who had received the loads in camp, fifty cuts each with a stick, whilst they were held down on the ground. He then gave to the man whom he accused of having lost the box a hundred lashes, asking him several times during the beating where the box was—the man each time still swearing that *his* box was in camp. He then chained and padlocked the chiefs all together, and accused me of losing three boxes of ammunition (which I flatly denied), and told me that in '77 it would have been death, and if it happened again we must part. If this sort of thing is to go on, and he speaks to me again as he did to-day before the men, I should not be sorry if we did part, for I certainly will not keep my temper again.

'Afterwards I went to his tent and asked him to explain his statement that I had lost three boxes of ammunition; and this he utterly failed to do. He said, "You have three times reported to me boxes lost." I then told him that the last time was only two days ago, when Dr. Parke and I had explained the matter to him, and Parke had handed over to me the box missing from my loads; and the only other time I had reported a load lost I had also reported to him its recovery. If he goes on much more like this, I shall get sick of the whole thing. He has failed to find out the man who lost the box, and has degraded three of my chiefs, who were simply the best men I have ever seen.'[1]

A significant sentence must here be quoted from Major Barttelot's diary. On April 11 he wrote:—

'Parke told me that the Zanzibaris had informed Stanley that we, the Europeans, had opened the Fortnum & Mason boxes; so Parke, in answer to Stanley, said, "Yes," but the only person who had had any of the contents was himself,

---

[1] *Story of the Rear-Column*, p. 24.

and that he should advise him to put a little trust in his officers, who were, at any rate, gentlemen, and not accustomed to be accused of that sort of thing.'[1]

Mr. Stanley assures us that on the journey to Stanley Pool he was 'very patient—it was too early yet to manifest even the desire to be otherwise;' and he adds, 'Fortunately for me personally there were good officers with me who could relieve me from the necessity of coming into contact with wilful fellows like the sulky, obstinate Soudanese. I reserved for myself the *rôle* of mediator between exasperated whites and headstrong, undisciplined blacks.'[2] But the facts do not bear out his statements. It is clear that even before he reached Stanley Pool he had deservedly lost all the respect of his white colleagues, and had forced them to treat with systematic cruelty the black men under them, much increasing their difficulties and promoting lawlessness by his ungenerous disparagement of them in the presence of the blacks.

The tramp of the ill-managed slave-gang to Leopoldville, over 235 miles of ground, occupied just four weeks. Many deserted during that time, others died, or, too ill to carry their loads, even under the influence of the stick, were left to die on the way—according to the rule with slave-gangs. When he reached Leopoldville, Mr Stanley found that besides sixty-three absentees, 'about a hundred men were useless as soldiers or carriers,' and that 'the Zanzibaris were observed to be weakening rapidly.' 'They have been compelled,' he said, 'to live on stinted rations lately, and their habit of indulging in

---

[1] *Diaries and Letters*, p. 83.
[2] *In Darkest Africa*, vol. i. p. 85.

raw manioc is very injurious.' But as the rice doled out to them was insufficient, and as the country traversed was too barren and desolate to yield much other food, either by purchase or by theft, the poor drudges can hardly be blamed for 'plucking up the poisonous manioc tubers and making themselves wretchedly sick.'[1]

At Leopoldville Mr. Stanley found, or received soon after his arrival, a large quantity of stores, separately brought up by native carriers under the care of Mr. Rose Troup, to be added to those with his own caravan. He had expected that the Congo State steamers would be in readiness to transport the whole Expedition along the Upper Congo from Stanley Pool to Yambuya, a distance of about 1,050 miles. In this he was disappointed. As he reported :—

'The same disposition that we found at Banana Point to obstruct our advance, and to glory in our misfortunes, was strongly manifest at Stanley Pool. The steamers promised by King Leopold were not ready, and, even with the best goodwill of the Commandant, M. Leibrichts, only the "Stanley" steamer was available, after a certain amount of repairs. . . . There remained the "Peace" steamer of the Baptist Mission, and the "Henry Reed" steamer of the Livingstone Inland Mission. But the missionaries were loth to lend their steamers. Meantime, I had the dissatisfaction of learning that a body of armed men, nearly 800 strong, had been invited by the sovereign of a State to march through a territory which was utterly unable to support its own soldiers, and that they were encamped at the *entrepôt* of the Upper Congo without the prospect of being furnished with even one meal from the country itself.

[1] *In Darkest Africa*, vol. i. p. 89.

Fortunately the stores of rice that I had caused to be sent up would suffice for nearly five days to provision the people, but the more we knew of the strange poverty of the country only deepened our anxiety.'[1]

His condition being desperate, Mr. Stanley considered himself justified in resorting to desperate measures to improve it.

'Various verbal and written messages passed between us and the missionaries respecting the situation, but I found that the more I pleaded the more the prospect darkened. As our necessities were so urgent, and immediate departure from the famine-stricken region was imperative if we were to be freed from the scandal of seeing these armed men, maddened by hunger, helping themselves, I compelled the Livingstone Inland Mission to sign a charter, and the Baptist Mission, probably fearing a similar high-handed measure, voluntarily offered the " Peace," by which means and by lighters which they towed we were enabled to advance up the Upper Congo.'[2]

It was fortunate that this high-handed arrangement was possible. The seizure of the 'Peace' and 'Henry Reed' was necessary to save the people from starvation; but, as Mr. Troup says, 'it should not be forgotten that before his arrival at Leopoldville Mr. Stanley knew the exact situation of affairs, and after his long experience we must credit him with the ability to foresee exactly what the consequences would be.'[3]

[1] *Parliamentary Papers*, C. 5906, pp. 4, 5.
[2] *Ibid.* p. 5. Before leaving England Mr. Stanley had sought permission from Mr. Robert Arthington, of Leeds, the donor of the 'Peace,' to make use of it; but his request had been refused.—*In Darkest Africa*, vol. i. p. 47.
[3] *With Stanley's Rear-Column*, p. 87.

Leaving Mr. Troup at Leopoldville to await the return of the 'Stanley,' and to take on in it the bulk of the stores and as many of the men as there was not room for in the first journey,' Mr. Stanley started on May 1 with about 500 of his followers, besides Tippoo-Tib's party. The next six weeks appear to have passed very pleasantly for him. 'Seated in an easy-chair,' he says, he 'forgot the lapse of time,' as he enjoyed 'delightful views of perfectly calm waters and vivid green forests,' and much else which 'will remain longer in his mind than the stormy aspects which disturbed the exquisite repose of nature almost every afternoon.'[1] Those 'aspects' included troubles with members of his company as well as the periodical thunder-storms.

Of the troubles we hear more from Mr. Stanley's colleagues than from himself. They were mainly caused by the necessity of obtaining food, which could only be done by buying or stealing from the natives in the villages by the river-side. 'The aborigines,' according to Mr. Stanley, 'were modest in their expectations, and in many instances they gave goats, fowls and eggs, bananas and plantains, and were content with "chits" on Mr. John Rose Troup, who would follow us later.'[2] Mr. Jameson's account is different. 'The natives are a bad lot,' he wrote on May 15, 'and I believe we will have to fight for food for the men by looting villages.'[3]

Some fighting occurred on the same day. Mr. Jameson proceeds :—

'We made fast to the shore at a village about twelve

[1] *In Darkest Africa*, vol. i. pp. 97, 98.   [2] *Ibid.* p. 99.
[3] *Story of the Rear-Column*, p. 43.

miles above Bolobo, and when Stairs and Nelson landed with the axe-men it seems the natives did not want to let them go through the village. Some of the men ran back yelling out that the natives were coming, and to bring all the guns. Barttelot thought they were being attacked, so he landed all the Soudanese and a box of ammunition, but on getting up into the village not a native was to be seen; they had all run away. When the Soudanese returned to the shore they made a rush across a small stream to the village on the opposite side, followed by the Zanzibaris, when an awful scene of loot commenced. They seized goats, fowls, bananas, manioc, spears, and everything that they could lay their hands on. I saw one man with an enormous wooden stool which he could not possibly have taken with him on the steamer, and I caught a Somali red-handed with an immense bundle of manioc and a spear. I smote him rather hard and he dropped the lot. The spear I attached to my person.'[1]

The sequel to that story is dated May 20:—

'This morning, I am sorry to say that the most disgraceful row I have ever heard of happened between Mr. Stanley and Jephson and Stairs. It appears that early this morning a number of the men and chiefs went to Mr. Stanley, and complained that the officers had flung away their rations for one day. Mr. Stanley sent for Stairs. The men swore they had bought the food from the natives last Sunday at the village they looted (for description of how they *bought* it, see diary of that day, May 15). Stairs told Mr. Stanley this, assuring him that only stolen stuff was taken away from them, and sent for Jephson, who gave the same testimony. It is still quite evident that Mr. Stanley takes the word of the Zanzibaris on every occasion before that of the white men, and when he saw that he had hold of rather the wrong end of the stick,

[1] *Story of the Rear-Column*, p. 44.

he attacked them about their tyranny to the men. He attacked them in a frantic state, stamping up and down the deck of the "Peace." He called Jephson all sorts of names: a "G—d d—n son of a sea-cook." "You d——d ass, you're tired of me, of the Expedition, and of my men. Go into the bush, get, I've done with you. And you, too, Lieutenant Stairs, you and I will part to-day; you're tired of me, sir, I can see. Get away into the bush." Then he turned round to the men (about 150) sitting down, and spoke Swahili, to the effect that the men were to obey us no more, and that if Lieutenant Stairs or Jephson issued any orders to them, or dared to lift a hand, they were to tie them up to trees. He had already told Stairs that he had only to lift his hand for the men to throw him into the sea. He lastly offered to fight Jephson: "If you want to fight, G—d d—n you, I'll give you a bellyful. If I were only where you are, I'd go for you. It's lucky for you I am where I am." Mr. Stanley was on the deck of the "Peace," Jephson on shore. All this was said before the missionaries, Tippoo-Tib, and everyone. As for Stairs or Jephson being tired of the Expedition, no men could work harder or have their hearts more in it. I should think a repetition of this kind of thing would make them both pretty sick of Mr. Stanley and the Expedition. He also called Jephson a "G—d d——d impudent puppy." Barttelot next interviewed him; and he told him that he was very sorry for Stairs, but had made up his mind they should stay where they were—that there was evidently a compact among us against him. Barttelot assured him that there was nothing of the kind. Stairs next went to him, and after a long interview it ended in Mr. Stanley taking him back, and telling him that he had given orders to the chiefs to obey him as before. Imagine this being necessary, simply from what he had himself said to them! Jephson went last, and the interview ended by Mr. Stanley apologising for the language he had used, and taking him back also. I had no idea until to-day what an extremely dangerous man Stanley was. Could there be anything more inciting to mutiny than what he had told the Zanzibaris? He forgets one thing, however: that if they dared to lift a hand to one of us there would be a terrible lot of them shot, which would rather weaken his Expedition. It is a curious fact, when one thinks over it, that the very men who complained to Mr. Stanley ought, by his own orders, issued when we left the Pool, to have been severely flogged.'[1]

Major Barttelot confirms and supplements this narrative:—

'I was astonished when Stairs and Jephson returned and told me about it, especially in Stairs' case, for no kinder officer to the men, or more zealous or hard-working officer, is there in the Expedition, besides being most efficient and capable. The missionaries, two of them, who heard the disturbance, and the captain and engineer of the "Peace," never heard such language or witnessed such a disgraceful scene before. I believe this is Stanley's method of carrying on in Central Africa, but I had judged him pretty well before, and was not surprised so much at his conduct. However, I gave him time to cool down, shaving in the meanwhile, and then went over to see him. We were lying 200 yards up-stream. On the way I met Parke, who told me that Stanley had called him on to the "Peace," and opined that we were talking about him; that it was apparent to him that we had formed a compact against him, and were tired of the Expedition, and only made a row to get sent back. Parke assured him of our loyalty and earnest wishes to carry on the work. I then saw Stanley, and told him I was sorry for what had happened, asking to know his wishes concerning Jephson and Stairs—whether they were really dismissed or not. He said they were.

[1] *Story of the Rear-Column*, p. 47.

Harped back on his old idea of the compact. I assured him to the contrary. He said he could carry on the Expedition without any of us. I asked him whether I was to tell Jephson and Stairs that his decision was irrevocable. He hesitated, and then said, "As regards myself it is." By that alone I knew he was blustering. I went away, and Jephson and Stairs came over, at my advice, and saw him, and squared it. It is a baddish look-out, for of course the seeds of mutiny have been sown against us, and may at any moment crop up.'[1]

Though he occasionally used strong language to them, Mr. Stanley was on better terms with Mr. Jephson, Lieutenant Stairs, and some others, than with Major Barttelot and Mr. Jameson. On his way up the Congo he arranged, if he had not long before decided, that at some convenient halting-place he would leave Barttelot in charge of the sick and worthless members of his party, with orders to await the arrival of Mr. Troup's cargo of stores, and to follow in due course with the help of the 600 carriers promised by Tippoo-Tib, himself hurrying on towards Wadelai with a picked body of men and so much of the stores as they could easily carry. 'His object,' Major Barttelot wrote on May 5, on this project being notified to him, 'is personal dislike to me and hatred of the Soudanese.'[2] Bolobo was at first thought of, and Mr. Stanley did leave there 125 men, 'who appeared weakest in body,' he said, ' to fatten up on the bananas and excellent bread and fish that were easily procurable.'[3] But this party was entrusted to the care of Messrs. Ward and Bonny, and Major Barttelot was taken on to

[1] *Diaries and Letters*, p. 97.   [2] *Ibid.* p. 91.
[3] *In Darkest Africa*, vol. i. p. 103.

Yambuya, where it was settled that he was to have charge of the 'entrenched camp' there to be set up, with Mr. Jameson as second in command.

Before reaching Yambuya, when the Expedition had gone as far as Bangala, a little to the east of the junction of the Aruwimi with the Congo, on May 30, Major Barttelot was told off to escort Tippoo-Tib to Stanley Falls. An episode in this mission must be taken account of, as it illustrates the state of affairs in the district shortly before Barttelot was left at Yambuya, under orders to remain on friendly terms both with Tippoo-Tib's Arabs and with the natives, and also to keep the peace between his Zanzibari and Soudanese followers and these Arabs and natives. On June 10 Tippoo-Tib wished to halt at the village of Mbunga in order to trade with the inhabitants. This was done after the villagers had consented and 'peace brotherhood' had been made with their chief. Major Barttelot proceeds :—

'All went well for an hour, and they were buying away. I was on shore, walking by myself, unarmed, towards the southern end of the village—I had already been to the other end—when suddenly I heard loud vociferations in front of me and voices raised as in anger. I hurried on to see, but before I could get there about twenty of Tippoo's men rushed past me, and two were wounded. I then met three of the Soudanese, who forced me to come back. All this while the natives were passing us by dozens, all shouting and flourishing their spears and knives; they never offered to touch me, though unarmed; in fact, they ran into the long grass on either side of the road to avoid me. About 200 yards from the ship I found one of Tippoo's men lying in the road stabbed in the back by a spear. We carried him on board, where I found Tippoo had six men and one woman wounded, and a Zanzibari of the ship's crew, Asani. I fell my men in, and went to the northern end of the village to look for the natives, Tippoo going to the southern, but they had all disappeared into the bush. So we burnt the southern and central part of the village. . . . About 4 P.M. we passed another village, where they were assembling, and Tippoo-Tib wished to put in, but I would not. He ordered my men to fire, but as Stanley told me on no account to have unnecessary rows with the villagers, I ordered them not to fire. This caused an estrangement between Tippoo-Tib and myself, who said, as I had refused to aid him, he would do nothing more for the Expedition. I explained to him how matters were, and that we had already punished one village, that I could not disobey Mr. Stanley's orders, and that my men could only take orders from me. He agreed to this, but was still angry with Stanley, and said he should refer it to him.'[1]

After conveying Tippoo-Tib to Stanley Falls, Major Barttelot steamed round to Yambuya, where he arrived on June 22, Mr. Stanley and the rest of his party having preceded him by a week. In the meantime Mr. Stanley had done some trading and quarrelling with the natives on his own account. A few of the villagers were hospitable. Others resented his approach—and not without reason, as the 'Stanley' was well known to them as a bearer of white men and Zanzibaris nearly as ready as Tippoo-Tib and the Arabs to attack them and burn their homesteads. 'They are anything but friendly,' Mr. Jameson wrote on June 11, 'as at nearly every village they yelled and shouted at us, shaking their spears and shields, and making signs of cutting

[1] *Diaries and Letters*, p. 104.

our throats, heaping all sorts of insults upon us. It is a bad look out for our chances of trading for food at the entrenched camp.' On June 14, however, some natives timidly consented to have dealings with the strangers. 'Just before we started,' according to Mr. Jameson, 'some of Mr. Stanley's company set fire to the huts—a most uncalled-for piece of devilment, and a thing to be regretted, as it is more likely to set the natives against us than anything.'[1]

Such were the conditions under which Mr. Stanley captured Yambuya, on the south side of the Aruwimi, with the intention of establishing there a camp for his rear-column. He had visited this place in 1883, as the 'founder' of the Congo Free State, and had then, as he says, 'attempted to conciliate the natives without any permanent result.' He now resolved to occupy it, 'if not with the natives' goodwill by fair purchase of the privilege, then by force.'[2] It is so far satisfactory that the force he soon thought proper to use was not attended with bloodshed. The natives, with whom he had a palaver on board the 'Peace,' protested against his landing amongst them. 'Camp on the opposite side if you will,' he reports that they said through their interpreter. 'We will bring you whatever we have to sell; but, if we permit you to land here, our village will become the common resort of the Arab slavers.' To this reasonable plea Mr. Stanley paid no attention. As he informed Sir William Mackinnon on June 19, in a letter which gives a different account from 'In Darkest Africa,' but one presumably more accurate :—

[1] *Story of the Rear-Column*, pp. 64–67.
[2] *In Darkest Africa*, vol. i. p. 109.

'We argued that if we were with them they need have no fear of the marauders; but we wasted our breath. We had been nearly two hours at this work of negotiating, and the natives, being addicted to palavers, would not have minded very much had the palavers lasted a week. We therefore signalled to the "Stanley" to appear with the troops. A few minutes later, at a second signal, both steamers set up a hideous steam whistling, under the protection of which the troops disembarked, and in a few seconds we were in possession of an empty village. There was no occasion to fire a shot, for the natives had disappeared as completely as the vapour of the steam whistling had dissolved. We have commenced the construction of a proper encampment. . . . We have to send out scouting parties in every direction to spy out the land, to discover the fields for future forage, if the natives should absolutely refuse to return and resume their old villages and possessions.' [1]

That successful trick was gone through in the early morning of June 16. When Mr. Stanley's men landed, as Mr. Jameson reported, 'not a native was to be seen, and the whole village was occupied in perfect peace.' 'We put up our tents,' he added, ' and destroyed the huts which were not required for our men.' [2] The natives established themselves on the other side of the Aruwimi, and Mr. Stanley endeavoured to open up trade with them, and with others in the neighbourhood, on what he considered to be generous terms. ' Several captures were made in the woods,' he says, ' and after being shown everything the natives were supplied with handfuls of beads, to convey the assurance that no fear

[1] *With Stanley's Rear-Column*, by J. Rose Troup, p. 136.
[2] *Story of the Rear-Column*, p. 68.

ought to be entertained of us and no harm done to them.'[1] Considering how they had been expelled from their village, the Yambuya people appear to have been very tolerant of the aggressors. 'Some natives,' Mr. Jameson wrote on the 21st, 'came into camp to have a palaver with Mr. Stanley. They proposed that we should send five Zanzibaris with them to the other side of the river to show confidence and make palaver. Stanley said no, but that they must send two goats and ten fowls to us, and then palaver.'[2]

Major Barttelot having arrived at Stanley Falls on the 22nd, and it having been finally decided that he should remain at Yambuya until he could follow with the rear-column, 'blood brotherhood' between him and the native chief was made on the 26th. 'Let us hope that it will induce them to bring us something to eat,' was Mr. Jameson's comment, and he added : 'Here are Major Barttelot and myself left absolutely without one atom of meat, tinned or fresh, for several months, and no *visible* means of obtaining any, for the natives have brought in nothing, and have removed everything from all the villages within reach of this camp. There is not a pound of game meat, either bird or animal, in the country round.'[3]

Two days later Mr. Stanley started on his journey to the Albert Nyanza, taking with him 383 picked men, the healthiest and trustiest, with Lieutenant Stairs, Captain Nelson, Mr. Jephson, and Dr. Parke—

---

[1] *In Darkest Africa*, vol. i. p. 112.
[2] *Story of the Rear-Column*, p. 73.
[3] *Ibid.* pp. 75, 76.

the only trained medical man in the Expedition; and leaving Major Barttelot and Mr. Jameson to hold the 'entrenched camp' with the 125 Zanzibaris and Soudanese who had been rejected as sickly and incompetent.

CHAPTER IV

SOME OF MR. STANLEY'S WANDERINGS

WHEN, in November 1886, Mr. Stanley offered to relieve Emin Pasha, and recommended the Congo route as 'the easiest and most feasible,' he declared that 'by this route Emin can be reached safely by the middle of June 1887, and Emin as well as the Relief Expedition could reach the sea by the middle of December 1887.'[1] On the eve of starting from Zanzibar, in February 1887, having modified his estimate, he wrote to inform Emin that he expected to be at Yambuya by June 18, and after that to have a fifty days' march to Kavalli's country, near the Albert Nyanza, whither he asked Emin to send word, 'informing me of your whereabouts.'[2] That is, his second promise was to 'relieve' Emin before the middle of August 1887. In spite of unlooked-for obstacles he was at Yambuya within the appointed limit of time; but it was not till the middle of December that he arrived at the Albert Nyanza, and only in the following April that he began to take steps for discovering Emin's 'whereabouts.'

His occupations during these nine and a half months and the four months following must now be briefly

---

[1] *Parliamentary Papers*, C. 5601, p. 7.
[2] *In Darkest Africa*, vol. i. p. 63.

reviewed. In doing that, however, we have to depend almost exclusively on such information as Mr. Stanley has himself furnished. There are no detailed reports from his colleagues which can be used in correcting or supplementing his sensational and disjointed confessions.

Leaving Yambuya on the morning of June 28, 1887, with an advance guard of fifty men bearing bill-hooks and axes as well as rifles, and with four companies of armed carriers, one under each of his English officers, making a party of nearly 400 in all, Mr. Stanley quickly entered the great forest which he was to spend five months in traversing; and when he was but four miles distant from Yambuya clear indication was given of the method of procedure which he deemed incumbent upon him. On the Aruwimi, along whose southern bank his pioneers were cutting a path, he saw a fleet of canoes. 'There was much movement and stir,' he says, 'owing, of course, to the alarm that the Yambuyas had communicated to their neighbours. . . . About a hundred canoes formed in the stream crowded with native warriors, and followed the movements of the column as it appeared and disappeared in the light and into the shadows, jeering, mocking, and teasing.' The 'alarm' was surely reasonable, as Mr. Stanley had a fortnight before ruthlessly expelled the Yambuya villagers from their homes. But he considered it foolish and strange; and when he advanced further and found that some 300 natives were not only preparing to defend their village of Yankonde, with drawn bows in their hands, but had actually planted sharp skewers on the road to it, in order to hamper his approach, he felt that he had indeed good cause to be indignant at 'the craft of these pure pagans,' and to fiercely resent it.

'Forming two lines of twelve men across the road, the first line was ordered to pick out the skewers, the second line was ordered to cover the workers with their weapons, and at the first arrow shower to fire. A dozen scouts were sent on either flank of the road to make their way into the village through the woods. We had scarcely advanced twenty yards along the cleared way before volumes of smoke broke out of the town, and a little cloud of arrows came towards us, but falling short. A volley was returned, the skewers were fast being picked out, and an advance was steadily made until we reached the village at the same time that the scouts rushed out of the underwood, and as all the pioneers were pushed forward the firing was pretty lively, under cover of which the caravan passed through the burning town to a village at its eastern extremity, as yet unfired. Along the river the firing was more deadly. . . . Very many, I fear, paid the penalty of the foolish challenge. The blame is undoubtedly due to the Yambuyas, who must have invented fables of the most astounding character to cause their neighbours to attempt stopping a force of nearly four hundred rifles.'[1]

Mr. Stanley takes no 'blame' to himself for this wanton slaughtering and village-burning. But his violence appears to have answered its purpose. The report of it going before him, he was able to march on for some time without much further resistance being offered, or any reason being found for fresh massacres. The natives dispersed as soon as they heard of his coming. His shoeless Zanzibaris had some trouble in avoiding the poisoned skewers with which 'the main

[1] *In Darkest Africa*, vol. i. pp. 136–138.

approaches to the many villages were studded.' But for three weeks he had comparatively safe travelling. Thus he reports that, on July 5, ' of course Bukanda had been abandoned long before we reached it, the village of cone huts was at our disposal, the field of manioc also;' that from seven villages at Gwengweré, on the 10th, ' all the population had fled, probably to the opposite main, or to the islands in mid-river, and every portable article was carried away except the usual wreckage;' and that, on the 11th, ' as we were disappearing from view of Gwengweré the population was seen skurrying from the right bank and islands back to their homes, which they had temporarily vacated for our convenience; it seemed to me to be an excellent arrangement; it saved trouble of speech, exerted possibly in useless efforts for peace and tedious chaffer.'[1]

So the narrative goes on, with occasional notes of kindlier intercourse where the natives were bold enough to face their visitors and meekly trade with them. At Mupé, for instance, on July 22, ' trifles, such as empty sardine boxes, jam and milk cans and cartridge cases, were easily barterable for sugar-cane, Indian corn and tobacco.' When Mr. Stanley deemed it convenient to regard the natives as human beings, they were for the most part friendly, and he was heralded by reports of his good as well as of his bad deeds. Thus, at My-yui, on July 29, ' It was not long before we struck acquaintance with this tribe. We quickly recognised a disposition on the part of the aborigines to be sociable. A good report of our doings had preceded us. Trade commenced very pleasantly.' In this case, however,

[1] *In Darkest Africa*, pp. 139, 145, 147, 148.

unpleasantness soon arose. The people objected to sell their wares on the terms offered, and as Mr. Stanley's men were 'ravenously hungry,' some of them dared to barter their ammunition to the natives for food. Thereupon, says Mr. Stanley, 'the natives were driven away; one of the chief's principal slaves was lifted out of his canoe by a gigantic Zanzibari, and word was sent to the natives that if there were no fair sales of food made as on the first day, the prisoner would be taken away and we should cross over and help ourselves.' That threat was acted on next day. 'We embarked at dawn on the 31st with two full companies, entered My-yui, and despatched the foragers. By 3 P.M. there was food enough in the camp for ten days.' But the stolen provision for ten days seems to have been exhausted in one. On August 4 Mr. Stanley complained that 'the results of three days' foraging' were only '250 pounds of Indian corn, eighteen goats, and as many fowls, besides a few branches of plantains.' 'A number of villages and settlements were searched, but the natives do not appear to possess a sufficiency of food. In such a region there were no inducements to stay.'[1]

Having plunged into the forest with nearly 400 hungry followers, for whom food had to be procured in some way, Mr. Stanley, of course, felt himself constrained to despoil and persecute the natives whenever they would not or could not supply what he wanted in exchange for the brass rods and beads he offered. He appears to have been at all times ready to purchase instead of to steal, provided the people were willing to sell to him on his own terms; but any resistance was

[1] *In Darkest Africa*, pp. 155, 161, 162, 166.

promptly dealt with by the Remington and Winchester rifles of his marauding host, or by the Maxim gun which he had brought from England, and never failed to use on the smallest provocation. That the natives should attempt to defend themselves, or in any way retaliate, seemed to him, if not a monstrous crime, at any rate the excess of folly.

He condemned his own followers as severely whenever they offended him. He says in one place :—

'The Zanzibaris persisted in exhibiting an indifference to danger absolutely startling, not from bravery, or from ignorance of fear, but from an utter incapacity to remember that danger existed, and from a stupid unconsciousness as to how it affected them. Animals are indebted to instinct as a constant monitor against danger, but these men appeared to possess neither instinct nor reason, neither perception nor memory. Their heads were uncommonly empty. The most urgent entreaties to beware of hidden foes, and the most dreadful threats of punishment, failed to impress on their minds the necessity they were under of being prudent, wary, and alert to avoid the skewers in the path, the lurking cannibal behind the plantain-stalk, the cunning foe lying under a log, or behind a buttress, and the sunken pit, with its pointed pales at the bottom. When the danger fronted them it found them all unprepared. A sudden shower of arrows sent them howling abjectly out of reach or under shelter ; and if the arrows were only followed by a resolute advance, resistance, by reason of excess of terror, would be impossible. . . . With an astounding confidence, they scattered along the road, and stretched the line of the column to three miles in length, but at sight of natives all sense was lost save that of cowardly fear. Out of 370 men at this time in the camp there were clearly 250 of this description, to whom rifles were of no use save as a clumsy, weighty club, which they would part with for a few ears of corn, or would willingly exchange for a light walking-staff if they dared.'[1]

With all his experience of Zanzibari carriers, during three earlier Expeditions in Central Africa, Mr. Stanley should not have been surprised by the demonstrations of their unfitness for the crusade on which he now employed them. And foolhardiness and cowardice were not the only offences of which he had to complain. Though the men who accompanied him in his forward march were chosen as the sturdiest and trustiest of the whole Expedition, many of them dared to fall ill and die, others to desert, and all to quarrel and fight with one another, and to steal from their masters as well as from the yet more barbarous people through whose countries they passed. The numberless floggings he administered were of no avail in making them honest. On September 19, after he had travelled about 380 miles in twelve weeks, and had lost sixty-two men by death and desertion, Mr. Stanley considered that unless he adopted 'the strongest measures' with what was left of his party, they would 'in a short time be compelled to retrace their steps, and all the lives and bitter agonies of the march would have been expended in vain.' Accordingly he extemporised a court-martial on three Zanzibaris who had 'absconded with their rifles.' He thus describes the proceedings :—

'In the morning "all hands" were mustered, and an address was delivered to the men in fitting words, to which all assented; and all agreed that we endeavoured our

[1] *In Darkest Africa*, vol. i. p. 176.

utmost to do our duty, that we had all borne much, but that the people on this occasion appeared to be all slaves, and possessed no moral sense whatever. They readily conceded that if natives attempted to steal our rifles, which were "our souls," we should be justified in shooting them dead, and that if men, paid for their labour, protected and treated kindly, as they were, attempted to cut our throats in the night, they were equally liable to be shot.

'"Well, then," said I, "what are these doing but taking our arms, and running away with our means of defence? You say that you would shoot natives, if they stood in your way preventing your progress onward or retreat backward. What are these doing? For if you have no rifles left, or ammunition, can you march either forward or backward?"

'"No," they admitted.

'"Very well, then, you have condemned them to death. One shall die to-day, another to-morrow, and another the next day; and from this day forward every thief and deserter who leaves his duty and imperils his comrades' lives shall die."

'The culprits were then questioned as to who they were. One replied that he was the slave of Farjalla-bill Ali, a headman in No. 1 Company; another that he was the slave of a Banyan in Zanzibar, and the third that he was the slave of an artisan at work in Unyanyembé.

'Lots were cast, and he who chose the shortest paper of three slips was the one to die first. The lot fell on the slave of Farjalla, who was then present. The rope was heaved over a stout branch. Forty men at the word of command laid hold of the rope, and a noose was cast round the prisoner's neck.

'"Have you anything to say before the word is given?"

'He replied with a shake of the head. The signal was given, and the man was hoisted up. Before the last struggles were over the Expedition had filed out of the camp.'[1]

The two other culprits were forgiven; and only twice afterwards did Mr. Stanley deem it necessary to kill any of his followers in cold blood.

The Expedition had now entered a region frequented by Arab or Manyuema slave-raiders, who had nearly exterminated the native population and exhausted the scanty food supplies. The Zanzibaris either fraternised with these marauders or were robbed and ill-treated by them. As he proceeded on his journey Mr. Stanley's troubles increased. On September 26, 'the people were so reduced by hunger, that over a third could do no more than crawl.' He was himself 'reduced to two bananas on this day from morning to night,' and 'some of our Zanzibaris had found nothing to subsist on for two entire days.' Luckily they captured a woman who guided them on the 27th to a plantain field, where they collected a store which, 'distributed impartially, ought to have served them for from six to eight days, but several sat up all night to eat.'[2]

Worse followed, with intervals of rest and refreshment for those who had strength to enjoy them, until December 2, when Mr. Stanley emerged from the forest with 173 of his followers. In September he had left fifty-six of his sick men at the station of Ugarrowwa, one of Tippoo-Tib's tributary slave-raiders, at the head of a company of Manyuema who made their head-quarters on the Aruwimi. These sick men Ugarrowwa had promised to take care of; 'but,' says Mr. Stanley, 'I

---

[1] *In Darkest Africa*, vol. i. p. 202.
[2] *Ibid.* pp. 207, 208.

G

doubted greatly whether he would trouble his head about any of them.' Thirty-three others he had left in October with Kilonga-longa, another Manyuema slave-raider. 'It was doubtful whether they were any better off in this Moslem settlement than in the uninhabited forest. Yet we had no other option, the ulcers were most rabid, a slight wound or a pimple in the foot or leg would develop in three or four days to the most ghastly sores, several inches in diameter, and penetrating to the bone. It was a terrible sight, and this ulcerous disease raged like an epidemic. Other diseases were rare, but next in order of importance was anæmia, engendered by poor diet or semi-starvation.'[1]

Except when he turned aside to visit the Manyuema settlements, or surprised some dwarfs in their concealed villages, Mr. Stanley met with very few human beings during the second half of his journey through the great forest; and the people of the settlements were too numerous for him to threaten or attack with prudence. So outnumbered was his party, and his Zanzibaris were such 'gaunt and craven wretches,' that on at least one occasion he was obliged to let them be 'scourged and speared' without more than a mild protest.[2] But he resumed his old policy as soon as he was again in open country. The first bunch of green grass seen by him on the skirts of the forest, he says, 'was hailed with devout raptures, as Noah and his family may have hailed the kindly dove with the olive-branch.'[3] He bore no olive-branch to the unfortunate savages through whose homes he marched on the rest of his

[1] *Parliamentary Papers*, C. 5906, p. 6.
[2] *In Darkest Africa*, vol. i. p. 284. [3] *Ibid.* p. 272.

way to the Albert Nyanza. More wanton cruelty seems rarely to have been shown by him during all his travels in Central Africa than he records with proud satisfaction concerning this march of fifty miles.

He halted on December 2 near the village of Indesura, to afford a little rest to the remaining half of his party; but no native was seen until, 'as a man went to draw water from the stream close by, an ancient crone stepped out of the bush.' Thereupon, 'the man dropped his water-pot and seized her.' 'She, being vigorous and obstinate, like most of her sex just previous to dotage, made a vigorous defence for her liberty. But the man possessed superior strength and craft, and hauled her into camp.' Instead of reproving the perpetrator of this outrage, Mr. Stanley, 'by dint of smiles and coaxing,' extracted from the captive some useful information about the district and its inhabitants, whom, with characteristic misuse of words, he calls 'aggressors.' 'Woe betide the native aggressor we may meet, however powerful he may be,' Mr. Stanley says, in reference to his exploits at this time, and with exultations at the revived 'spirit' of his followers. 'With such a spirit the men will fling themselves like wolves on sheep.'

He tells us that he did mildly reprove four of his scouts, who on the following day 'captured twenty-five goats by a ruse;' but he saw nothing wrong in other and more extensive thefts. 'A happier community of men did not exist on the face of the round earth than those who rejoiced in the camp of Indesura,' he says. 'Their pots contained generous supplies of juicy meat; in the messes were roast and boiled fowls, corn mush, plantain-flour porridge, and ripe bananas.'[1] All this luxurious fare, which the long-starved wanderers fully deserved, might easily have been bought with a few of the brass rods and beads of which Mr. Stanley had such abundance and had made so little use on his journey; for, as he found, only a few months afterwards, and when he had given them good reason for hating him, the natives were quite ready to be his friends. But Mr. Stanley preferred quarrelling and stealing. Instead of allaying the natural alarm of the people at the advent of so many strangers, he courted their resentment, and, as on former occasions, caused the report of his approach to be regarded with terror.

On December 4 he led his party eastward until he found a suitable spot at which to halt for the night. 'Relieved from their burdens,' he reports, 'a few tireless fellows set out to forage in some villages we had observed far below our line of march in the valley. The suddenness of their descent among the natives provided them with a rich store of fowls, sugar-canes and ripe branches of bananas.'[2]

Next day, still moving eastward, Mr. Stanley did not leave 'a few tireless fellows' to do all the thieving. Doubtful as to his whereabouts, he marched stealthily up to a village. 'In a few seconds the natives were warned of our approach, and fled instinctively, and, Parthian like, shot their long arrows. The scouts dashed across every obstacle, and seized a young woman and a lad of twelve, who were the means of instructing

---

[1] *In Darkest Africa*, vol. i. pp. 272, 274, 275; also Mr. Stanley's report to the Emin Relief Committee, in the *Times*, April 3, 1889.
[2] *In Darkest Africa*, vol. i. p. 278.

our poor ignorance'—although Mr. Stanley complains of his captives for not 'confining themselves to monosyllables which we might easily have understood.' In this village 'our people obtained a large quantity of ripe plantains and bananas; a few goats were also added to our flock, and about a dozen fowls were taken.' Then the march was resumed, and, 'the wretched woman and boy,' who had been seized, serving as guides, the populous district of the Babusessé was reached in the afternoon.

'Before entering the banana shades we repaired our ranks and marched in more compact order. A strong body of men armed with Winchesters formed the advance guard; a similar number of men armed with Remingtons, under the command of Stairs, closed the rear of the column. But however well cautioned the men were against breaking rank, no sooner had the advance guard passed safely through a dangerous locality than the main body invariably despatched scores of looters into huts and granaries to hunt up booty and fowls, bananas, goats, sugar-cane, and trivia articles of no earthly use. These plantations hid a large number of natives, who permitted the advance to pass because their files were unbroken, and their eyes on the watch, but those straggling looters soon gave aborigines the opportunity. Some arrows flew well aimed; one pinned a man's arm to his side, another glancing from a rib admonished its owner of his folly. A volley from rifles drove the men away from their covert without harm to any of them. At the easternmost settlement we camped.'[1]

That night Mr. Stanley's only discomfort arose from some feeble efforts by the natives to expel the usurpers, and from the wounding by them of one or two of his

[1] *In Darkest Africa*, vol. i. pp. 279-281.

'incorrigible looters,' to whom, he says, he 'had not the moral courage to apply the screw of discipline.' On the following day, too, when he crossed the Ituri, and on the day after that, he was able to continue his raiding without serious opposition. 'The Abunguma shook their spears bravely at us; the Babusessé occupied every prominent point on the right side of the river. It appeared once or twice as if our manhood was about to be tested on an important scale. . . . But though we were prepared for a demonstration, the natives remained singularly quiet.'[1]

It was not till December 8, and when he reached the foot of the Mazamboni range of mountains, that Mr. Stanley had to fight. There he saw 'one mass of plantations, indicative of a powerful population,' and found that these people, the Mazamboni, had been joined by the Abunguma, whom he had driven from their own settlements, and who had gone eastward 'in order to join this numerous tribe and meet us with a fitting reception.' Resolved to camp for the night on one of the hills, Mr. Stanley, 'with a view of not provoking the natives,' took a south-east tract, to skirt the districts in which many of them were assembled.

'On entering this rich, crop-bearing valley a chorus of war-cries pealing menacingly above our heads caused us to look up. The groups had already become more and more numerous, until there were probably 300 warriors with shield, spear, and bow, shaking their flashing weapons, gesturing with shield and spear, crying wrathfully at us in some language. Waxing more ungovernable in action, they made a demonstration to descend; they altered their intentions, returned to the summit, and kept pace with us—we

[1] *In Darkest Africa*, vol. i. pp. 283-285.

along the base, they along the crest of the fore hills, snarling and yelling, shouting and threatening, which we took to be expressive of hate to us and encouragement to those in the valley.'[1]

Battle soon arose. Some of the mountaineers, whom Mr. Stanley estimated at 'over 800' in all, began to descend. Four of the Zanzibari scouts 'delivered their fire harmlessly,' and then ran away.

'This was a bad beginning for our side; the natives accepted it as a favourable omen to them, and yelled triumphantly. To check this glow, our riflemen sought cover, and seriously annoyed the natives. Some at the extremity of the hill of Nzera Kum did execution among the mountaineers on the slope of the range opposite at 400 yards distance; others crept down into the valley towards the river, and obtained a triumph for us; others again, working round the base of Nzera Kum, effected a diversion in our favour. Saat Tato, our hunter, carried away a cow from her owners, and we thus obtained a taste of beef after eleven months' abstinence. As night fell, natives and strangers sought their respective quarters, both anticipating a busy day on the morrow.'[2]

That is part of Mr. Stanley's later and more picturesque account of his fighting on December 8. An earlier narrative is briefer and, except as regards the result to his commissariat, different. 'Such natives as were too bold we checked with but little effort,' is his prosaic report to the Emin Relief Committee; 'and a slight skirmish ended in us capturing a cow, the first beef tasted since we left the Ocean.'[3]

[1] *In Darkest Africa*, vol. i. pp. 287, 289.
[2] *Ibid.* 290, 291.
[3] *The Times*, April 3, 1889.

After his supper of stolen beef, Mr. Stanley read his Bible 'as usual;' and in the chapter he read were the 'fine lines' addressed by Moses to Joshua, 'Be strong, and of a good courage; fear not, nor be afraid of them; for the Lord thy God, He it is that doth go with thee; He will not fail thee, nor forsake thee.' Those words Mr. Stanley accepted as a direct and special utterance to himself. 'I could almost have sworn I heard the voice,' he assures us. Yet, he adds, 'before I slept, though I certainly never felt fitter for a fight, it struck me, that both sides were remarkably foolish, and about to engage in what I conceived to be an unnecessary contest.'[1] It might even have struck Mr. Stanley, as it must strike others, that the remarkable foolishness, or remarkable criminality, was all on the side of the unscrupulous and vainglorious filibuster who had provoked a wholly 'unnecessary contest' with the rightful occupants of the hills and plains over which he was forcing his way.

There was no fighting next day. To his surprise, Mr. Stanley received overtures of peace from Mazamboni, and sent him a present of two yards of cloth and eighteen-pennyworth of brass rods, for which it was promised that the chief would return thanks in person. But on the morning of the 10th the natives who had been expected to prostrate themselves before the white men made hostile demonstrations. After a messenger had delivered a long speech, 'loud responsive yells rose from the valley in hideous and savage clamour, and then from every mountain top, and from the slopes there was a re-echo of the savage outburst.' A

[1] *In Darkest Africa*, vol. i. pp. 291, 292.

'treacherous fellow' even dared to discharge his arrows. 'There was then no alternative but to inflict an exemplary lesson upon them; and we prepared to carry it out without losing a moment of time, and with the utmost vigour, unless checked by proffers of amity.' Mr. Stanley mustered his forces, and assigned fifty rifles to Lieutenant Stairs, thirty to Mr. Jephson, and twenty to one Zanzibari captain, and ten to another.

'In a few minutes Stairs' company was hotly engaged. The natives received our men with cool determination for a few minutes, and shot their arrows in literal showers; but the lieutenant, perceiving that their coolness rose from the knowledge that there was a considerable stream intervening between them and his company, cheered his men to charge across the river. His men obeyed him, and as they ascended the opposite bank opened a withering fire which in a few seconds broke up the nest of refractory and turbulent fellows who had cried out so loudly for war. The village was taken with a rush, and the banana plantations scoured. The natives broke out into the open on a run, and fled far northward. Lieutenant Stairs then collected his men, set fire to the village, and proceeded to the assault of other settlements, rattling volleys from the company announcing the resistance they met.'[1]

Meanwhile Mr. Jephson attacked another group. 'The Winchesters were worked handsomely,' and, with the Remingtons, 'had such a disastrous effect on the nerves of the natives, that they fled furiously up the slopes.' More than once, however, the natives had the effrontery to rally and rush on their opponents.

'Until the afternoon the contest continued; the natives were constantly on the run, charging or retreating. By

[1] *In Darkest Africa*, vol i. pp. 294, 295.

evening not one was in sight, and the silence around our camp was significant of the day's doings. The inhabitants were on the mountains, or far removed on the eastward and northward. In the valley around us there was not a hut left standing to be a cover during the night. The lesson, we felt, was not completed. We should have to return by that route. In the natural course of things, if we met many tribes of the quality of this, we should lose many men, and if we left them in the least doubt of our ability to protect ourselves, we should have to repeat our day's work. It was, therefore, far more merciful to finish the affair thoroughly before leaving a tribe in unwhipped insolence in our rear. ... We were compelled to root out the idea that they could harm us in any way.'[1]

That evening Mr. Stanley was again able to sup off stolen beef, and doubtless considered himself more than ever a modern Joshua, strong and of good courage, because the Jewish 'God of Battles' was with him.

The following day was spent in skirmishing and 'foraging.'

'At one time it appeared as though the day would end with reconciliation, for a native stood on a high hill above our position, after all had reached camp, and announced that he had been sent by Mazamboni to say that he received our gifts, but that he had been prevented from visiting us according to promise by the clamour of his young men, who insisted on fighting. But now, as many of them had been killed, he was ready to pay tribute and be a true friend in future. We replied that we were agreeable to peace and friendship with them, but as they had mocked us, kept our peace presents, and then scornfully called us women, they must purchase peace with cattle and

---

[1] *In Darkest Africa*, vol. i. p. 296.]

goats, and if they held up grass in their hands they could approach without fear.'[1]

But no such submission was made before the morning of the 12th, when Mr. Stanley deemed it safest and most convenient to resume his march. He was followed by 'mobs' of natives, 'making demonstrations, and annoying us with their harsh cries and menaces,' which were only resented by a few stray shots, until nine miles had been traversed and a suitable camping-place had been found. Then, says Mr. Stanley, 'to punish them for four hours' persecution of us, we turned about and set fire to every hut on either bank'—that is, to punish Mazamboni's people for daring to object to his raiding and slaughtering among them, Mr. Stanley destroyed the villages of Gavira's people, nine miles distant. Gavira's people had naturally 'gathered to oppose' the intruders; but, as Mr. Stanley boasts and sneers, 'the instant the flames were seen devouring their homes the fury ceased, by which we learnt that fire had a remarkable sedative influence on their nerves.'[2]

December 13 was the last day of Mr. Stanley's long march to the Albert Nyanza, and when the lake was sighted, 'upon every man's lips was the pious ejaculation, "Thank God!"' But that day, too, had its share of killing, stealing, and other exploits, not generally reckoned Christian. As the caravan moved on, 'our long serpent-like line of men was soon detected, and hailed with war-cries, uttered with splendid force of lungs, that drew hundreds of hostile eyes burning with ferocity and hate upon us.' Mr. Stanley, however,

[1] *In Darkest Africa*, vol. i. p. 297.
[2] *Ibid.* pp. 300, 301.

anxious to reach his goal, pushed forward, leaving 'village after village untouched,' although, as he reports, 'we felt it in our veins that we were being charged with weakness.' He only sanctioned one bout of 'good practice with the rifles,' until he was on a knoll from which he thought that he could with best advantage baffle the 'supreme effort about to be made.'

'As we arrived at the summit of the knoll, the head of the native army, streaming thickly, was at the foot of it on the other side, and without an instant's hesitation both sides began the contest simultaneously, but the rapid fire of the Winchesters was altogether too much for them, for, great as was the power of the united voices, the noise of the Winchesters deafened and confused them, while the fierce hissing of the storm of bullets paralysed the bravest. The advance guard rushed down the slopes towards them, and in a few seconds the natives turned their backs and bounded away with the speed of antelopes. Our men pursued them for about a mile, but returned at the recall, a summons they obeyed with the precision of soldiers at a review, which pleased me more even than the gallantry they had displayed.'[1]

In praising his men for obedience to orders Mr. Stanley makes himself responsible for all the murderous work they did; and more followed before the day was over. Having quitted the first battle-field, Mr. Stanley proceeded along the table-land till he was on the edge of the slope leading down to the lake :—

'After a halt of about twenty minutes we commenced the descent down the slopes of the range. Before the rear-guard under Lieutenant Stairs had left the spot, the natives had gathered in numbers equal to our own, and before the

[1] *In Darkest Africa*, vol. i. pp. 302, 303.

advance had descended 500 feet, they had begun to annoy the rear-guard in a manner that soon provoked a steady firing. We below could see them spread out like skirmishers on both flanks, and hanging to the rear in a long line up the terribly steep and galling path. . . . Though the firing was brisk, there was but little hurt done; the ground was adverse to steadiness, and on our side only one was wounded with an arrow, but the combat kept both sides lively and active. Had we been unburdened and fresh, very few of these pestilent fellows would have lived to climb that mountain again. The descent was continued for three hours, halting every fifteen minutes to repel the natives, who, to the number of forty, or thereabouts, followed us down to the plain.'

There Mr. Stanley pitched his camp and a final 'fusillade' against the small groups of natives prowling around 'ended a troublous day, and the rest we now sought was well earned.'[1]

Next day Mr. Stanley walked to the shore of the lake, guided by natives whose kindly bearing when he expected they would need to be shot down amazed and disconcerted him. 'Wondering at their extraordinary manner, and without a single legitimate excuse to quarrel with them, we proceeded on our way meditatively, with most unhappy feelings,' is his shameless confession.[2]

Reaching the Albert Nyanza, but at a point considerably to the south of that at which he had requested Emin Pasha to meet him, and six months after the first date, four months after the second that he had named, Mr. Stanley looked to see whether Emin was there waiting for him, in all readiness to be 'relieved.'

---

[1] *In Darkest Africa*, vol. i. pp. 307, 308.   [2] *Ibid.* p. 310.

To his great chagrin no White Pasha was to be discovered, even with help of a powerful field-glass. More than that, and worse, the people in the neighbourhood—to whom were addressed 'our cajolings and our winsomest smiles,' although 'the harsh, rasping language of Unyoro grated horribly on the hearing,' could give him no news of Emin Pasha, or of any later white visitor to their country than Mason Bey, who had been there in 1877. Mr. Stanley felt that he had reason to be angry. He says:—

'From the date of leaving England, January 21, 1887, to this date of December 14, it never dawned on us that at the very goal we might be baffled so completely as we were now. There was only one comfort, however, in all this: there was henceforward no incertitude. We had hoped to have met news of the Pasha here. A governor of a province, with two steamers, lifeboats, and canoes, and thousands of people we had imagined would have been known everywhere on such a small lake as the Albert, which required only two days' steaming from end to end. He could not, or he would not, leave Wadelai, or he knew not of our coming.'[1]

The last suspicion was more charitable and reasonable than either of the others. As it happened, the only 'knowledge' Emin Pasha had of Mr. Stanley's coming was the promise or assumption that he would follow the route proposed by Dr. Junker and Dr. Schweinfurth, and would approach Wadelai from the eastern, not the western side of the lake. In November 1887 he wrote to Dr. Felkin: 'All well; on best terms with chief and people; will be leaving shortly for

[1] *In Darkest Africa*, vol. i. pp. 310, 311.

Kibiro on east coast of Lake Albert. Have sent reconnoitring party to look out for Stanley, which had to return with no news yet.'

As, however, Emin Pasha was not waiting for him on the spot he had chanced to reach at the moment of his tardy arrival, Mr. Stanley felt that he had come on a fool's errand; and that was the case, though for the folly Emin Pasha was in no way responsible.

None the less was Mr. Stanley's situation pitiable, in so far as pity may be joined with scorn at the failure which an utterly reckless adventurer had brought upon himself.

Pushing on to 'relieve' Emin, Mr. Stanley had left Yambuya on June 28 with nearly four hundred picked carriers and soldiers, and what he thought an ample store of ammunition. He had arrived at the Albert Nyanza with about 170 men, the rest having died, deserted, or been left as invalids on the road under the care of Dr. Parke and Captain Nelson. He had also left behind him the steel boat and the Maxim gun which he had been unable to drag all through the forest. Of the seventy-seven cases of ammunition which he appears to have had when he left Yambuya he had wasted thirty in cruel warfare against the natives. He reckoned that whereas he might have been able with his steel boat to reach Wadelai in four days, the journey by land would occupy twenty-five days, in which he would have 'to expend twenty-five cases in fighting, assuming that the tribes were similar to those in the south'—that is, if he chose to quarrel with them and shoot them down in like fashion. He also reckoned that, as he would have to fight his way back to Yambuya, or any place at which he might find the rear column consigned to Major Barttelot's care, ten cases of ammunition was a very moderate allowance for the enterprise, and this would leave only twelve cases for Emin Pasha's use, which would be ' quite an inadequate supply.' 'This,' he says, 'was a mental review of our position as we trudged northward along the shore of the Albert.'[1] In other words, having satisfied himself that in his present straits it was impossible for him to be of any service to Emin, and thinking in his present mood that the man who had not come up to be 'relieved' at a place and date of which he had no warning was not worth troubling about, Mr. Stanley straightway resolved that he would hurry back to rescue, if he could, some of the men he had all but abandoned, or at any rate to pick up the steel boat and the Maxim gun which might help him in further wanderings in Central Africa.

Therefore, after two days waiting and a little fighting by the Albert Nyanza, Mr. Stanley retraced his steps.

It is not necessary here to detail his movements during the next twelve months, these not differing much in character from those we have already reviewed. But one instance must be given of the way in which his cruel policy towards the natives had pernicious effects and, in his opinion, necessitated more and more cruelties. On December 17 he passed through a district which he had already done what he could to desolate. The natives, alarmed at his return, naturally sought 'to gratify their spleenish hate,' as he called it. They

[1] *In Darkest Africa*, vol. i. pp. 311, 312.

threatened his rear-column, and, it was supposed, captured a sick Zanzibari, who 'either purposely lagged behind or felt his failing powers too weak to bear him further, and laid down in the grass.' Of the natives he said:—

'On this afternoon I reflected upon the singularity that savages possessing such acute fear of death should yet so frequently seek it. Most men would have thought that the losses which had attended their efforts on the 10th, 11th, 12th, and 13th would deter such as these from provoking strangers who had proved themselves so well able to defend themselves. At one time we had almost been convinced that fire would teach them caution; we had also thought that keeping in a quiet line of march, abstaining from paying heed to their war-cries and their manœuvres, and only act when they rushed to the attack, were sufficient to give them glimpses of our rule of conduct. But this was the fifth day of our forbearance. . . . I resolved, then, that the next day we should try to find what effect more active operations would have on them, for it might be that, after one sharp and severe lesson and loss of their cattle, they would consider whether war was as profitable as peace. Accordingly, next day, before dawn, I called for volunteers. Eighty men responded with alacrity. The instructions were few. "You see, boys, these natives fight on the constant run; they have sharp eyes and long limbs. In the work of to-day we white men are of no use. We are all footsore and weary, and we cannot run far in this country. Therefore you will go together with your own chiefs. Go and hunt those fellows who killed our sick men yesterday. Go right to their villages and bring away every cow, sheep, and goat you can find. Don't bother about firing their huts. You must keep on full speed, and chase them out of every canebrake and hill. Bring me some prisoners that I may have some of their own people to send to them with my words." . . . At five in the afternoon the band of volunteers returned, bringing a respectable head of cattle, with several calves. Six bulls were slaughtered at once, and distributed to the men according to their companies, who became nearly delirious with happiness.'[1]

The victims of this and previous raids were members of the extensive Wahuma tribe, of whom Mr. Stanley wrote at a later date that they are 'fine-featured, amiable, quiet, and friendly people, with whom we have never exchanged angry words, and who bring up vividly to the mind the traits of those blameless people with whom the gods deigned to banquet once a year upon the heights of Ethiopia.'[2]

Going back to the skirts of the great forest, Mr. Stanley entrenched himself on January 8, 1888, at a place which he called Fort Bodo, and thence sent Lieutenant Stairs with a party of ninety-eight 'to extricate Nelson and Parke from the clutches of the Manyuema, also to bring up the convalescents, the "Advance" steel boat, Maxim machine-gun, and 116 loads stored at Iporto.' That commission was executed in twenty-five days, 'with a sacred regard to his instructions and without a single flaw'; and Lieutenant Stairs was on February 16 despatched on a longer errand. This time he was to recover the other sick men left at Ugarrowwa's settlement, and to set on their way twenty couriers, with letters and a map, in search of the rear-column left at Yambuya. We must not suppose that this rear-column, to which Mr. Stanley had promised to return in the previous November, if it did not sooner come up to him, had been quite neglected; for Mr.

[1] *In Darkest Africa*, vol. i. pp. 321, 323.
[2] *Ibid.* p. 371.

Stanley informs us that sometimes 'his thoughts were filled with visions of Barttelot and Jameson struggling through the forest overwhelmed with their gigantic task.' Meanwhile, Mr. Stanley and his garrison of about seventy, including three cooks, 'revelled in abundance' at Fort Bodo throughout ten weeks, to the enjoyment of which there was a drawback to Mr. Stanley when he 'fell ill of a stomach disease.'[1]

When Mr. Stanley recovered, the date he had fixed for Lieutenant Stairs' return with such sick men as he could find, and, if procurable, some news about Major Barttelot, was overpast, and he felt 'anxious to depart and be doing something towards terminating his labours.' Accordingly, leaving Captain Nelson and a portion of the garrison at Fort Bodo to wait for Lieutenant Stairs, he started on April 2 on another journey to the Albert Nyanza. On this occasion he was accompanied by Dr. Parke and Mr. Jephson, and an augmented force carrying considerable stores, his steel boat and his Maxim gun. On this second excursion his mode of travelling was so far altered that he was inclined to treat Mazamboni and the other chiefs on the road as friends instead of enemies, and either fear or unusual magnanimity prompted the chiefs and their people to reciprocate his advances, though not with the enthusiasm he looked for.

'We discovered that the chiefs, as well as the lesser folk, were arrant beggars, and too sordid in mind to recognise a generous act. Though a peace was strenuously sought by all, yet the granting of it seemed to them to be

---

[1] *In Darkest Africa*, vol. i. pp. 321, 340, 337, 331, 338; *Parliamentary Papers*, C. 5906, p. 7.

only a means of being enriched with gifts from the strangers. Mazamboni, even after a long day's work, could not be induced to give more than a calf and five goats as a return for a ten-guinea rug, a bundle of brass wire, and ivory horns from the forest. The chief of Urumangwa and Bwessa, that flourishing settlement which in December had so astonished us with its prosperity, likewise thought that he was exceedingly liberal by endowing us with a kid and two fowls.'[1]

Mr. Stanley takes no account of all his killing and stealing among these poor savages four months before; nor does he appear to feel any shame in thus acknowledging that all the trouble he had gone through was the result of his own wantonness :—

'As we traversed the smiling land, hailed, and greeted, and welcomed by the kindly Bavira, we could not forbear thinking how different all this was from the days when we drove through noisy battalions of Bavira, Babiassi, and Balegga, each urging his neighbours, and whooping and howling everyone to our extermination, with a quick play of light on crowds of flashing spears, and yard-long arrows sailing through the air to meet us; and now we had 157 Bavira actually in front of the advance-guard, as many behind the rear-guards, while our 90 loads had been distributed among voluntary carriers who thought it an honour to be porters to the same men whom they had hounded so mercilessly a few months previous.'[2]

On the road Mr. Stanley heard that during his absence from the Albert Nyanza 'a white man called Maleju, or the Bearded One, in a big canoe all of iron,' had visited the part of the lake at which he had himself

---

[1] *In Darkest Africa*, vol. i. pp. 350–361.   [2] *Ibid.* p. 366.

halted for two days, and that a 'mysterious packet' was waiting for him at Kavalli's settlement, the place at which he had requested Emin Pasha to look for him. He could not therefore be in doubt that the 'Bearded One' was Emin, and, indignant as he still was with Emin for not having 'taken the trouble' to divine his plans and meet him in February at another than the appointed spot,[1] he so far altered his route as to proceed to Kavalli's. There he found a letter from Emin, and shortly afterwards, in response to his answer, received a visit from the Pasha. What followed upon these communications will be commented on hereafter.

Having left Mr. Jephson to look after Emin's affairs, Mr. Stanley returned to Fort Bodo, intent on other and more urgent 'relieving' work. Arriving at Fort Bodo on June 8, he found that in his absence Lieutenant Stairs had brought up 'to exhibit their nude bodies disfigured by the loathliest colours and effects of chronic disease,' fifteen wretched Zanzibaris, all the survivors save four of the fifty-six whom he had left with Ugarrowwa on his way from Yambuya. 'I had estimated that out of the fifty-six, boarded out at our expense, at least forty convalescents would be ready, fit for marching,' Mr. Stanley says, forgetting that he had previously 'doubted greatly whether Ugarrowwa would trouble his head about any of them.'[2] Neither his doubts nor his estimates seem to have resulted in any self-reproach respecting this particular item of wreckage in bi wrecked Expedition.

[1] See Mr. Stanley's ungenerous sneers and false assumptio In Darkest Africa, vol. i. p. 357.
[2] Ibid. p. 428; Parliamentary Papers, C. 5906, p. 6.

The next item of wreckage with which he concerned himself was the rear-column under Major Barttelot, which, as it now occurred to him, was 'labouring under God alone knew what difficulties,'[1] having been left at Yambuya in June 1887, with a promise that it should not be left there more than five months, but which had already been neglected for nearly twelve.

With a party of more than 200 men, chiefly Madi carriers procured for him at the Albert Nyanza by Emin Pasha, Mr. Stanley left Fort Bodo on June 16. On the way he found some of the couriers whom he had previously despatched to Major Barttelot, but who had been unable to reach their destination. At Banalya, about ninety miles to the east of Yambuya on the Aruwimi, he met Mr. Bonny, from whom he heard 'as deplorable a story as could be rendered of one of the most remarkable series of derangements that an organised body of men could possibly be plunged into.'[2]

That was on August 17, 1888. We must now go back a year and seven weeks to see something of the 'deplorable story' of which Mr. Bonny gave his version to Mr. Stanley.

[1] *In Darkest Africa*, vol. i. p. 431.   [2] *Ibid.* p. 468.

CHAPTER V

THE REAR-COLUMN

ON June 24, 1887, four days before he started for Lake Albert Nyanza, leaving 125 of the most incapable of his carriers and soldiers at Yambuya, Mr. Stanley handed to Major Barttelot a formal 'letter of instructions,' part of which must be quoted. After referring to the men and loads which it was expected that Messrs. Troup, Ward, and Bonny would bring up before August 10, and to the 'strong reinforcement' of carriers promised by Tippoo-Tib, Mr. Stanley proceeded to say :—

'Pending the arrival of our men and goods, it behoves you to be very alert and wary in the command of this stockaded camp. Though the camp is favourably situated and naturally strong, a brave enemy would find it no difficult task to capture if the commander is lax in discipline, vigour, and energy. Therefore I feel sure that I have made a wise choice in selecting you to guard our interests here during our absence.[1] . . . I hope you will spare no

[1] Compare with this Mr. Stanley's statement in a lecture at New York on December 3, 1890 : ' Several days after he had set out I was told by General Brackenbury that Barttelot would be sure to give me trouble. He furnished me with some instances of his conduct. I then resolved within myself, as it was too late to recall him, and it would be a pity to dismiss him for anything he had done in the

pains to maintain order and discipline in your camp, and make your defences complete, and keep them in such a condition that, however brave an enemy may be, he can make no impression on them .... For, remember, it is not the natives alone who may wish to assail you, but the Arabs and their followers may, through some cause or other, quarrel with you and assail your camp. .... It may happen, should Tippoo-Tib have sent the full number of adults promised by him to me, viz., 600 men (able to carry loads), and the "Stanley" has arrived safely with the 125 men left by me at Bolobo, that you will feel yourself sufficiently competent to march the column with all the goods brought by the "Stanley" and those left by me at Yambuya, along the road pursued by me. In that event, which would be very desirable, you will follow closely our route, and before many days we shall most assuredly meet. ... It may happen also that, though Tippoo-Tib has sent some men, he has not sent enough to carry the goods with your own force. In that case you will, of course, use your discretion as to what goods you can dispense with to enable you to march.'[1]

At Zanzibar, it will be remembered, Mr. Stanley had arranged with Tippoo-Tib that, in consideration of the latter being appointed Governor of the Stanley Falls District of the Congo Free State, and being taken by sea and land to his seat of office, he should befriend the Emin Relief Expedition, and provide it with 600 carriers. Having escorted Tippoo-Tib to Stanley Falls, Major Barttelot wrote in his diary on June 17:—

past, that I would take precautions to prevent his committing outrages under the impulse of his passionate temper. As far as Yambuya I saw no sufficient reason to dismiss him. ... Not wishing to deal harshly, I allowed him to remain.'—*New York Tribune*, Dec. 4, 1890.

[1] *In Darkest Africa*, vol. i. pp. 115, 116.

'I had a palaver with Tippoo. He is evidently a bit sore with Stanley about the men he promised to give him, for Stanley promised he would supply them with ammunition; and to the best of my belief the ammunition is left behind, to come up by the next trip. Tippoo-Tib must have been told this by Stanley, and asked to supply it, to be repaid hereafter; but he thinks it a breach of contract, and also says his men have no powder. I effected a sort of compromise, by making him half promise to supply, at any rate, 200 men with ammunition, to be repaid. This will suit me admirably, because then, directly Ward and Troup come up, I can cut on, unless Stanley changes his mind again.'[1]

A month later Barttelot said in one of his letters from Yambuya:—

'Part of the agreement on which Tippoo-Tib was to let him have the men was, that on arrival here he should supply them with caps and powder; these have all been left behind, and Tippoo-Tib knew it. When I was at the Falls, Tippoo told me he thought Stanley had broken faith with him, and that the men would not come till the ammunition had arrived. On arrival here I told Stanley this, and he got into an awful rage, and said all sorts of things, because he knew that what I said was true. I was two days later arriving here from the Falls than he expected. He was in such a state about this, that he was going to send off Stairs to look for me, and you never saw such a letter of instructions as he gave him. To this effect: that Tippoo-Tib had seized the steamer, or that the Soudanese had mutinied and held her, or that on my own account I had a row with the natives, and they possessed the steamer. I was naturally angry at this, and went and told him I had read his letter to Stairs, and thought it absurd. In the first place, he had allowed me a margin of two days, and I

[1] *Diaries and Letters*, p. 108.

had not exceeded it. Secondly, as to Tippoo-Tib, Stanley himself had said he would as soon trust Tippoo-Tib as any white man. Concerning the Soudanese, that was equally absurd; and my making a raid was absurd, when I had plenty of food. My having seen Stairs' letter, which he knew was full of the lowest suspicion, annoyed him, and my catching him out at every point still more, and there was a row. He said to Stairs, when he gave him the letter, that if any of us got into danger through foolhardiness or want of proper caution, he would not move a hand's-breadth to help him. It shows you what a suspicious fellow he is. . . . This has been a doleful letter, but I write to you because I think one of the family should know how we are situated. I have never been on such a mournful, cheerless trip as this. The harder we worked, the glummer Stanley looked. After a long march, no smile from him or word of any sort, except to say, " You have lost a box," or some sneer of that sort.'[1]

The stormy interview occurred on June 24, shortly after Major Barttelot had received the written orders from Mr. Stanley to remain at Yambuya till he could follow with the expected stores and reinforcements of men. Mr. Stanley describes it in different terms,[2] but Major Barttelot's account is manifestly more truthful.

Though they shook hands at parting, it is quite clear that Mr. Stanley's and Major Barttelot's dislike of one another had by this time reached an acute stage. 'Stanley and I were never on good terms,' Barttelot wrote. 'He could not threaten me, and threats are his chief mode of punishment.' Mr. Jameson also was quite out of favour. 'He (Mr. Stanley) is always suspecting us, and has constantly called us all mutineers,

[1] *Diaries and Letters*, p. 119.
[2] *In Darkest Africa*, vol. i. pp. 117-126.

and threatened to treat us as such,' Barttelot said in another letter. 'It is my belief, if he thought he could get rid of us, he would; he sticks at nothing.'[1] It is possible that these two English gentlemen judged their leader too harshly; but they certainly had no reason to be grateful to him for placing them and leaving them in the irksome and inglorious position they had to occupy at Yambuya.

However, they may have erred, and whatever faults they may have committed in endeavouring to adapt themselves to the distressing and degrading conditions of life imposed upon them by their chief, they cannot be charged with disloyalty to him or any neglect of his instructions. Under those instructions they were to remain at Yambuya until the additional stores and men arrived from the Upper Congo; and after that, in the event of carriers being supplied by Tippoo-Tib, they were to follow in the direction of the Albert Nyanza, if they felt 'sufficiently competent to march the column.' It was left to Major Barttelot's discretion whether he should start after two months' necessary delay or await Mr. Stanley's return. But it was clearly implied that, if no help came from Tippoo, he should remain quietly at Yambuya, and it appears that Mr. Stanley, who says that he never really counted on the fulfilment of Tippoo's promise, expected him to do that. 'Good-bye, Major; shall find you here in October when I return,' were his last words as he walked off into the forest.[2]

Messrs. Troup, Ward, and Bonny reached Yambuya, with the men and stores in their charge, on August 14. But repeated applications made to Tippoo-Tib were of

[1] *Diaries and Letters*, pp. 114, 118.   [2] *Ibid.* p. 116.

no avail till the following June. Long before that, however, Tippoo had sent or encouraged large parties of so-called Arabs to settle or hover about in the neighbourhood, partly to watch and hamper Major Barttelot's movements, partly to carry on their persecution of the natives. The meddling of these people, as will be seen, greatly increased Barttelot's difficulties in dealing both with his own Zanzibaris and Soudanese and with the unfortunate aborigines.

The conditions under which Mr. Stanley left his rear-column at Yambuya on June 28, 1887, have already been indicated. He had driven away the rightful owners of the district, and, although he went through a form of peace-making with their chief, he had been unable to force them to furnish the newcomers with food. Food, of course, was indispensable. Except that Major Barttelot and Mr. Jameson were each supplied with $2\frac{1}{2}$ lbs. of coffee, $1\frac{1}{2}$ lbs. of tea, 4 tins of condensed milk, 3 small tins of butter, $1\frac{1}{2}$ tins of sardines, $1\frac{1}{2}$ tins of sausages, 4 pots of Liebig's Extract, and a few other articles in like meagre proportion, as rations for six months, they, as well as their black followers, had to depend entirely on what they could pick up, or steal, or buy. To each man a brass rod, called a 'matako'—costing three-halfpence in England—and six cowries were doled out every week in order that they might, if they could, buy 'fish, &c.'[1] There were, it is true, large stores of what may be considered luxuries in Major Barttelot's custody, but, as he had strict orders to keep these in reserve for use of the whole Expedition, he loyally abstained from touching

[1] *Diaries and Letters*, pp. 116, 139.

them. There were also some sacks of rice and a few biscuits, available for emergencies, but these were for the most part mouldy, and, such as they were, reserved for the white men's consumption. The blacks had to support themselves wholly with such manioc and other unwholesome food as they could find. If they, and their officers too, were driven to base methods of keeping themselves alive, Mr. Stanley has no right to reproach them. It was he who took them to Yambuya. It was he who left them there to starve. It was he who encouraged and compelled them to resort to all the pitiful and reprehensible expedients that are recorded in the letters and diaries of Major Barttelot, Mr. Jameson, Mr. Ward, and Mr. Troup.

We read of nothing worse during the first ten days than the flogging of night sentries for sleeping at or deserting their posts—a severity that may have been excusable, as Major Barttelot had less than eighty capable men to protect his camp. 'It is sickening, this continual flogging,' Mr. Jameson wrote on July 6; 'but there is no help for it.' Next day he reported as a strange occurrence: 'No sentries asleep; so no flogging this morning, thank goodness!'[1]

Presently the need of food, which the natives, called Washengis, refused to sell at the price offered, led these young English gentlemen to adopt a mean device. On July 9 the villagers, who had been driven to the other side of the river, sent to ask leave to gather some of the manioc they had left behind. The messenger was told that, if he would bring two goats, 'he could take the manioc in peace.' This he promised to do. 'He

[1] *Story of the Rear-Column*, pp. 80, 81.

has, however, not turned up,' wrote Mr. Jameson, 'so I am going to show them that we are in earnest, to-morrow morning, by taking twenty-five of the Soudanese with me, and stopping all the river paths to the manioc fields. I will try and capture a woman, and then they will come to terms I think.'[1] The threat was acted upon. According to Major Barttelot, 'We found out where and what time they landed, and lay in wait for them, and caught two women, and a baby and one boy. We could have caught men, but did not want them, only the women, as we knew they would pay a ransom for them. The boy we let go, but the women we kept until they were ransomed.'[2] After a week's detention one of the women escaped. The other with her baby was ultimately bartered for 'two goats, nine fowls, and some fish, with a promise that they will trade.' That was on July 17. But on the 20th Mr. Jameson reported, 'One miserable canoe, with some stale fish for sale, was the only sign of trade to-day;' and on the 21st, 'I see no chance of getting any more, for the natives do not trade, or offer to, in the least; as a last resource we must catch some more of their women.'[3]

For several days less barbarous stealing, or efforts to steal, sufficed. On August 1 we read: 'The natives have deserted all the villages for miles round, and gone over to the other side of the river, unfortunately taking all their goats and chickens with them. So there is no loot of any kind, although we continually make long excursions, seeking what we may devour.

[1] *Story of the Rear-Column*, pp. 82, 83.
[2] *Diaries and Letters*, p. 125.
[3] *Story of the Rear-Column*, pp. 83, 90, 92.

We sometimes come suddenly upon a large village, and find not a living thing in it, although the fires are still smoking, and it has evidently been full of life only a few minutes before. How they know we are coming often puzzles me.'[1]

The arrival in the neighbourhood of some of Tippoo-Tib's followers, early in August, if productive of fresh trouble in many ways, was so far advantageous to Major Barttelot's party that it induced the natives to seek his protection. Some of them returned to their old homes near Yambuya, and brought provisions for sale. Among the rest was the husband of the ransomed woman. 'He seems to bear us no ill-will for having taken his wife and child, but was as merry as possible,' Mr. Jameson wrote on the 9th. Mr. Ward, who arrived with Messrs. Troup and Bonny on the 14th, confirms Mr. Jameson's impression. 'It is quite true,' he says, 'that women were captured for the purpose of their being ransomed for food, but this was the sum total of the matter. The proceeding may seem very horrid and very harsh to gentle readers in England, but with us in Africa, following the custom of the country to this extent, the manœuvre was regarded in quite an ordinary light. This proceeding, however, only took place on two occasions. No harshness was used. The natives brought the food to ransom their women in the most matter-of-fact way, and laughed heartily with us over the whole transaction.'[2]

The bringing up of the men and stores from the west by Mr. Ward and the others raised the strength

[1] *Story of the Rear-Column*, p. 100.
[2] *My Life with Stanley's Rear-Guard.* By Herbert Ward, p. 158.

of the Yambuya garrison to 246, of whom 165 were Zanzibaris in sufficient health to carry loads; but as there were 660 or more loads to be carried, it was not possible for Major Barttelot to leave Yambuya unless he threw away three-fourths of his baggage, or obtained the carriers promised by Tippoo. He was beginning to lose hope of Tippoo's keeping his bargain, but he wisely resolved to send Messrs. Jameson and Ward to Stanley Falls, to put pressure on the agent of Mr. Stanley and the Congo Free State. 'Should they eventually come,' he said in a letter addressed to Sir William Mackinnon on August 15, 'I should march at once on Mr. Stanley's track. If, however, they do not, I shall be compelled to stay here till November, when Mr. Stanley expects to return, or till such time afterwards as he may return.'[1]

Mr. Jameson, who at Stanley Falls received much barbaric courtesy from Tippoo-Tib, and plenty of food, but only empty promises about the 600 carriers, returned to Yambuya on September 12, Mr. Ward having already gone back. In his absence difficulties had increased at the entrenched camp. The marauding Arabs had gathered round in greater numbers, and their treacherous show of friendship led to renewal and aggravation of troubles between Major Barttelot and the natives. On September 3 he gave to the Arabs, whose worthlessness and mischievousness were not at this time fully apparent to him, two canoes which the natives had left behind them when they were driven out of Yambuya. This entry in his diary for the 4th illustrates the general state of affairs.

[1] *Diaries and Letters*, p. 133.

'The two canoes I gave the Arabs were anchored at the top of our path to the river. The sentry had orders to fire upon anyone trying to take them away. The natives tried to take them during the night; the sentry fired and wounded one man. About 8 A.M. the Arabs took their canoes away, but the natives captured one, and the Arabs came back and complained to me. I promised to get it back for them on condition they did not molest the natives till I had done so. A chief came in, so I made him a prisoner, and told him he would be a dead man if the canoe was not returned in twenty-four hours. The canoe was returned in the afternoon, and I let him go, cautioning him that if he and his men did not sell us fish as usual, I would no longer protect him from the Arabs.'[1]

Some of the complications that followed these proceedings—high-handed and impolitic, but apparently inevitable in the circumstances—may be learnt from later passages in Major Barttelot's diary, which also show that Mr. Bonny, to whom had been assigned the task of collecting food for the white officers, quickly repeated and improved upon Mr. Jameson's exploit in woman-stealing.

'*Sept.* 10.—The chiefs have been deceiving us, so Bonny caught eight women and a baby to-day as their punishment.'

'*Sept.* 11.—Had a palaver with natives about their women, but as they chose to show independence no arrangement was come to. The native chief came over, bringing the rifle the natives had stolen from the Zanzibaris, seven fowls, and some fish. For them we let him take one woman.

'*Sept.* 14.—Ingungo brought us heaps of splendid fish, and we gave him back one woman.

[1] *Diaries and Letters*, p. 153.

'*Sept.* 20.—The Washengis came in, and we exchanged a woman for eight fowls and some fish.'[1]

Ingungo or Ngungu, the Washengi chief, seems to have kept the English officers well supplied with food while he ransomed his eight women, one by one. Meanwhile, he and his people were being so grossly illtreated by their Arab persecutors as to provoke some pity from his English tormentors. Mr. Troup wrote on September 15: 'Heard shots on the other side, and found that the Arabs, who are camped further up— Abdallah's lot—had been over. Beastly shame, after their promise to us, and we had given them presents so they should not molest the natives whilst we are here. Natives are clearing out from the other side after the firing, a general stampede.'[2]

On the 18th Major Barttelot wrote: 'Ingungo came to see us, and brought two huge pots of honey. Poor chaps! the Arabs have treated them very badly; the scene yesterday was disgraceful. They shot the poor fellows in the water. I remonstrated with Salem Mohammed; he promised to stop it, and sent a canoe across for that purpose. There has been no shooting here to-day, though early in the morning there was a disturbance in the Arab camp.'[3]

Of Ngungu Mr. Troup said on the 30th :—

'He told us that he had nearly all his people killed by Tippoo-Tib's men down the river, where they had gone to take shelter, when Abdallah fired on them. He has no regular home now, and sleeps in different places every

---

[1] *Diaries and Letters*, pp. 154–156.
[2] *With Stanley's Rear-Column*, p. 158.
[3] *Diaries and Letters*, p. 156.

night. I felt very sorry for him, poor chap ; it is too bad—these Arabs have broken faith with us all round. It is, I consider, a most deplorable position to be in. We have to be friendly with the Arabs, as we expect them to get men for the Expedition ; and, although we have told them to leave the people alone here, they have not done so, and it is impossible for us to force them to obey us in any way. First, we cannot afford to fall out with them ; and, secondly, if we did, they could give us a good licking in the long run ! All the same, it goes against one's feelings altogether to see these poor people hunted to death. We asked Ngungu over and over again to bring the remnant of his people to the fort and live with us, promising him protection in every way ; and, although he says he will come, we see nothing of him. He is mistrustful of everyone—and no wonder, after all he has gone through lately.'[1]

So the wretched story goes on. Any sympathy the white men showed to the natives under the cruelty of the Arab intruders was futile, and the natives suffered all the more from Arab cruelty in consequence of the English occupation of Yambuya. They also suffered not a little from the rough treatment of the Englishmen and their Zanzibari and Soudanese followers. For this treatment some allowance must be made, as, however much the natives were entitled to humane consideration, their cannibal propensities necessarily rendered them repulsive to the white visitors. Many of the so-called Arabs were also cannibals, and dreadful stories are told of their revolting practices and their general lawlessness. Major Barttelot was practically at the mercy of these followers of Tippoo-Tib. 'It must be remembered,' says Mr. Troup, ' that had the

[1] *With Stanley's Rear-Column*, p. 162.

Arabs in anger taken matters into 'their own hands, they could have quickly made an end of our portion of the Expedition, either by starving us out, or by an attack on our not too strongly fortified and none too well garrisoned camp.'[1]

And Major Barttelot's difficulties were greatly increased by the insubordination of his own people, and the excessive severity by which he strove to check it. There can be no doubt that he found himself in a position for which he was by nature unfitted. 'He viewed things,' says Mr. Ward, 'through the strict, stern, rigid spectacles of discipline, and with the autocratic manner of a British officer. He was a stranger to African manners and speech, with the ever-present suspicion of everyone and everything which this disadvantage must always excite. As a consequence of all this, the black people with whom he was brought into contact were to Barttelot an unknown quantity, and the contempt and disdain natural to the highly strung officer, who believed that nothing was equal to the British soldier, gained full and unfortunate sway. He had been used to the plain and upright dealings of the white man, and, if trickery, such trickery as he could understand. He was completely at sea when dealing with the black, whose word is so frequently a lie.'[2] 'It did not take me long,' says Mr. Troup, 'to discover that he had an intense hatred of anything in the shape of a black man, for he made no disguise of this, but frequently mentioned the fact.'[3]

---

[1] *With Stanley's Rear-Column*, p. 176.
[2] *My Life with Stanley's Rear-Guard*, p. 30.
[3] *With Stanley's Rear-Column*, p. 145.

These estimates of Major Barttelot are in accordance with what is known of his antecedents; but we must not forget that it was Mr. Stanley who, setting them an example of brutality, compelled Barttelot and his colleagues to kick and flog the men under them on the smallest provocations. Floggings began almost on the first day of the encampment at Yambuya, and were then limited to the comparatively mild punishment of 25 lashes for sleeping while on sentry duty. Penalties multiplied and became harsher when the Zanzibaris and Soudanese were detected in cheating their masters and plotting against them with the Arabs. Two Zanzibaris, for instance, named Msa and Bartholomew, were suspected of stealing from Mr. Jameson, whom they accompanied as his servants on his first journey to Stanley Falls. He wrote, on September 1 : ' This morning I wanted one or two matakos to make a present to a girl who brought back one of my tortoises which had strayed. Upon asking Bartholomew for them he at first pretended not to understand, and then could not answer at all. He confessed to having received 70, and, upon adding up all that had been spent, I found it was only 13, so that he must have stolen 57. When I accused him of it he did not even deny it.' On the 2nd he reported : ' We found upon examination that a piece of cloth had been stolen; so I asked Tippoo-Tib to put Bartholomew and Msa in chains, as I felt sure they would attempt to escape. They had, I afterwards discovered, told Tippoo-Tib they meant to run away, but he declined to connive at their escape, so the two gentlemen are now in irons.'[1] Next day they broke

[1] *Story of the Rear-Column*, pp. 128, 129.

loose; but they were caught by Tippoo-Tib's men and taken to Yambuya on the 25th, when Major Barttelot had them 'chained and padlocked in the guard-room.'[1] 'This morning,' Mr. Jameson wrote on the 27th, 'justice was meted out to Bartholomew and Msa, the deserters and thieves. They were flogged in front of all the men, Bartholomew receiving 150 lashes, and Msa 100. The former kept calling out "I die to-day, I die to-day," in a prolonged howl.' On October 19, though they had been sent to work in chains, they contrived to escape again. Captured again, they were chained up for a fortnight longer, and on November 5, as Mr. Jameson reported, 'the Major left it to Troup, Bonny, Ward and myself to try, and pass sentence on, Msa and Bartholomew. I proposed working them hard every day in chains, as I am sick of flogging; but the other three proposed 150 lashes each, and as they are in the majority, that sentence will be administered.' On the 7th 'Msa took his 150 lashes, Bartholomew only 75, as he is still tender from his last flogging.'[2]

Another poor wretch whose case must be cited was named Burgari Mahommed. On December 2 he stole half a goat from Mr. Ward. 'This,' wrote Mr. Jameson, 'is the most daring robbery they have yet attempted.' For the offence he was flogged on the 4th. 'The Soudanese are wonderfully plucky in bearing pain,' according to Mr. Jameson, 'for although he received 150 strokes, which cut him up very much, he never uttered a sound.'[3] As Burgari had falsely accused

---

[1] *Diaries and Letters*, p. 156.
[2] *Story of the Rear-Column*, pp. 142, 152, 153, 159, 161, 162.
[3] *Ibid.* pp. 164, 165.

another of being the thief, he was on the 5th sentenced to forfeit his pay for nine months, and was promised 'another flogging later on.'[1] Meanwhile he was kept in chains, 'doing walking punishment every day,' until February 4, when he 'escaped from the guard-house, taking with him the sergeant's rifle and twelve cartridges.'[2] 'He is a very hardened scoundrel,' wrote Mr. Ward, ' and I should not be surprised if he has concealed himself near by in the forest, so as to have a shot at one of us as we walk up and down in the evening after dinner outside the fort.' It appears that Burgari had told one of the Arabs 'that his life was not worth living, marching up and down in the sun all day, and that he knew that he would be shot when caught, and that he intended shooting Barttelot dead before he would be captured.'[3] On the 9th, however, he was caught and 'sentenced to death,' after a sham court-martial, thus described by Mr. Troup:—

'The case of the Soudanese deserter came up for discussion after luncheon to-day, and we had to decide what punishment should be meted out to him. It was argued that the Zanzibari deserters had been flogged, and that this man ought to receive the same punishment. But it was held by some of the officers that the Soudanese were engaged as soldiers, and were under military discipline, therefore this case should be dealt with as desertion in an enemy's country. The end of the discussion was that two of us (I being one) held that he should not be shot, but the others, being in the majority, carried their point, and he was therefore condemned to suffer the extreme penalty.'[4]

[1] *Diaries and Letters*, p. 170.
[2] *Story of the Rear-Column*, p. 204.
[3] *My Life with Stanley's Rear-Guard*, pp. 75, 77.
[4] *With Stanley's Rear-Column*, p. 203.

The following is Mr. Jameson's report of the affair :—

'Troup and I were the only ones who thought the extreme penalty might be mitigated. No one can deny that, according to military law on active service, he ought to be shot, and there is no doubt it ought to have a very good effect on the others; but when one thinks what a miserable, poor wretch he is, and from what a miserable existence he tried to escape, one cannot help pitying him. It is a long time now since he stole the meat out of Ward's house, which was the offence for which he was punished originally. I think, all things taken into consideration, a little leniency to such a poor wretch would not be flung away.'

On the 10th Mr. Jameson added :—

' Burgari was shot this morning, and all the men in camp were paraded to witness it. He was tied up to the flogging-post on the road outside the camp, and eight Soudanese formed the firing party. Death was instantaneous, one bullet going through the backbone and another through the heart. He took the whole thing quite coolly, without the sign of a tremble or an utterance of any kind, and waited quietly, with his head slightly bent, for the signal to fire.'[1]

The killing of Burgari, in accordance with the vote of Major Barttelot, Mr. Ward and Mr. Bonny, appears to have been illegal; but there was much more form of law in this case than in some of Mr. Stanley's summary executions, and perhaps it was kinder than the further flogging Messrs. Jameson and Troup recommended. Moreover, the treatment he received was humane in comparison with that accorded some of his companions: to a Zanzibari named John Henry, for instance, who

[1] *Story of the Rear-Column*, p. 207.

'bolted' with Major Barttelot's revolver on April 16. He was caught on the 20th, and on the 22nd Barttelot ordered that he should be shot on the morrow. All the other Zanzibaris having threatened to 'desert in a body' if John Henry was shot, the sentence was commuted to one of 300 lashes. It was carried out on the 23rd, and the poor Zanzibari endured two days of agony. 'I heard that John Henry died yesterday,' Barttelot wrote on the 26th, 'but I am certain he must have been shot or hung sooner or later, for he was a monstrous bad character.'[1]

It is evident there was appalling demoralisation in the Yambuya camp, steadily increasing throughout the weary months in which Major Barttelot waited vainly for Mr. Stanley's return and vainly applied for the carriers promised by Tippoo-Tib. In the hope of obtaining these carriers, Major Barttelot, having sent Mr. Jameson to Stanley Falls in August, went thither himself with Mr. Troup in October, and again with Mr. Jameson in February. As on the latter occasion he found that Tippoo-Tib was at Kassongo, a place not far from Lake Tanganyika, and the head-quarters of Tippoo's old government, he sent Mr. Jameson there to offer on their joint liability any amount of money that King Leopold's Arab viceroy wanted as recompense for the help sought from him. Yet no good resulted from all these efforts. Tippoo did, from time to time, send several of his followers to Yambuya, but they were useless as carriers, being trained not for that work but for slave-hunting and ivory-raiding, and their presence in

---

[1] *Diaries and Letters*, pp. 227-231 : *With Stanley's Rear-Column*, pp. 247, 248.

the neighbourhood, with a great many others about whom there was no pretence of their serving Major Barttelot, was only a source of new troubles and dangers. Most of them were Manyuema, the same debased and vicious horde of tributaries to Tippoo as Mr. Stanley found himself unable to cope with in his journey through the forest. Mr. Stanley described these people in the letter to Major Barttelot which he sent by couriers from Fort Bodo, in February, but which never reached its destination:—

'We first met the Manyuema on the last day of August, and parted from them January 6. In the interval we have lost 118 through death and desertion. In their camps it was as bad as in the wilderness, for they ground us down by extortion so extreme that we were naked in a short time. They tempted the Zanzibaris to sell their rifles and ammunition, ramrods, officers' blankets, &c., and then gave food so sparingly that these crimes were of no avail. Finally, besides starving them, tempting them to ruin the Expedition, they speared them, scourged them, and tied them up, until in one case death ended his miseries. Never were such abject slaves of slaves as our people had become under the influence of the Manyuema.'[1]

It is noteworthy that in this letter Mr. Stanley warned Major Barttelot against the Manyuema, and instructed him, rather than fall a prey to these people, to take the very course that he afterwards blamed him for taking. He wrote:—

'Before you get near the Arab influence, where your column will surely break up if you are alone, I order you to go to the nearest place (Mugwye's, Aveysheba, or Nepoko confluence) that is to you, and there build a strong

[1] *Diaries and Letters*, p. 188.

camp and wait for us. . . . If you come near Ugarrowwa's you will lose men, rifles, powder, everything of value. Your own boys will betray you because they will sell food so dearly that your people, from stress of hunger, will steal everything.'[1]

The perils that Mr. Stanley bade Major Barttelot keep clear of, if he was able to make any progress towards the Albert Nyanza—and many more besides—befel him and his comrades while they struggled on at Yambuya and in its neighbourhood. Let these extracts from one of Mr. Jameson's letters to his wife, written from Stanley Falls on March 17, help to explain their position and to extenuate any faults they may have committed.

'On August 23, the men from Tippoo-Tib never having arrived, Barttelot sent me off to Stanley Falls to interview Tippoo-Tib personally on the subject, and I did not return until September 12. My interview with him was most satisfactory; he made the most plausible excuses for the non-arrival of his men, and gave the most gushing promises of instant aid. The result of all these promises was that after many weeks 64 men arrived, which small number was not of the slightest use to us. Barttelot then went in October to Stanley Falls, and there saw Tippoo-Tib, who informed him that he could not get the men there, and must go to Kassongo to obtain them. He left for that purpose early in November, but up to the present date he has only sent us 200 men altogether. You can imagine how utterly helpless we are, and how utterly dependent upon Tippoo-Tib, when I tell you that we have already lost fully one-third of our entire force at Yambuya camp from sickness, and that I do not believe we could produce 80 really sound carriers to-morrow, and yet we have between

[1] *Diaries and Letters*, p. 191.

600 and 700 loads there. This hope deferred, and weary waiting, month after month, with no brighter outlook, is horrible work—far, far worse than any amount of hardship and fighting. . . . Ever since Mr. Stanley's non-arrival in November there has been a sort of gloom over all of us in Yambuya camp, sometimes brightened up by the news of approaching help from Tippoo-Tib, only to be made darker by the help being put off for indefinite months. It is a sad, sad sight to see men dying round you every day and not to be able to put out a hand to save them. Without a single fight, we have lost close upon 70 men out of our small force, and there are many more who, I am sorry to say, will never leave the camp, or, if we leave it, must be left there to die.'[1]

A few weeks earlier Mr. Ward had written :—

'There are about 30 men who are simply skin and bones, unable to walk; and to see the poor dying wretches, their great hollow eyes staring at vacancy, sitting naked on the dusty ground, propped up by their elbows, with drooping heads, gradually dying—it is a hard sight. Poor devils! they do not seem to care an atom about death; in fact, they seem apparently to look forward to it as a relief to their sufferings. They are nearly all slaves. They have lived hard, worked hard, and are now dying hard—it's hard luck indeed! . . . This eternal waiting is awful. Day after day passes; we see no strange faces, we hear no news; our men are daily growing thinner and weaker, except in a few cases. It was a truly pitiable sight, a few days ago, to see an emaciated skeleton crawl, with the aid of a stick, after a corpse that was being carried on a pole for interment. He staggered along, poor chap, and squatted down alongside the newly-made grave, watching the proceedings with large, round, sunken eyes, knowing it was only a matter of a few days and he himself

[1] *Story of the Rear-Column*, pp. 224, 225.

would be laid in the sod. He told me in a husky, hollow voice, "He was my friend." One poor fellow in particular—he is a mere mass of bones—persists in doing his work, and every evening he staggers into camp. He has been told to lie up and his manioc shall be provided for him, but he refuses. He said to me, in reply to my expression of sympathy on observing how thin he was, "Only a short time more, master!" Death is written in plain letters on many faces in this camp. Almost as many lives will be lost over this philanthropic mission as there are lives to save of Emin's people.'[1]

It was while Mr. Jameson was with Tippoo-Tib in May, on their way back from Kassongo, that he witnessed the act of cannibalism on account of which, painful as it is, he has been most cruelly traduced. His own report of the affair is manifestly truthful.[2] He was an unwilling participator in a hideous ceremony, for which he was in no way responsible, and which it would have been impossible for him to avert.

There can be no doubt, however, that while showing much sympathy for the suffering of those around them, Mr. Jameson and his comrades came to regard it with some callousness. Of that there is accumulated and distressing evidence in their severity to both natives and Zanzibaris, which is frankly recorded in their own letters and diaries. But how many average Englishmen, forced to pass a year in such surroundings, with nothing ennobling in their tasks, little that was not degrading in the few poor mockeries of pleasure or of relief from their constant misery which were within

[1] *My Life with Stanley's Rear-Guard*, pp. 77, 80.
[2] *Story of the Rear-Column*, pp. 290, 291. It has been so often quoted that it need not be here repeated.

their reach, would have acted better? 'Let him that is without sin among you'—and that has resisted like temptations—'cast the first stone.' And what were all the errors into which Major Barttelot and Mr. Jameson fell, under conditions recklessly imposed on them by Mr. Stanley, in comparison with the errors and worse of Mr. Stanley himself, the organiser and controller of the whole abortive Expedition of which the Yambuya arrangements, appointed and made necessary by him, were the greatest abortion?

On March 24 Major Barttelot returned from one of his visits to Stanley Falls, intending to await the result of Mr. Jameson's excursion to Kassongo, yet resolved that in any case he would not remain much longer in the neighbourhood, but would, at whatever risk, make an effort to follow Mr. Stanley. On his way back he was, as he recorded in his diary, on one day 'prostrate with fever;' on another 'weak from fever and having hardly eaten anything for the last three days;' on another 'completely worn out;' on another 'shattered and weak.' 'They thought I was a ghost,' he wrote when he arrived; and on the next day, 'I was prostrate, and opportunity was taken to play me false;' on the next, 'I find they have been playing the mischief since I have been away;' on the next, 'I am much upset at what I find.'[1] It is plain that by this time his health was thoroughly broken down, and the suspicions with which, rightly or wrongly, he regarded some of his colleagues, were in keeping with the increased violence that he used towards his unmanageable followers. It must be remembered that, though Mr. Stanley had left

[1] *Diaries and Letters*, pp. 212, 213.

at Yambuya all the men who were then sickly, he had taken with him his only qualified medical officer. For some time Mr. Jameson was amateur doctor to the garrison. He was afterwards relieved or assisted by Mr. Bonny. The other Englishmen also had turns at prescribing for one another and for themselves. But it was no fault of theirs if all of them blundered, or if no proper precautions were taken—if it was possible to take any precautions—to guard against the mental effects common to the tropical fevers that repeatedly attacked them.

Ill and harassed as Major Barttelot was, he made careful arrangements for going in search of Mr. Stanley as soon as he could obtain the 400 men whom he had at length had some reason to expect. Acting as far as he could on the instructions left with him a year before by his chief, and knowing that it would be impossible for him to carry all the stores in his charge, he detached the portions that, in his opinion, could best be spared. These he sent to Bangala by the 'Stanley,' which visited Yambuya early in June, in order that they might be taken charge of by Mr. Ward, who had previously gone down the Congo with a telegram to be forwarded to the Emin Relief Committee, notifying to it Major Barttelot's plans, and inviting its approval.[1] He also allowed Mr. Troup, who had for some time been dangerously ill, to proceed homewards in the 'Stanley.' Thus the only Englishmen left with him

---

[1] Mr. Stanley's unreasonable and ungenerous complaints about the wrongful disposal of the stores are sufficiently dealt with by Captain Walter Barttelot in *Diaries and Letters*, pp. 246-253; and by Mr. Herbert Ward in *My Life with Stanley's Rear-Guard*.

were Mr. Jameson, now returned from his long journeying in search of Tippoo-Tib, and Mr. Bonny.

Tippoo-Tib had at length supplied 400 carriers, in consideration of a payment of 1,000*l.*; but troubles with them began at the moment of their arrival. The men were Manyuema, as worthless and mischievous as Mr. Stanley had declared the race to be, and Muni Somai, the chief appointed for them by Tippoo-Tib, was a fit servant of such a master. Before he had been many hours on the road, and even before he started, Major Barttelot had evidence that, had he been in a state of mind to weigh it, might have convinced him of the impossibility of forcing a way through the forest with such helpers and with the residue of sickly and demoralised Zanzibaris and Soudanese left to him. He must not be blamed, however, for doing his best. He had been waiting at Yambuya six irksome months after the date at which Mr. Stanley had promised to return. He had heard nothing but vague and contradictory rumours about Mr. Stanley, whose absence and silence warranted the fear that he was either dead or himself in need of the relief he had gone to convey to Emin Pasha. Of the Yambuya garrison more than half had died; the rest were dwindling every day. As soon as he obtained the Manyuema, whose services were bought with his own and Mr. Jameson's money, he felt it his duty to go forward. If his present enterprise was rash, one that would have been doomed to failure in the hands of a much stronger man than he was after his year of misery, we must none the less honour him for his courage and his loyalty.

The Expedition that left Yambuya on June 11, 1888,

consisted of 430 Manyuema, 115 Zanzibaris, and 22 Soudanese. Each day there were desertions and thefts, insubordination on the part of the Zanzibaris, and defiance of orders by the Manyuema, who were under Muni Somai's independent control. On the 22nd Mr. Jameson, who was detached from Major Barttelot's party to keep a watch on Muni Somai, wrote in his diary :—

'What a chapter might be written on the starts and delays ever since we have been in Yambuya camp! Muni Somai told me to-day that the Manyuema were not men, but simply "meat-like beasts"; for, said he, "how can they be men, and yet love to eat men as they do? If there were two goats and one man offered them to choose from for food, they would take the man; all they think of now is what a lot of natives they will eat further on." He added, "The first lot of natives that they fight, they will eat as many as they can, and when their stomachs are full they will then catch others to carry their loads."'[1]

On the 23rd Major Barttelot made this record :—

'I punished my boy Soudi for idiocy in the morning, and, when I returned towards evening, found he had deserted, and no news of the other deserters. My revolver and seventy-five rounds of ammunition were gone, also my table-knife. The poor little beggar only took what he considered absolutely necessary, and was advised to it by the men. On being informed that they all knew where he was, I offered a reward for him, but no one responded. I was told that many others intended to desert. I fell them all in, and took away all the arms from the Zanzibaris, and their ammunition. The Soudanese are faithful. I told Bonny I should go to the Falls the next day and get some

[1] *Story of the Rear-Column*, p. 319.

chains, and that I would not return the rifles to the Zanzibaris for some lengthened period. He thought it good.'[1]

There can be small doubt that Major Barttelot had by this time fallen into such a state of feverish excitement that he was no longer responsible for his actions.[2] His disarming of the Zanzibaris on June 23, with the intention of putting them all in chains, was a measure that would have been fatal to the success of the Expedition if it had not already been in a hopeless state. And madder mistakes followed. On his way to Stanley Falls he wrote to Mr. Jameson, who was with Muni Somai following a somewhat different route through the forest, bidding him seek from the Arab chief 'sixty men, good men, to help bring up the loads and rifles' of the disgraced Zanzibaris, and to 'act as guards to them'—as if he had not seen how much worse were Muni Somai's Manyuema than his own mutinous Zanzibaris! In the same letter he said, 'I am going to ask Tippoo either for sixty Manyuema or for slaves.'[3] The Zanzibaris, it is true, were slaves in effect, and Muni Somai's Manyuema were certainly no better; but it was a new phase in the history of the luckless enterprise for slaves to be avowedly bought or borrowed by its English leader.

Major Barttelot was not alone, however, in proposing to purchase slaves. According to Mr. Jameson, slaves were actually bought by Mr. Bonny, who was in charge of the Zanzibaris during Major Barttelot's absence,

[1] *Diaries and Letters*, p. 328.
[2] See the strange letters written by him to Mr. Ward on March 30 and June 6.—*My Life with Stanley's Rear-Guard*, pp. 101, 121.
[3] *Story of the Rear-Column*, p. 390.

Mr. Jameson going across to look after them as often as he could. On June 28 Mr. Jameson wrote: 'Bonny says that five Manyuema people from the village of Mampuya came in yesterday, and he succeeded in buying from them a man as carrier and guide;' and on July 5, 'Bonny had not been able to buy any carriers, as they only brought in two small boys, for whom they wanted a gun, and two girls for a gun each.'[1]

In unprofitable and reprehensible negotiations with Tippoo-Tib, and in journeying to and fro, Major Barttelot occupied more than three weeks. He had directed that all his people should assemble at Banalya, sometimes called Unaria, on the Aruwimi, and there await his arrival from Stanley Falls. Mr. Bonny was at that place with the Zanzibaris and Soudanese on July 15, and most of Muni Somai's men came up on the 16th and 17th; but as Mr. Jameson had to look after the rear of the Manyuema and the loads left behind, he only reached Banalya on the 22nd, and then by a hurried march which he made alone. On the previous day he had received news from Mr. Bonny that Major Barttelot, having resumed the command on the 17th, had been killed on the 19th.

There have been much exaggeration and perversion of what seem to have been the facts as regard the way in which Major Barttelot met his death. Arriving at Banalya without the slaves he had sought, but with letters from Tippoo-Tib ordering Abdullah, the local chief, to provide them, he found Muni Somai's followers in a very riotous condition. They were recklessly firing off their guns and wasting the material needed for future

[1] *Story of the Rear-Column*, pp. 326, 332.

use. The noise and disorder utterly unnerved the already over-excited Major, and on the morning of the 19th he was further distracted by the drum-beating and howling of some women of the party. The orders he sent out that this performance should cease being disregarded, he rushed out of his hut, exclaiming, as Mr. Bonny avers, 'I will stop this and shoot the first man I catch firing.' All he did, however, was to threaten one of the women beating the drum, whereupon her husband retaliated by sending a bullet through his heart. His death was instantaneous. That he acted indiscreetly in approaching the women at all may be taken for granted; but only those who prefer to think ill of a man whose life was sacrificed in vain attempts to perform tasks that were beyond his strength will accept as true the cruel gossip which Mr. Bonny, the only other Englishman on the spot, detailed to Mr. Stanley, and which Mr. Stanley has since elaborated in various forms.[1]

Kindlier and juster critics may endorse the words written by Mr. Jameson as soon as he heard of the blow that deprived him of the friend with whom he had endured terrible hardships throughout more than a

[1] See Mr. Bonny's statement in the 'Log' printed in the *Times* of November 19, 1890. Mr. Stanley's remark on an incident in his return journey to Fort Bodo is significant. 'Among the Manyuema,' he says, 'were two insane women, or rather, to be quite correct, two women subject to spasms of hysterical exaltation, possessed by "devils," according to their chiefs, who prevented sleep by their perpetual singing during the night. Probably some such mania for singing at untimely hours was the cause of the Major's death. If the poor Major had any ear for harmony, their inharmonious and excited madhouse uproar might well have exasperated him.'—*In Darkest Africa*, vol. ii. p. 20.

year. 'He was a straightforward, honest, English gentleman, his only fault being a little too quick-tempered. He loved plain, straightforward dealing far too much ever to get on well with the Arabs. He hated their crafty roundabout way of doing everything, and showed it to them, and, of course, was disliked in turn. He was far too good a man to lose his life in a miserable way like this, and God knows what I shall do without him.'[1]

Mr. Jameson lived only four weeks longer. After attending to the affairs of his dead comrade, and making arrangements for the remnant of the Expedition, deserted by Muni Somai and his Manyuema, to be cared for in his absence by Mr. Bonny, Mr. Jameson had left Banalya on July 25 and proceeded to Stanley Falls. There he sought and obtained the trial and punishment of Major Barttelot's assassin; but he was chiefly occupied in zealous endeavours to procure from Tippoo-Tib fresh carriers, to enable him still to push on in search of Mr. Stanley. But Tippoo declined to help him unless he was paid 20,000*l*. for the work. Even with that preposterous demand Mr. Jameson was willing to comply, until he found that one of Tippoo's conditions was that the journey should be made by way of Kassongo and Lake Tanganyika, instead of by the route Mr. Stanley had prescribed. Thereupon he decided that he would travel by canoe to Bangala, thence communicate with the Emin Relief Committee in order to ascertain its wishes, and, if it sanctioned acceptance of Tippoo's proposals, to return at once and do his utmost in getting them carried out. There was no breach of

[1] *Story of the Rear-Column*, p. 338.

duty in this, only a last desperate effort to perform the task which he considered still incumbent upon him, slight as were the chances of his succeeding in face of all the appalling difficulties consequent on the overwhelming disasters that had beset him and his comrades. With that resolve he left Stanley Falls on August 9. On the way he was stricken with fever. He reached Bangala on the 16th to be tended by Mr. Ward. Next day he died.[1]

On that same day, August 17, Mr. Stanley arrived at Banalya from Fort Bodo. There he found all that was left of the rear-column and was made acquainted with the 'tragedies and catastrophes which,' he says, 'reduced a completely equipped and well-organised column of 271 men rank and file to 102 meagre, starved, and anæmic souls.'[2] He took no blame to himself for its miserable condition and the misfortunes that had attended it. He blamed only the men he had betrayed. To Mr. Jameson—of whose death, of course, he was not then aware—he wrote an angry letter, of which the following are some sentences:—

'Bonny showed me your letter of the 12th inst., wherein you stated it to be your purpose to go to Bangala. I cannot make out why the Major, you, Troup, and Ward, have been so *demented*—demented is the word. You understand English; an English letter of instructions was given you. You said it was intelligible—yet for some reason or another you have not followed one paragraph. You paid 1,000*l.* to go on this Expedition; you have voluntarily thrown your money away by leaving the Expe-

---

[1] *Story of the Rear-Column*, pp. 338–374.
[2] *Parliamentary Papers*, C. 5906, p. 10.

dition. Ward is not a whit better; he has acted all through, as I hear, more like an idiot than a sane being. You have left me naked. I have no clothes, no medicine; I will say nothing of my soap and candles, photograph apparatus and chemicals, two silver watches, a cap, and a score of other trifles. You believed I was dead, yet you brought along my boots and two hats and a flannel jacket. . . . Though, as reported to me, you, and all of you, seem to have acted like madmen, your version may modify my opinion.'[1]

Mr. Stanley also wrote a long report to the Emin Relief Committee, in which he said :—

'My personal kit, medicines, soap, candles, and provisions were sent down the Congo as "superfluities!" Thus, after making this immense personal sacrifice to relieve them and cheer them up, I find myself naked and deprived of even the necessaries of life in Africa. But, strange to say, they have kept two hats, four pairs of boots, a flannel jacket, and I propose to go back to Emin Pasha, and across Africa, with this truly African kit. . . . Livingstone, poor fellow, was all in patches when I met him, but it will be the reliever himself who will be in patches this time.'[2]

On his own showing, Mr. Stanley's wrath and despair, consequent on the discoveries he made at Banalya, arose much less from the miseries that had befallen the men under Major Barttelot's care than from the accident that had reduced his reserve of medicines, soap, candles, trousers, and other personal property. For the real cause of the real misfortunes he acknowledged no responsibility.

[1] *Story of the Rear-Column*, p. 365.
[2] *The Times*, April 3, 1889.

That cause was his recklessness in leaving Major Barttelot without making proper arrangements to enable the rear-column to follow him. He does, in one place, admit that the mischief was partly due 'to the breach of contract by Tippoo-Tib, and to his method of prevarication and dissimulation, to which crooked manners the young officers of the rear-column were strangers.'[1] But he does not admit that he was himself in fault.

Tippoo-Tib, it must be noted, complained that there was breach of contract on Mr. Stanley's part. He had been appointed Governor of the Stanley Falls District under King Leopold, and had promised to furnish Mr. Stanley with 600 carriers; but before Mr. Stanley left Yambuya in June 1887 it was brought to his notice that Tippoo-Tib required the supply of ammunition promised for his men before he was willing to furnish them, and he was excusably annoyed by the failure of the Congo State authorities to put in force the agreement as regards his governorship which had been made at Zanzibar.

On the latter point Major Barttelot wrote in March 1888 to Sir William Mackinnon: 'It should be remembered that Tippoo is an officer of the State, but that up to the present no notice has been taken of him at all, and he feels justly aggrieved. Besides, there are certain loads of his left by him at the Pool to be forwarded by the State, which have never been forwarded.'[2] And Mr. Jameson reported in his diary a conversation he had in May with Tippoo, who then complained to him that 'the Belgians have never communicated with me

[1] *Parliamentary Papers*, C. 5906, p. 10.
[2] *Diaries and Letters*, p. 220.

since I came up to Stanley Falls last year.'[1] 'He has written to the King of the Belgians,' Mr. Jameson added, 'asking him to send two officers and about thirty men to the Falls, not to assist him in any fighting, but as visible authority on behalf of the State during his own stay there, and in case of his absence at any time; but ever since the despatch of this letter, about a year ago, not a word have they sent him to the Falls. The way the Belgians have treated Tippoo-Tib seems very strange. He is extremely anxious to have a definite settlement made about the matter, and they have kept him for a whole year without any communication whatever. Tippoo-Tib naturally cannot understand this way of doing things, and looks upon it as a decided slight upon himself.'[2]

One of the duties assigned to Mr. Ward when he was sent down the Congo in March was to represent to the Belgian authorities the importance of doing something to prove the reality of Tippoo's new office. He found that there was some excuse for the delay. One of the two Belgian officers appointed to reside with Tippoo died on the way, and the other, falling ill, had to be sent to Europe. It was not till June that it was convenient to fill their places; but arrangements for that were being made before Mr. Ward reached Leopoldville, and with one of the three officers now designated for Stanley Falls, Lieutenant Baert, he had some interesting talk on April 14. Mr. Ward noted in his diary that :—

'During a conversation with M. Baert upon the Arab

[1] *Story of the Rear-Column*, p. 293.
[2] *Ibid.* p. 294.

situation up in the country about the Falls, he said: "Among us [Belgian officers in the Congo Free State and in Brussels] it was pronounced very short-sighted policy on Stanley's part appointing Tippoo-Tib to be chief of the Falls." "But stay," said I, "Stanley only suggested such an action, for before finally settling anything at Zanzibar, the agreement, &c., was sent home to His Majesty the King of the Belgians, to be ratified and sanctioned; therefore Stanley cannot be in any way blamed." "No, but if he is not legally accountable, he is at least morally responsible. It was Stanley who brought the Arabs to the Falls eleven years ago, and he is really the cause of their being where they are to-day." I stated that if the State officers who are going up to the Falls only temporise and are politic, there would be no trouble.'[1]

There can be no doubt that Mr. Stanley's arrangement with Tippoo-Tib, though sanctioned by King Leopold, was not approved by his subordinates in the Congo State, who shrewdly perceived that the nominal enlistment of Tippoo in the service of the State was actually a further recognition of his pretensions to complete and uncontrolled authority. The Congo officials, or their superiors in Brussels, were not at all eager to confirm the arrangement; hence, in part, the long delay in sending up ostensible advisers to Tippoo. When at length Captain Van Géle brought Lieutenant Baert and his colleagues, they were not able to exercise any real influence. Tippoo continued to be, as he still is, absolute master in the country, and the farcical 'contracts' entered into with him by Mr. Stanley in February 1887, only encouraged him in defiance and contempt, both of the Congo Free State, for which

[1] *My Life with Stanley's Rear-Guard*, p. 119.

Mr. Stanley was spokesman, and of the Emin Relief Expedition, of which Mr. Stanley was leader.

It is quite likely that, had he seen any advantage in doing so, Tippoo-Tib would have supplied the promised carriers long before June 1888, when the Belgian officials assisted at the formal agreement under which Muni Somai was sent to assist Major Barttelot. But his Arab chiefs and their Manyuema serfs were until then more profitably employed in raiding for slaves and ivory than it was thought that they could be in conveying Mr. Stanley's stores to the Albert Nyanza. Accordingly Major Barttelot was left in the lurch, and Mr. Stanley seems at no time to have seriously expected that his bargain with Tippoo would be kept.

On his arrival at Banalya in August 1888 Mr. Stanley wrote a very friendly letter to Tippoo, in which he described his journeys across the forest and back, but made no complaint of Tippoo's 'breach of contract,' and only mildly suggested that he might now be inclined to co-operate with him. Here is the material part of the polite epistle :—

'And now, my friend, what are you going to do? We have gone the road twice over. We know where it is bad and where it is good. We know where there is plenty of food and where there is none, where all the camps are, and where we shall sleep and rest. I am waiting to hear your words. If you go with me, it is well. If you do not go with me, it is well also. I leave it to you . . . . Whatever you have to say to me, my ears will be open with a good heart, as it has always been towards you.'[1]

Mr. Stanley, it is true, bitterly denounced Tippoo-

---

[1] *My Life with Stanley's Rear-Guard*, p. 139.

Tib at a later date, and even threatened him with legal proceedings for his 'breach of contract'; but it is not unreasonable to suppose that there was never any seriousness in the threat, and that the denunciations were merely intended to divert attention from Mr. Stanley's own wrong-doing. That, at any rate, was undoubtedly the purpose of the angrier and more cruel abuse with which he has recently assailed the memories of the two men, Major Barttelot and Mr. Jameson, who died in his service, and the characters of two others, Mr. Ward and Mr. Troup, who live to defend themselves.

Mr. Stanley's later slanders and falsifications need not be answered. They only emphasise and aggravate his offence, great and unpardonable enough in itself, in having caused the wreck of his rear-column.

CHAPTER VI

THE 'RELIEF' OF EMIN

MR. STANLEY'S first serious effort to 'relieve' Emin Pasha was made in January 1889, two years after he had left England, promising to do the work with as little delay as possible. For much of the delay that occurred he is entitled to excuse on the plea that he was hindered by stupendous difficulties, which overtaxed even his talents as an adventurer and the resources at his disposal.

As the Congo route was chosen with the approval of his employers and at the request of one of them, they must share with him the blame for that choice, and probably neither he nor they foresaw the obstacles in his path. It was doubtless thought that he would have easy sailing up the Congo and easy marching afterwards. It was taken for granted that Tippoo-Tib would promptly supply the 600 carriers partly paid for in advance. When Mr. Stanley hurried on from Yambuya to the Albert Nyanza, it seems to have been expected that Major Barttelot would quickly follow with all the stores left in his charge, either with or without the promised carriers. It was not supposed that Mr. Stanley would have to cut and fight his way through a dismal forest and through tribes made hostile by his treatment of them, and would only emerge five months later with his forces reduced by nearly half through death and desertion, and with so little of the ammunition consigned to Emin Pasha that he considered every pound of it to be necessary for his own use. It was also an unlooked-for contingency that, when he was within four days' sail of Wadelai, he had no boat in which to make the voyage, and no Maxim gun with which to clear a road by land; and no one could have anticipated that, after these had been recovered, he would have more pressing work to do in 'relieving' the sick men he had left behind him, and especially the disorganised residue of his 'rear-column,' abandoned for a year in the neighbourhood of Stanley Falls, than in concerning himself about Emin. In all his emergencies Mr. Stanley evidently did what he deemed best under the lamentable circumstances in which he found himself, and he must be blamed rather for creating those circumstances than for any blunders he committed in preventing them from overwhelming him.

But the fact remains that, having pledged himself to 'relieve' Emin Pasha by June, or at any rate by August or September 1887, he was only in a position to take effective measures to that end in the early part of 1889.

The material portions of the letter which he wrote to Emin from Zanzibar on February 23, 1887, should here be quoted:—

'DEAR SIR,—I have the honour to inform you that the Government of His Highness the Khedive of Egypt, upon receipt of your urgent letters soliciting aid and instructions, have seen fit to depute me to equip an Expedition to proceed to Wadelai to convey such aid as they think you require, and to assist you in other ways agreeably with the written instructions which have been delivered to me for you.

'Having been pretty accurately informed of the nature of your necessities from the perusal of your letters to the Egyptian Government, the Expedition has been equipped in such a manner as may be supposed to meet all your wants. As you will gather from the letters of His Highness and the Prime Minister of Egypt to you, and which I bring with me, all that could possibly be done to satisfy your needs has been done most heartily. From the translation of the letters delivered to me, I perceive that they will give you immense satisfaction. Over 60 soldiers from Wady Halfa have been detailed to accompany me in order that they may be able to encourage the soldiers under your command and confirm the letters. We also march under the Egyptian standard.

'The Expedition includes 600 Zanzibari natives, and probably as many Arab followers from Central Africa. . . .

'Besides abundance of ammunition for your needs, official letters from the Egyptian Government, a heavy mail from your numerous friends and admirers, I bring with me personal equipments for yourself and officers suitable to the rank of each.

'Trusting that I shall have the satisfaction of finding you well and safe, and that nothing will induce you to rashly venture your life and liberty in the neighbourhood of Uganda, without the ample means of causing yourself and men to be respected which I am bringing to you, I beg you to believe me

'Yours very faithfully,
'HENRY M. STANLEY.' [1]

We have seen that Mr. Stanley had not quite for-

[1] *In Darkest Africa*, vol. i. p. 62.

gotten Emin in the interval; but in order to estimate the value of the 'relief' he afforded we must now follow the story consecutively.

Having in December 1887 reached the Albert Nyanza at a point where he had not told Emin Pasha to look for him, and not seeing him there, Mr. Stanley hurried west again as far as Fort Bodo. That step may have been reasonable, as humanity and self-interest made other claims upon him more urgent, and as he then had no 'relief' whatever to offer. Yet it seems strange that, having directed Emin to communicate with him at Kavalli's settlement, he did not take more pains to apprise the Pasha of his arrival, and that he went back so quickly by the route he had just taken, in order to wreak vengeance on the natives who had resented his previous slaughterings.

He did visit the Kavalli district, however, on April 16, 1888, and then he received the following letter from Emin, dated March 25 :—

'DEAR SIR,—Rumours having been afloat of white men having made their apparition somewhere south of this lake, I have come here in quest of news. A start to the furthest end of the lake, which I could reach by steamer, has been without success, the people being greatly afraid of Kabba Rega's people, and their chiefs being under instructions to conceal whatever they know. To-day, however, has arrived a man from Chief Mpigwa, of Nyamsassi country, who tells me that the wife of the said chief has seen you at Undussuma, her birthplace, and that his chief volunteers to send a letter of mine to you. I send therefore one of our allies, Chief Mogo, with the messenger, to Chief Mpigwa's, requesting him to send Mogo and his letter, as well as an Arabic one, to you, or to retain Mogo and send the letter ahead. Be pleased, if this reaches you, to *rest where you are*, and to inform me by letter, or one of your people, of your wishes. I could easily come to Chief Mpigwa's, and my steamer and boats would bring you here. At the arrival of your letter or man, I shall at once start for Nyamsassi, and from there we could concert our further designs. Beware of Kabba Rega's men! He has expelled Captain Casati.—Believe me, dear sir, to be

'Yours very faithfully,
'Dr. Emin.

'Tunguru, Lake Albert.'[1]

On receiving that letter, says Mr. Stanley, his men 'became mad with enthusiasm,' and he condescended to reply to it. He sent Mr. Jephson, with fifty men and the steel boat 'Advance,' to the shore of the Albert Nyanza, with orders to proceed in search of Emin, and to deliver a letter inviting him, 'if he was willing to leave Africa,' to come at once.

'I await your decision at Nyamsassi. As it is difficult to supply rations to our people on the Nyanza plain, I hope we shall not have to wait long for it. On the plateau above there is abundance of food and cattle, but on the lower plain, bordering the Nyanza, the people are mainly fishermen.

'If this letter reaches you before you leave your place, I should advise you to bring in your steamer and boats rations sufficient to subsist us while we await your removal, say about 12,000 or 15,000 lbs. of grain, millet, or Indian corn, &c., which, if your steamer is of any capacity, you can easily bring.

'If you are already resolved on leaving Africa, I would suggest that you should bring with you all your cattle, and every native willing to follow you. Nubar Pasha hoped you

[1] *In Darkest Africa*, vol. i. p. 367.

L

would bring all your Makaraka, and leave not one behind if you could help it, as he would retain them all in his service.

'The letters from the Ministry of War, and from Nubar Pasha, which I bring, will inform you fully of the intention of the Egyptian Government, and perhaps you had better wait to see them before taking any action. I simply let you know briefly about the intentions of the Government, that you may turn the matter over in your mind, and be enabled to come to a decision.

'I hear you have abundance of cattle with you; three or four milk cows would be very grateful to us if you can bring them in your steamer and boats. . . .

'We shall have to forage far and near while we await your attendance at Nyamsassi, but you may depend upon it we shall endeavour to stay here until we see you.'[1]

On April 29 Mr. Jephson returned, accompanied by Emin Pasha and some of his officers, and though Mr. Stanley was annoyed at seeing that the Governor of the Equatorial Province had 'a small, spare figure,' instead of the 'tall, thin, military-looking figure' for which he had brought a pair of trousers from which 'about six inches had to be cut off the leg before they fitted'— with a face, too, on which 'there was not a trace of ill-health or anxiety; it rather indicated good condition of body and peace of mind'—he welcomed his guests and toasted them in 'five half-pint bottles of champagne.'[2]

Next day they talked business, and presumably Mr. Stanley then handed to Emin the credentials he had with him. Mr. Stanley says:—

[1] *In Darkest Africa*, vol. i. p. 369.
[2] *Ibid.* pp. 374–376.

'I had an idea that I might have to wait about two weeks, when we would all march to the plateau and occupy a suitable spot in Undusuma, where, after seeing everything done for complete security and comfort, I could leave him to return to the assistance of the rear column. On being re-united, we could resume our march within a few days for Zanzibar; but the Pasha's manner is ominous. When I propose a return to the sea to him, he has the habit of tapping his knee, and smiling in a kind of "we shall see" manner. It is evident he finds it difficult to renounce his position in a country where he has performed vice-regal functions.'[1]

Mr. Stanley gives what purports to be an exact report of the conversations that ensued; and this, whether accurate or not, is very instructive. In the first place, he says, he urged Emin Pasha to at once abandon the Equatorial Province, and accept the escort to Egypt offered him.

'"Were I in your place, I would not hesitate one moment what to do."

'"What you say is quite true," replied the Pasha; "but we have such a large number of women and children, probably 10,000 people altogether! How can they be all brought out here? We shall want a great many carriers."

'"Carriers for what?"

'"For the women and children. You surely would not leave them, and they cannot travel."

'"The women must walk; for such children as cannot walk, they will be carried on donkeys, of which you say you have many. Your people cannot travel far during the first month, but little by little they will get accustomed to it. Our women, on my second expedition, crossed Africa; your women, after a little while, will do quite as well."

[1] *In Darkest Africa*, vol. i. p. 377.

'"They will require a vast amount of provisions for the road."

'"Well, you have a large number of cattle, some hundreds, I believe. Those will furnish beef. The countries through which we pass must furnish grain and vegetable food. And when we come to countries that will accept pay for food, we have means to pay for it, and at Msalala we have another stock of goods ready for the journey to the coast."

'"Well, well. We will defer further talk of it till to-morrow."'[1]

Emin evidently did not like the notion of abandoning the people dependent on him, and he may be excused for questioning the possibility of driving a herd of cattle, large enough to feed 10,000 people, for several months, and the honesty of stealing 'grain and vegetable food' on the way.

On May 1 he informed Mr. Stanley that 'he had resolved to leave Africa, if his people were willing; if not, he would stay with them.' But on May 3, Mr. Stanley says, the Pasha told him that, though the Egyptians would probably be glad to return to their own country, and he should be glad to get rid of them, he felt sure that his other people would refuse to leave their homes. Thereupon Mr. Stanley gave him a choice of two remarkable proposals. One 'comes from the King of the Belgians,' he said :—

'He has requested me to inform you that in order to prevent the lapse of the Equatorial Provinces to barbarism, and provided they can yield a reasonable revenue, the Congo State might undertake the government of them if it could be done by an expenditure of about 10,000*l.* or

[1] *In Darkest Africa*, vol. i. p. 379.

12,000*l*. per annum ; and, further, that His Majesty, King Leopold, was willing to pay a sufficient salary to you—1,500*l*. as governor, with the rank of general—in the belief that such employment agrees with your own inclination. Your duty would be to keep open the communications between the Nile and Congo, and to maintain law and order in the Equatorial Provinces.'

The other was as follows :—

'If you are convinced that your people will positively decline the Khedive's offer to return to Egypt, that you accompany me with such soldiers as are loyal to you to the north-east corner of Victoria Nyanza, and permit me to establish you there in the name of the East African Association. We will assist you to build your fort in a locality suitable to the aims of such an association, leave our boat and such things as would be necessary for your purpose with you, and then hasten home across the Masai-land, lay the matter before the East African Association, and obtain its sanction for the act, as well as its assistance to establish you permanently in Africa. I must explain to you that I have no authority to make this last proposition, that it issues from my own goodwill to you, and with an earnest desire to save you and your men from the consequences of your determination to remain here. But I feel assured that I can obtain its hearty approval and co-operation, and that the Association will readily appreciate the value of a trained battalion or two in their new acquisition, and the services of such an administrator as yourself.' [1]

Mr. Stanley need not be charged with treachery to the Egyptian Government in making these alternative offers, and he deserves credit for the shrewdness with which he endeavoured to render Emin of service to at

[1] *In Darkest Africa*, vol. i. p. 387.

least one of his two European employers, and left Emin to choose which of the two he would serve. This was only in keeping with the two chief original purposes, not altogether conflicting, of the so-called Emin Relief Expedition.

Let it be remembered that the nominal area of the Congo Free State extends eastward nearly to the borders of the Equatorial Province. The charter of the Imperial British East Africa Company empowers it to stretch out from the Zanzibar coast, in a north-westerly direction, as far as it can, provided it does not encroach on German, French or Italian 'spheres of influence.' Mr. Stanley, being under great obligations to both King Leopold and Sir William Mackinnon, was naturally anxious to be of use to one of them.

We learn from him that Emin Pasha at once rejected the first proposal, saying, 'While I am here, the Provinces belong to Egypt, and they remain her property until I retire. When I depart they become "no man's land." I cannot strike my flag in such a manner, and change the red for the blue. I have served the first for thirteen years;[1] the latter I never saw. . . . I do not think that proposition, with all due gratitude to His Majesty King Leopold, can be entertained.' But the other proposal was received by him with some favour. Provided his people consented to leave the Equatorial Province, as the Egyptian Government wished them to do, and were willing to settle elsewhere, Emin saw no objection to the arrangement, and advantages in it.

[1] Mr. Stanley writes 'thirty years'—evidently a mistake for thirteen.

'"I do not think that my people would object to accompanying me to the Victoria Nyanza, as their objection, so far as I know, only applies to going to Egypt. Assuming that the people are willing, I admire the project very much. It is the best solution of the difficulty, and by far the most reasonable. For, consider that three-fourths of the 8,000 people are women, children, and young slaves. What would the Government do with such a mass of people? Would it feed them? Then think of the difficulty of travel with such an army of helpless people. I cannot take upon myself the responsibility of leading such a host of tender-footed people to die on the road. The journey to the Victoria is possible. It is comparatively short. Yes, by far, the last proposition is the most feasible."

'"There is no hurry, since you are to await the arrival of the rear column. Turn the matter over in your mind while I go to bring the Major up. You have certainly some weeks before you to consider the matter thoroughly. . . . If you absolutely decline to serve the King of the Belgians, and you are resolved to stay in Africa, you must trust in my promise to get a British Company to employ you and your troops, which probably has by this time been chartered with the purpose of constituting a British possession in East Africa."'[1]

On one of the few pages of 'In Darkest Africa' in which Mr. Stanley makes the least approach towards speaking justly of Emin Pasha he thus sums up the situation at this time:—

'Those who are interested in motives will not find it difficult to understand the apparent hesitation and indecision that he seemed to labour under when questioned by me as to his intentions. For nothing could have been more unexpected and unwelcome than the official letters

[1] *In Darkest Africa*, vol. i. pp. 392, 393.

from the Khedive and Nubar Pasha, which declared their resolve to abandon the Province, except the absolute silence of British officials, or British philanthropists, or commercial companies, respecting the future of the country wherein he had spent so many years of his life in contentment, if not in peace. In lieu of what he had expected, I had only the offer of the King of the Belgians to make to him, to which were attached certain conditions that appeared to him to render the offer of no value. He could not guarantee a revenue—possibly because he knew better than anyone else that there was neither Government nor Province, and that, therefore, revenue could not be collected. It was then I proposed to him, solely on my own responsibility, that he should take service with the British East Africa Association, because the copy of his letter to Sir John Kirk informed me that it approached nearer to his own proposition than the other. As I could not guarantee the engagement without authority, and could only promise that I would do my utmost to realise my ideas, I could but extract a declaration of his preference that the second offer was more congenial to him than retreat to Egypt or service with the Congo State. Yet, as we know, he could definitely accept neither, inasmuch as he did not know whether his rebellious officers would consent to depart from the Province, even as far as the Victoria Nyanza.'[1]

So matters stood, it appears, when Mr. Stanley parted amicably from Emin on May 24, although he says that before then he had begun to lose confidence in the Pasha. For one thing, Emin gave him a pound of tobacco, a bottle of pickles, and a pair of shoes, and also made presents to Mr. Jephson and Dr. Parke. 'These gifts,' wrote Mr. Stanley, 'reveal that he is not in the extreme distress we had imagined, and that there

[1] *In Darkest Africa*, vol. ii. p. 421.

was no necessity for the advance to have pressed forward so hurriedly.' For another thing, Emin was heard preferring a request courteously—' and rather pleasantly, I thought '—to one of his officers. 'There is something about this that I do not understand,' wrote Mr. Stanley; 'it is certainly not like my ideal governor, vice-king, or leader of men, to talk in that strain to subordinates.'[1]

For all that, on returning to Fort Bodo in order that he might go thence in search of Major Barttelot and the rear column, Mr. Stanley left Mr. Jephson and three Soudanese with Emin, it having been arranged that Mr. Jephson, armed with Nubar Pasha's and the Khedive's letters and a proclamation from Mr. Stanley, should accompany Emin on a round of visits to the stations in the Equatorial Province, there to ascertain the wishes of the people as regarded returning to Egypt. The steel boat 'Advance' was also left for Mr. Jephson's use, and, as an instalment of the 'relief' to be afforded to Emin, 'thirty-one cases Remingtons, two boxes Winchesters, one box of brass rods, lamp and sounding iron' were handed over to him.[2]

This was certainly but a small part of the 'abundance of ammunition for your needs,' and 'personal equipments for yourself and officers, suitable to the rank of each,' which Mr. Stanley, writing from Zanzibar in February 1887, had told Emin to expect in the following August, and considerably less than the Emin Relief Committee had undertaken to send out; yet it was evidently as much as Mr. Stanley could deliver in

[1] *In Darkest Africa*, vol. i. pp. 398, 399.
[2] *Ibid.* p. 403.

May 1888. It may have been his misfortune more than his fault that so much of the large store of ammunition and other articles with which he started had been used, lost, wasted, or left behind during his twelve months' wanderings; but so it was.

It must be clearly understood that in May 1888 Mr. Stanley was in no position to 'relieve' Emin Pasha. He had not with him either the promised quantity of fighting material, or anything like the '600 Zanzibari natives, and probably as many Arab followers from Central Africa,' besides 'over sixty soldiers from Wady Halfa, detailed to accompany me in order that they may be able to encourage the soldiers under your command,' mentioned in his announcement to Emin of 'the ample means of causing yourself and men to be respected, which I am bringing to you.' 'With 126 men,' he wrote in March 1888, 'I attempt the relief of Emin Pasha the second time,' his flying visit to the Albert Nyanza in December 1887 being the first attempt. In addition to these 126, he had a 'garrison' of forty-nine men at Fort Bodo, which, he wrote, 'consists of all those who suffer from debility, anæmia, and leg sores, some of which are perfectly incurable.'[1] His whole available 'force,' sick and well, therefore numbered 175. Had Emin accepted his offer, and come out at once with any of his people who chose, to remain in camp near the Albert Nyanza until the rear column had been rescued, they would have been in sorry plight as regards defence, and in sorrier plight as regards food. The food supplies at Fort Bodo, even with the help of constant raiding on the natives

[1] *In Darkest Africa*, vol. i. p. 348.

around, were inadequate for the few scores actually detained there. Had the number been raised to several hundreds, not to speak of the 8,000 or 10,000 of Emin's estimate, terrible famine must have ensued. It is true that the Fort Bodo garrison afterwards grew crops for themselves, but these were not planted at this time, and consequently would not be ready for Emin's followers; and even Mr. Stanley cannot have seriously imagined that Emin's two steamers could bring up the 'hundreds' of cattle requisite for their sustenance.

Let it be noted that this 'second relief of Emin Pasha,' while it was utterly inadequate for Emin's relief by Mr. Stanley, had for one of its results the relief of Mr. Stanley by Emin. Emin procured 130 Madi carriers [1] for Mr. Stanley to take with him to the Congo, and use in bringing up some of the stores left with the rear column.[2] The other results were altogether mischievous.

The suggestion that Mr. Stanley should depute one of his companions to remain with Emin and to act as a spokesman for the whole Relief Expedition came from the Pasha. Mr. Jephson, to whom the office was assigned, wrote in his journal:—

'It appears Emin told Stanley that his officers were exceedingly sceptical about us, and did not believe we came from Egypt. He has therefore asked Stanley to leave one of his officers with him until Stanley's return here with the

---

[1] *In Darkest Africa*, vol. i. p. 403.

[2] They were not, however, equal to the heavy tasks imposed on them by Mr. Stanley. Seventy-three died of exhaustion or were shot for desertion on the journey to Banalya, and thirty-one perished on the journey back. Of the 130 engaged in May only twenty-six returned in December.—*In Darkest Africa*, vol. ii. pp. 14, 105.

rear column. He would wish this officer to be his guest, to go round with him to all his stations throughout the Province, and address the people, explaining to them who we were and the reason we had arrived here. He would wish this officer to read the letters of the Khedive and Nubar Pasha at each station, also a proclamation from Stanley to the soldiers. The people would be drawn up to hear what was said, and could ask Stanley's representative any question they pleased about the road, &c., and he could answer them. Emin thinks that this alone would satisfy them and convince them that we came from Egypt. It could then be seen if the people were willing or not to come out with us; and, in the event of his people refusing to leave, and he himself coming out with us, it could never be said of him that he had deserted his people.'[1]

The suggestion was reasonable, as affording a chance —the only one left—of persuading the people that the Relief Expedition was a reality. Although Mr. Stanley affected to be ignorant of the state of affairs in the Equatorial Province when he met Emin in May 1888, his letter of February 1887 showed that he was at that time aware of the difficulties by which Emin was even then and had been for some time nearly overwhelmed. The avowed purpose of the Expedition was to enable Emin either to quell the turbulence of his troops and hold the Equatorial Province against Mahdist encroachments, or to withdraw safely from it. The Egyptian Government had favoured the latter alternative, but Emin was left free to adopt the former if he chose; and that was the course he desired to take. Only when affairs were at the worst with him, and when he saw no

[1] *Emin Pasha and the Rebellion at the Equator*, by A. J. Mounteney Jephson, p. 31.

prospect of continuing his work, did he entertain the thought of quitting the field of his long and zealous labours; and as often as there was the least sign of improvement the wish to remain and continue the task gained fresh strength. 'If Stanley does not come soon we are lost,' he wrote on March 25, 1888,[1] soon after hearing for the first time that his 'deliverer' was near; but even then he believed that he would be supplied with means of crushing the mutiny that was growing, and had no idea of scuttling in the way proposed by Mr. Stanley. The utmost he consented to do, or that ought to have been expected of him, was to take counsel with all the people who recognised his Government, and propose to them the same honourable method of withdrawal which he was prepared himself to accept.

And for that, if for nothing else, he needed 'the ample means of causing himself and his men to be respected,' which Mr. Stanley had written to say, 'I am bringing to you.' Instead of that, Mr. Stanley brought him in May only thirty-three cases of ammunition and a few other stores. Instead of the imposing party of sixty Soudanese, led by Mr. Stanley himself in a dignified march to Wadelai, all that Mr. Stanley could provide him with was a party comprising Mr. Jephson and three Soudanese as Mr. Jephson's personal attendants. If when he courteously thanked Mr. Stanley for this small measure of relief it did not occur to Emin that his people would not be satisfied or overawed by it, he was soon made aware of its insufficiency.

Returning to his Province with Mr. Jephson and the three Soudanese, Emin Pasha promptly made

[1] Quoted by Mr. Stanley from *The Gotha Geographical Journal*

arrangements for the contemplated visits to his different stations. At each a meeting was to be called, and after addresses by Emin and Mr. Jephson, the Khedive's and Nubar Pasha's letters and Mr. Stanley's proclamation were to be read out. In his proclamation Mr. Stanley said, among other things:—

'I have come expressly at the command of the Khedive Tewfik to lead you out of this country and show you the way to Egypt. . . . At the same time the Khedive says that if you think the road is too long, or are afraid of the journey, you may stay here, but that if you do so you are no longer his soldiers and your pay stops at once, and that if any trouble befall you hereafter you are not to expect any help from him. Should you decide to obey him and follow me to Egypt, I am to show you the way to Zanzibar, and there put you on board a steamer and take you to Suez, and thence to Cairo, and your pay continues until you arrive in Egypt, and all promotions made here may be secured to you, and all rewards promised you here will be paid in full. I send one of my officers, Mr. Jephson, to read you this message, and that you may know that he comes from me, I lend him my sword. I now go back a little way to collect all my people and goods, and bring them here. After a few months—Inshallah—I shall return to hear what you have to say. If you say, "Let us go to Egypt," I will then show you a safe road, and will accompany you and not leave you until you stand before the Khedive. If you say, "We shall not leave this country," then I will bid you farewell and return to Egypt with my own people, and give the Khedive your answer.'[1]

The ceremony was first gone through on June 6, before a small assembly at Tunguru on the way to Wadelai, and the answer Mr. Jephson received from

[1] *Emin Pasha, &c.* p. 48.

the soldiers was that 'if the Pasha stayed, they stayed; if the Pasha went, they went.' But 'it was plain to me,' says Mr. Jephson, 'that the feeling of these people was not for going to Egypt'; and he gives good reasons for it.

'The Khedive's letter only promised to give them their pay up to the time they arrived in Egypt, and said nothing whatever about future employment. Moreover, most of these so-called Soudanese had been recruited from the Dinka, Madi, Boru, Shefalu, Niam-Niam, Bongo, Makraka, Monbuttu, or Moru tribes, and the country was more or less like their own homes, where they could keep up large households and live on the fat of the land. Even if they had been promised employment in Egypt, they could never have supported their people on their pay, and they would never be willing to get rid of their women and children. Egypt offered no attractions for them whatever, so it was hardly surprising when they answered that they wished to follow their Governor, who had looked after and clothed them all these years.'

Mr. Jephson adds significantly, with reference to the officer in charge at Tunguru—and the statement here made to him was several times confirmed at other places:—

'Suliman Aga afterwards suggested that it would be a good thing, if this country was no longer considered tenable, that the people with their Governor should be conducted to a country within reach of the sea, and left to settle there. It was peculiar that he should have thought of this plan, for Emin had made it himself in one of his letters to Nubar Pasha some months before. Stanley, when he reached the lake, had made three propositions to the Pasha, one of which was a suggestion that Emin should take his people and settle them in Kavirondo, on the Victoria

Nyanza, if they did not wish to go to Egypt. This plan, therefore, of Suliman Aga's agreed with both, but I did not say anything about it, as I had been strictly enjoined to understand that our first duty was to the Khedive.'[1]

It is a pity that Mr. Jephson was not at liberty to take counsel with Emin's people on the project which Mr. Stanley had broached to Emin, and which many of them would evidently have approved. It seems that they might easily have been induced to migrate to the east side of Victoria Nyanza, only a few weeks' journey from Wadelai, whereas they naturally objected to be conveyed to Egypt and exposed there to all sorts of unknown risks.

It may here be explained that 'Emin's people' comprised two battalions of regulars and a number of irregulars, numbering about 1,500 in all, together with the natives clustered round the stations and there engaged in various trades and manufactures under Emin's direction. The troops, as Mr. Jephson says, were recruited from different parts of the Equatorial Province and its surroundings, and were chiefly officered by Egyptians. For a long time they had practically been without ammunition, and restricted to the use of native weapons, and at all times they were more like an unwieldy police force than a well-disciplined and efficient army. The first battalion of the regulars had virtually revolted in 1884, at the time when Emin was constrained to retire from his northern districts, and from Rejaf, its head-quarters, had maintained communications with the Mahdists. Emin believed that the second battalion, distributed over the southern stations, was

[1] *Emin Pasha, &c.* pp. 52, 53.

loyal to him, though many of its officers defied his orders whenever they deemed it convenient to do so.

Soon after his arrival at Wadelai with Mr. Jephson, Emin received a message from the officers of the first battalion, to the effect that 'hearing that an expedition had arrived at the south end of the lake with ammunition from Egypt to the people, they were now convinced that their Governor had been right, and wished to apologise for what they had done, and make their submission to him.' At Mr. Jephson's intercession, as he tells us, Emin readily forgave them, though, as events proved, this was only a ruse. The purpose of the malcontents of the first battalion was to secure a share of the expected ammunition, and, if possible, to obtain the co-operation of the second battalion in placing Emin at their mercy. In this second project they succeeded before long, and for a time; but in the meanwhile Mr. Jephson visited several stations, and there produced Mr. Stanley's proclamation and the other documents, while at others, at which he thought it unsafe to appear in person, he caused the papers to be read by deputy. In most cases he received vague answers, as at Tunguru; but in none did he obtain any assurance that the soldiers really desired or intended to be conveyed to Egypt. At length a crisis, which might have been foreseen, arose. Mr. Jephson was at Laboré with the Pasha on August 12. As he reports:—

'I read the Khedive's and Stanley's letters, and explained as usual everything connected with the Expedition. Whilst I was speaking I noticed that the soldiers were not as attentive as was generally the case, and that there was a good deal of whispering going on amongst them. A large crowd of people too, men, women, and children, had gathered in dense masses on a little bluff above the place where the soldiers were drawn up in line, and there was an uneasy stir amongst them, as if something unusual was going to happen. After I had finished speaking, Emin, as was his custom, added a few words to what I had said. Whilst he was speaking, a big, bull-headed, sullen-looking Soudanese stepped out of the ranks and exclaimed, "All you have been telling us is a lie, and the letter you have read out is a forgery, for if it had come from Effendina he would have *commanded* us to come, and not have told us we might do as we please. You do not come from Egypt. We know of only one road to Egypt, and that is by Khartoum. We will either go by that road or will live and die in this country."'[1]

Those outspoken words were doubtless but an expression of the opinions held by most of the people at the other stations; and there was much excuse for them. Mr. Jephson and his three Soudanese attendants were not sufficiently authoritative representatives of the Khedive to convince the discontented and suspicious soldiers. In sending such an embassage Mr. Stanley only prejudiced Emin, and discredited himself and his errand. It is quite clear that Mr. Jephson's mission hastened on, and gave form to, the long-growing disaffection which had caused Emin to appeal repeatedly to Europe for help.

The disloyal speech of the 'big, bull-headed, sullen-looking Soudanese' at Laboré was the signal for a general mutiny. 'The whole people were ripe for rebellion,' says Mr. Jephson.[2] Seeking safety in Dufilé,

---

[1] *Emin Pasha, &c.* p. 145.
[2] *Ibid.* p. 155.

Emin and Mr. Jephson were there made prisoners on August 18, 'which, when we think of it,' Mr. Stanley remarks, 'is the day after Jameson's sad death at Bangala, and after our arrival at Banalya.'[1] One of the reasons offered for the arrest Mr. Jephson tells us was that :—

'They thought that there would be an attempt on the part of the Governor and Stanley to compel them to leave the country. They would not be able to carry their women and children and goods with them; moreover, they knew nothing of a road to Egypt viâ Zanzibar, and did not really believe that Khartoum had fallen. . . . As for me, they said they had nothing personally against me except that I was an envoy of Stanley, and was helping the Pasha and him to carry out their plans of forcing the people to leave the Province. But they supposed I was only obeying orders. I was free to go about the station, but I should be followed by sentries who would report to them all that I did.'[2]

The sequel only so far concerns us as it bears upon the question of Emin Pasha's responsibility to the people of whom a dominant faction had cast him off. He was formally deposed by a council of rebel leaders on September 24; but a few days after that the Mahdists, apparently encouraged by the news of the disturbances in the Province, entered it from the north and easily captured three of the stations. So much alarm was thereby caused that Emin was liberated on November 17, and invited, though not by the leaders who had deposed him, to resume his functions as Governor. This offer he declined. Yet he still considered himself bound in honour to do what he could

---

[1] *Parliamentary Papers*, C. 5906, p. 11.
[2] *Emin Pasha, &c.* p. 164.

for the majority of the people who were still loyal to him. Here he differed from Mr. Jephson. 'All he has now to do,' in Mr. Jephson's opinion, 'is to get out of the country with the few faithfuls, and not trouble his head about the rest. If they want to follow let them do so by all means, but they must take all the trouble on their own shoulders.'[1] Not sharing this view, Emin stayed on until, when it was feared that Dufilé would be captured by the Mahdists, he and Mr. Jephson retreated, with a large part of the population of Wadelai and many others, to Tunguru. There they were on January 26, 1889, when authentic news reached them about Mr. Stanley.

Mr. Stanley had in the meanwhile accomplished his journey in search of the rear column, and brought back all that remained of it to Fort Bodo. Arriving at that place on December 20, he expected to find Mr. Jephson and Emin, and all who wished to be relieved, awaiting him. Not seeing them, he started with commendable promptitude for the Albert Nyanza. At Kandekoré, on the road thither, he left with Lieutenant Stairs and Dr. Parke 124 men too weak and diseased to travel. On January 16, with about 270 Zanzibaris and Manyuema, he encamped about a day's march from the lake, in, as he reports, 'one of the old villages which was once burnt by us, and which was again clean and new and prosperous.' There a parcel of letters was handed to him, which produced 'a complete mental paralysis for the time, and deadened all the sensations except that of surprise.'[2]

[1] *Emin Pasha, &c.* p. 294.
[2] *In Darkest Africa,* vol. ii. p. 109.

These letters, written at different times, were from Emin and Mr. Jephson, and told something of the troubles they had gone through. 'Mr. Jephson will tell you what has happened,' Emin had written pathetically on September 2 from Dufilé, where he was a close prisoner, scarcely hoping that Mr. Stanley would make an effort to rescue him, 'and is able to give you the benefit of his experience, and to make some suggestions, should you decide to come here as people wish. Should you, however, decide not to come, I can only wish you a good and safe return to your own country'; and on November 6 he stated that, if the Mahdists' progress continued, they might have only a few hours left for escape. On November 7, in a letter which Emin endorsed, Mr. Jephson explained the situation more fully:—

'Our position here is extremely unpleasant, for since this rebellion all is chaos and confusion; there is no head, and half a dozen conflicting orders are given every day and no one obeys; the rebel officers are wholly unable to control the soldiers. We are daily expecting some catastrophe to happen, for the Baris have joined the Donagla, and if they come down here with a rush nothing can save us. After the fall of Rejaf, the soldiers cursed their officers and said, "If we had obeyed our Governor and had done what he told us we should now be safe; he has been a father and mother to us all these years; but instead of listening to him we listened to you, and now we are lost."

'The officers are all very much frightened at what has happened, and we are now anxiously awaiting your arrival, and desire to leave the country with you, for they are now really persuaded that Khartoum has fallen and that you have come from the Khedive. The greater part of the officers and all the soldiers wish to reinstate the Pasha in his place, but the Egyptians are afraid that if he is reinstated vengeance will fall on their heads, so they have persuaded the Soudanese officers not to do so. The soldiers refused to act with their officers, so everything is at a standstill, and nothing is being done for the safety of the station either in the way of fortifying or provisioning it. We are like rats in a trap; they will neither let us act nor retire, and I fear, unless you come very soon, you will be too late, and our fate will be like that of the rest of the garrisons of the Soudan. Had this rebellion not happened the Pasha could have kept the Donagla in check for some time, but as it is he is powerless to act.

'I would make the following suggestions concerning your movements when you arrive at Kavalli's, which, of course, you will only adopt if you think fit.

'On your arrival at Kavalli's, if you have a sufficient force with you, leave all unnecessary loads in charge of some officers and men there, and you yourself come to Nsabé, bringing with you as many men as you can; bring the Soudanese officers, but not the soldiers, with you.

'Despatch natives in a canoe to Mswa with a letter in Arabic to Shukri Aga, telling him of your arrival, and telling him you wish to see the Pasha and myself, and write also to the Pasha or myself, telling us the number of men you have with you; it would perhaps be better to write to me, as a letter to him might be confiscated.

'On no account have anything to do with people who come to you unaccompanied by either the Pasha or myself, whoever they are, or however fair their words may be. Neither the Pasha nor I think there is the slightest danger now of any attempt to capture you being made, for the people are now fully persuaded you come from Egypt, and they look to you to get them out of their difficulties; still, it would be well for you to make your camp strong.'

This letter of Mr. Jephson's from Dufilé was supplemented by one dated from Wadelai on November 24, and another from Tunguru on December 18. In the second we read :—

'Dufilé is being evacuated as fast as possible, and it is the intention of the officers to collect at Wadelai, and to decide on what steps they shall next take. The Pasha is unable to move hand or foot, as there is still a very strong party against him, and the officers are no longer in immediate fear of the Mahdi's people.

'Do not on any account come down to Nsabé, but make your camp at Kavalli's ; send a letter directly you arrive, and as soon as we hear of your arrival, I will come down to you. I will not disguise the fact from you that you will have a difficult and dangerous task before you in dealing with the Pasha's people.'

And on December 21 Emin wrote :—

'Although for a moment there happened a movement in my favour, the officers, elated with their victory, soon were just as bad as they were in the beginning of this comedy. Everyone is now fully decided to leave the country for finding a shelter somewhere. Nobody thinks, however, of going to Egypt, except perhaps a few officers and men. I am, nevertheless, not without hope of better days ; but I join my entreaties with those of Mr. Jephson, asking you to stay where you are, viz., at Kavalli's, and to send only word of your arrival as quickly as you can.' [1]

Receiving all these letters on January 16, 1889, Mr. Stanley replied very angrily.

Though Mr. Jephson was still addressed as 'My dear fellow,' he was none the less held responsible, with Emin, for the disasters consequent on and largely caused by Mr. Stanley's own proceedings as a 'reliever' unable to afford any relief. Mr. Stanley, however, still

[1] *In Darkest Africa*, vol. ii. pp. 110-114.

declared himself willing to help, in his own way, these untrustworthy and self-ruining friends. 'If you are still victims of indecision,' he replied to Mr. Jephson on January 17, 'then a long good-night to you all. But, while I retain my senses, I must save my Expedition; you may be saved also if you are wise.' In that case Mr. Jephson was ordered—'if you consider yourself still a member of the Expedition subject to my orders'—to meet Mr. Stanley either with or without Emin Pasha at Kavalli's settlement in six days' time.

'You will understand that it will be a severe strain on Kavalli's resources to maintain us with provisions longer than six days, and if you are longer than this period we must retire to Mazamboni's, and finally to our camp on the Ituri ferry. Otherwise we must seize provisions by force, and any act of violence would cut off and close native communication. This difficulty might have been avoided had the Pasha followed my suggestion of making a depôt at Nyamsassi. The fact that there are provisions at Mswa does not help us at all. There are provisions in Europe also. But unfortunately they are as inaccessible as those of Mswa.'

In a postscript Mr. Stanley said he might be able to wait as long as ten days.

'Now don't you be perverse, but obey; and let my order to you be as a frontlet between the eyes, and all, with God's gracious help, will end well.

'I want to help the Pasha somehow, but he must also help me and credit me. If he wishes to get out of this trouble, I am his most devoted servant and friend; but if he hesitates again, I shall be plunged in wonder and perplexity. I could save a dozen Pashas if they were willing to be saved. I would go on my knees to implore the Pasha to be sensible in his own case. He is wise enough in all things else except in his own interest. Be kind and good to him for many virtues, but do not you be drawn into that fatal fascination which Soudan territory seems to have for all Europeans of late years. As soon as they touch its ground they seem to be drawn into a whirlpool, which sucks them in and covers them with its waves. The only way to avoid it is to obey blindly, devotedly, and unquestioningly, all orders from the outside. . . . This time there must be no hesitation, but positive yea or nay, and home we go.'

To Emin Mr. Stanley wrote more bluntly:—

'I have the honour to inform you that the second instalment of relief which this Expedition was ordered to convey to you is now in this camp, ready for delivery to any person charged to receive it by you. If you prefer that we should deposit it at Kavalli, or at Kyya Nkondo's, on the lake, we shall be ready to do so on the receipt of your instructions.

'This second instalment of relief consists of sixty-three cases Remington cartridges, twenty-six cases of gunpowder, each forty-five lbs. weight; four cases of percussion caps, four bales of goods, one bale of goods for Signor Casati—a gift from myself; two pieces of blue serge, writing paper, envelopes, blank books, &c.

'Having, after great difficulty—greater than was anticipated—brought relief to you, I am constrained to officially demand from you receipts for the above goods and relief brought to you, and also a definite answer to the question if you propose to accept our escort and assistance to reach Zanzibar, or if Signor Casati proposes to do so, or whether there are any officers or men disposed to accept of our safe conduct to the sea. In the latter event, I would be obliged to you if you would kindly state how those persons desirous of leaving Africa can be communicated with. I would respectfully suggest that all persons desirous of leaving with me should proceed to and form camp at Nsabé, or at Kyya Nkondo's, on the lake, with sufficient stores of grain, &c., to support them one month, and that a note should be sent to me informing me of the same, *via* Kavalli, whence I soon may receive it. The person in charge of the people at this camp will inform me definitely whether the people are ready to accept of our safe conduct, and, upon being thus informed, I shall be pleased to assume all further charge of them.

'If, at the end of twenty days, no news has been heard from you or Mr. Jephson, I cannot hold myself responsible for what may happen.'[1]

Mr. Stanley reports that Emin was 'very much offended' by the terms in which he was addressed. 'Yet I fail to see,' he says, 'how the officially worded letter could have wounded the most delicate susceptibilities.' Afterwards, when Mr. Jephson was with him, Mr. Stanley wrote another letter to Emin, at which, 'when Jephson heard it read, he affected to be aghast'; whereupon another letter was substituted for it, written 'after a style which probably Chesterfield himself would have admitted was the proper thing, which my friend Jephson pronounced was "charming" and "nice" and "exquisitely sweet."'[2] Unfortunately neither the Chesterfieldian epistle nor the document it replaced has been published, and we are left to guess at the difference between them. But there can be no question that Mr. Stanley's blustering and disparaging tone towards the sensitive and high-minded Pasha, his habit of always thinking the worst and coarsely uttering his

[1] *In Darkest Africa*, vol. ii. pp. 115–119.
[2] *Ibid.* pp. 119, 131.

thoughts, began to make mischief long before the open breach that took place at Zanzibar.

Mr. Jephson obeyed orders as soon as he could, though he was not able to be with Mr. Stanley before February 6. Then he explained the state of affairs in a way which, if not altogether satisfactory to Mr. Stanley, secured forgiveness; and forgiveness was the more readily obtained, perhaps, because, as Mr. Stanley says, Mr. Jephson had 'contracted during his compulsory residence with the Pasha one confirmed habit which provoked a smile; and that was, while saying several crushing things about the Province, he interlarded his clever remarks with "Well, you know, the poor, dear Pasha!" "He is a dear, old fellow, you know." "'Pon my word, I can't help but sympathise with the Pasha, he's such a dear, good man," &c., &c.' [1]

Mr. Jephson brought with him a letter from Emin, thanking Mr. Stanley for the 'second instalment' offered, and saying that there were 'lots of people' besides himself anxious to be rescued, but that as Mr. Stanley's letter had taken nine days to reach him it would not be possible for him to bring up his party in the eleven days remaining out of the twenty allowed. 'As probably I shall not see you any more,' Emin thanked Mr. Stanley for his intentions, and asked him 'to transmit my everlasting gratitude to the kind people who sent you to help us.' [2]

But Mr. Stanley extended the limit of time; and Emin, apparently on receipt of the Chesterfieldian letter, filled his two steamers with 'a first lot of people

[1] *In Darkest Africa*, vol. ii. p. 131.
[2] *Ibid.* p. 128.

desirous to leave the country.' These he conveyed to the side of the lake near which Mr. Stanley was encamped. In his party were twelve officers and forty soldiers. 'They have come,' he wrote, 'under my orders to request you to give them some time to bring their brothers—at least such as are willing to leave—from Wadelai, and I promised them to do my best to assist them. Things having to some extent now changed, you will be able to make them undergo whatever conditions you see fit to impose upon them.'[1]

Mr. Stanley says he believed from the first that the officers and soldiers, both these and the others they represented, were still rebels at heart, in spite of their verbal assurances of penitence and loyalty, and were plotting his ruin as well as Emin's. 'They conceived,' he averred, 'that it would be a grand idea if, by a *coup*, they could effect the splendid capture of the Expedition, with all its members, arms, and property, and present it to the Khalifa at Khartoum, and derive glory, honour, and profit by so doing.'[2] If Mr. Stanley really thought this, and had good grounds for his surmise, he showed considerable boldness in allowing nearly two months to be occupied in collecting the people who declared themselves willing to accompany him to Zanzibar. The delay was undoubtedly irksome, and there may have been warrant for some of the blame thrown upon Emin for vacillation and dilatoriness. But as during this time nearly all the 'rebel' troops remained quietly at Wadelai and thereabouts,

[1] *In Darkest Africa*, vol. ii. p. 135.
[2] *Parliamentary Papers*, C. 5906, p. 11.

and as on April 5 a muster showed that Emin's party at Kavalli's consisted of only 126 men and nearly four times as many women and children, events in no way justified Mr. Stanley's fears of treason.

The muster of April 5 was accomplished with difficulty, and under conditions that proved how little sympathy there was between the 'relieved' and the 'relievers.' In the morning, Mr. Stanley says, he paid a visit to Emin, and complained to him that there was no prospect of the soldiers and others still expected from Wadelai arriving in reasonable time, and that meanwhile he had evidence of mutinous plans at Kavalli's.

'There was an attempt made last night to appropriate our arms. Three separate times they entered the Zanzibaris huts and tried to abstract the rifles; but, acting after my instructions, the Zanzibaris tied their rifles to their waists, and when they were pulled, they were wakened, and the intending thieves decamped. . . . The attempt to rob us of our arms of defence failed last night. They will try again, and perhaps succeed, for I credit them with being clever enough, and it is quite clear that they have a design of some kind. Of course, if they succeed in appropriating even one rifle, the punishment will be summary, for I shall then forget what is due to them as your people and my guests. But this is what I wish to avoid. I should be loth to shed their blood, and create scenes of violence, when a better way of safeguarding our arms and ammunition, and effecting a quiet and peaceable departure from here, can be found.

'I propose to you one of two things. Sound the signal to muster all the Arabs and Soudanese with you, and then find out gently who is willing to leave with you. Those who are not willing I shall order to leave the camp. If they do not obey, then it will be for me to employ compulsion. But as these people despise our Zanzibaris, they may very probably attempt resistance. Well, in a land where there is no appeal but to our firearms, it will certainly end violently, and we shall both regret it afterwards.

'The other proposal is much more effective and more bloodless. Do you order your baggage to be packed up quietly, and at dawn my people shall all be ready to escort you to a camp about three miles from here. From that camp we shall issue a request that those who intend following you shall come in and be welcome, but no other person shall approach without permission on pain of death.'

Emin being slow in arriving at a decision, Mr. Stanley took the matter in his own hands:—

'I rose and sounded the signal for a general muster under arms. Myself and officers armed, and the Zanzibaris, Manyuema, Soudanese, and natives, seeing us assume our weapons, knew that the case was urgent, and hastened to the square with wonderful celerity. The natives of Kavalli passed the alarm, and some hundreds came rushing up to take their share in what they believed was a coming struggle.

'Within five minutes the companies were under arms and stood attentive along three sides of the great square. The Pasha, seeing that I was in earnest, came out, and begged me to listen to one word.

'"Certainly; what is it?" I asked.

'"Only tell me what I have to do now."

'"It is too late, Pasha, to adopt the pacific course I suggested to you. The alarm is general now, and therefore I propose to discover for myself this danger and face it here. Sound the signal, please, for the muster of your Arabs before me."

'"Very good," replied the Pasha, and gave the order to his trumpeter.

'We waited ten minutes in silence. Then, perceiving that not much attention was paid to the signal, I requested Mr. Jephson to take No. 1 Company, arm the men with clubs and sticks, and drive every Arab, Egyptian, and Soudanese into the square, without regard to rank, to search every house, and drag out every male found within.

'The Zanzibaris were deployed across the camp, and, advancing on the run, began to shower blows on every laggard and dawdler they came across.'[1]

Those who had not answered to the summons, as Mr. Stanley said in his first report to the Emin Relief Committee, afterwards modified, 'were secured in their huts and brought to the camp square, where some were flogged and others ironed and put under guard.'

Thus it was ascertained that about 570 men, women, and children were with Emin by the Albert Nyanza; and in that way Mr. Stanley took charge of them. 'Now, Pasha,' he said, 'this business having been satisfactorily ended, will you be good enough to tell these officers that the tricks of Wadelai must absolutely cease here, and that in future they are under my command. If I discover any treacherous tricks I shall be compelled to exterminate them utterly. No Mahdist, Arabist, or rebel can breathe in my camp. Those who will behave themselves and are obedient to orders will suffer no harm from their fellows or from us. My duty is to lead them to Egypt, and until they arrive in Cairo I will not leave them. Whatever I can do to make them comfortable I will do, but for sedition and theft of arms, there is only death.'[2]

[1] *In Darkest Africa*, vol. ii. pp. 181–183.
[2] *Ibid.* p. 185.

On April 10 Mr. Stanley began his march to Zanzibar; but two days later he became so ill that he had to halt for four weeks, and after that to proceed for some time by slow stages. The delay afforded an opportunity, of which they did not avail themselves, for more of Emin's people to overtake him. It also served, as he says, to convince him of the 'hatred, sullenness, or discontent' of which he saw evidence in the bearing of the few followers of Emin who were with him. The leader of a mutiny that broke out was tried by court-martial and hanged in due course; but many of those allowed to live were, he considered, 'permeated and saturated with mutiny, rebellion and treason.'[1] Mr. Stanley resolved, if the laggards did overtake him, to at once disarm them and, if they objected, to attack them as foes. Happily that was not necessary, and he resumed his march on May 8.

Besides Emin Pasha's people, who were virtually prisoners, he had with him 230 survivors of the expeditionary force of nearly 700 with which he had left Zanzibar more than two years before. There were also in the cavalcade, as soldiers and carriers, 130 of the Manyuema he had brought from Banalya, and about 550 natives hired in the neighbourhood. The whole company numbered more than 1,500.

When Mr. Stanley was really in a position to do something towards the 'relief' of Emin Pasha, no mention appears to have been made of the project for transferring him and his loyal people to some district near the Victoria Nyanza. Mr. Stanley seems to have himself abandoned it, and perhaps on good grounds.

[1] *Parliamentary Papers*, C. 5906, p. 13.

With his 230 Zanzibaris, and even his 130 Manyuema added to them, he evidently was not strong enough to escort a caravan of 8,000 or 10,000 men, women and children, with all their household goods, over any large tract of country and to establish them as a new colony.

Still less, however, would he have been able to conduct them all the way to Zanzibar. The 570 or more actually in his charge were too many for him to take care of; and it is quite clear that he was much aggrieved at the burden that he considered the Pasha had laid upon him. With whatever purposes he left London or Zanzibar, as the reliever or rescuer of Emin, he had so miscalculated his strength and so wasted his material, that when he reached the Albert Nyanza for the third time—which was the only time when he could be of any service at all—he was not competent to do much more than assist or compel Emin himself, with a small personal following, to run away from the scene of his labours. That was not what Emin had asked for, or, notwithstanding the greater difficulties that had come upon him while Mr. Stanley was dawdling and wandering, what he could cheerfully accept when it was forced upon him as the only course left open.

Poor Emin deserves much more sympathy than he has received from Mr. Stanley and Mr. Stanley's friends. The relief that he expected and that the Relief Expedition was intended to afford never reached him; and such 'relief' as was afforded was accompanied by sneers and insults, misrepresentations and misjudgments, which cannot but have wounded him all the more because he was too mild-mannered and generous to openly resent them. After a grudging acknowledgment of Emin's virtues, Mr. Stanley says, 'We dare not treat these features of a truthful, loving nature like that of Emin Pasha with an insolent levity.'[1] On his own showing he persistently did that, and on one occasion he tells us he went so far as to give him ' a little lecture upon the mode of conduct becoming a Pasha and a gentleman.'[2]

[1] *In Darkest Africa*, vol. ii. p. 217.
[2] *Ibid.* p. 423.

CHAPTER VII

MR. STANLEY'S LATER WANDERINGS

MR. STANLEY'S contributions to Central African geography, ethnology, and kindred studies do not here concern us. The ample records he has given of visits to places and people scarcely, if at all, known previously to Europeans are interesting; and others may be left to estimate the accuracy of the reports he has published. But it should here be pointed out that, whatever the scientific value of his explorations, they were never serviceable, and were often hindrances, to the particular work undertaken by him—the 'relief' of Emin Pasha. If this was especially the case as regards his seven months' wanderings, over 1,200 miles, from the Albert Nyanza to the Zanzibar coast, we must not suppose that all his earlier journeyings after leaving the mouth of the Congo, which he reckons at 4,800 miles, were undertaken solely on Emin's behalf, or were necessary consequences of the initial blunder of his plan for reaching Emin by way of the Congo.

Having spent more than five months of 1887 in travelling from Yambuya to the Albert Nyanza, with only a third of his stores and less than two-thirds of his followers, and sacrificing many of both on the way, it was of course incumbent on him to use the greater part of

1888 in returning to the neighbourhood of Stanley Falls and travelling back again, in order that he might recover the fragments remaining of the dropped portions of his Expedition; and his second and third journeys through the great forest were certainly performed with nearly as much speed as was possible, each in about three and a half months. Yet he claims great credit for having taken advantage of the opportunities thus afforded for studying the strange regions he traversed and their strange inhabitants; and he finds in the discoveries he made some compensation for the hardships to which he was himself exposed, and for the appalling loss of life among his followers. For his killing of natives by the way, and for his 'splendid captures'[1] and ill-usage of dwarfs in the forest, he does not consider that any apology or compensation was needed.

As one of the purposes of the Emin Relief Expedition was to supplement the work Mr. Stanley had previously done, as the agent of King Leopold, in 'opening up to civilisation' the western half of the Congo Free State, by visiting and describing portions of its eastern half, his wanderings along the course of the Aruwimi and about the great Upper Congo Forest may not have been wholly in vain. There was also an apparent reason for what would otherwise seem to be the unnecessary lengthening of his journey towards Zanzibar after Emin had been relieved. Though nothing came of Mr. Stanley's suggestion to the Pasha in April 1888, that a colony from the Equatorial Province should be planted near the Victoria Nyanza,

[1] *In Darkest Africa*, vol. i. p. 352.

under the auspices of the Imperial British East Africa Company, there was important work to be done on behalf of that company. In the first annual report of its directors to the shareholders we read:—

'In May 1889 Mr. H. M. Stanley, on his way to the coast, came into communication with the chiefs of many of the states through which he passed, and obtained from them the cession of their sovereign rights respectively, in consideration of the protection he afforded them against the attacks of the King of Unyoro. All these rights Mr. Stanley has patriotically transferred to the company, and your directors deem this a fitting opportunity to acknowledge with gratitude the valuable services rendered to them on all occasions by the illustrious explorer. The states and territories thus brought into affinity with the company are Mpororo, Ankori, Kitagwend, Unyampakado, Ukonju, Undussuma, Usongora, the Semliki Valley, and the territory between the Albert Nyanza and the Ituri river.'

That catalogue, read backwards, indicates part of the zigzag route taken by Mr. Stanley on his way to the coast, and the route enabled him to carry out some important geographical researches, as well as to negotiate some valuable treaties. His treaty-making, indeed, had already begun before he left Mazamboni's district, as the time passed in waiting for Emin Pasha was partly utilised in converting that chief and others in the neighbourhood into vassals of the British East Africa Company.

Hindered for nearly a month by his illness, Mr. Stanley's march properly began on May 8. As he proceeded in a southerly direction, he had before him the great Ruwenzori range which he had dimly seen from afar on a clear day in December 1887, and which, having heard of it from the natives, and doubtless remembering Speke's hypothesis identifying this range with the Mountains of the Moon, spoken of by ancient writers, he had all along intended to 'discover.'

First, however, he had to overcome some opposition from the Wara Sura, the soldiers of Kabba Rega, King of Unyoro, a corner of whose territory he had to cross. Kabba Rega's long hostility to foreigners, although for some time he maintained friendly relations with Emin Pasha, had been in 1886 adduced by Mr. Stanley as a sufficient obstacle to taking the short route from Zanzibar, through his country, to the Equatorial Province. Yet his defiance was not now found to be very terrible. On May 10 there was a battle between a few Soudanese, caught bathing, and some Wara Sura, in which one of the former and three of the latter were killed; but 'on the approach of the Zanzibaris the Wara Sura fled and were pursued for three miles.' There was another encounter on the 18th, while Mr. Stanley's caravan was crossing the Semliki. 'A body of fifty of the Wara Sura,' he reports, 'stole up to within 250 yards of the ferry, and fired a volley at the canoes while in mid-river. Iron slugs and lead bullets screamed over the heads of the passengers, and flew along the face of the water, but fortunately there was no harm done. We heard a good deal of volleying, but the chase and retreat were so hot that not a bullet found its purposed billet.'[1]

Mr. Stanley's chief trouble was with the Egyptians, whom the Zanzibaris drove before them like cattle.

[1] *In Darkest Africa*, vol. ii. pp. 233, 238.

'Words availed nothing, reason could not penetrate their dense heads,' he complains. 'Their custom was to rush at early dawn along the path, and, after an hour's spurt, to sit down, dawdle, light a fire and cook, and smoke and gossip; then, when the rear-guard came up to urge them along, assume sour and discontented looks, and mutter to themselves of the cruelty of the infidels.' Especially offensive to him were the Egyptian babies. 'These wee creatures must have possessed irascible natures, for such obstinate and persistent caterwauling never tormented me before.'[1]

Mr. Stanley spent four weeks in exploring the Ruwenzori, the northern slopes of Lake Albert Edward Nyanza, and the country round about. At first and for some time the natives fled at his approach, believing his soldiers to be Wara Sura; but they left plenty of food behind them. 'Ten battalions would have needed no commissary to provide their provisions; we had but to pluck and eat.'[2] Therefore the unwieldy caravan suffered much less than might have been expected from this remarkable delay in completing the 'rescue' of Emin. As, moreover, Mr. Stanley did no worse than help himself and his followers to the food they found, and even offered to pay for it, the natives soon discovered that the new-comers were not Wara Sura, but kindlier intruders. Nay more, though he gives us very few details and records no casualties, Mr. Stanley says that he had several encounters with Kabba Rega's people. 'Our march into Ukonju instantly caused the Wara Sura to evacuate the plain of Makara, and our approach

---

[1] *In Darkest Africa*, vol. ii. pp. 243, 244.
[2] *Ibid.* p. 247.

to Katwé caused a speedy flight of Rukara'—Kabba Rega's general—'and his army of musketeers and spearmen.'[1] As over these and neighbouring territories Kabba Rega usurped sovereignty, their chiefs appear to have welcomed Mr. Stanley's proposal that they should transfer their allegiance to him or his nominees, and in this way some of the 'treaties' he 'patriotically' handed over to the Imperial British East Africa Company were obtained.

Advantageous as was this scientific and political excursion in some respects, it was attended by disasters. The members of Emin Pasha's party whom Mr. Stanley was conducting to Zanzibar were ill-prepared for the unnecessary travelling forced upon them as participators in the crusade. According to Mr. Stanley, 'they had led such a fearful life of debauchery and license in their province that few of them had any stamina remaining, and they broke down under what was only moderate exercise to the Zanzibaris.' But the Egyptians were not alone in their misery. On June 27, among 200 sick people, 'blacks of Zanzibar, Soudan, and Manyuema were moaning and sorrowing over their sufferings'; and the list included Dr. Parke, Mr. Jephson, and Mr. Stanley himself—who, at any rate, must not be charged with having led 'a fearful life of debauchery and license,' and who was for some days 'as prostrated as any person.'[2]

There was terrible sickness all along the route, but throughout July Mr. Stanley was able to continue his triumphal march southward, receiving homage from the

[1] *In Darkest Africa*, vol. ii. pp. 321-324, 316.
[2] *Ibid.* pp. 324, 325.

chiefs or kings of the populous districts of Ankori and Mpororo, who welcomed him as a possible deliverer from the raids of the Wara Sura, and agreed to the treaties he proposed. He was also able to pursue his geographical inquiries and to collect much information useful and instructive to others besides Sir William Mackinnon and his colleagues. At about this time he was able to discharge the Albert Nyanza natives whom he had hired, and also, apparently, the residue of the Manyuema who had attended him from Banalya and who were now near their own homes. In August he passed through Karagwé, where he was less hospitably received, and where he had less reason for halting, as it and all the country south and east are now within the German 'sphere of influence;' and on the 28th of the month he reached Msalala, the mission-station to which Mr. Mackay had retired after his escape from Uganda. There he camped and was entèrtained until September 17. 'On the Europeans of the Expedition,' he says, 'the effect of regular diet and well-cooked food, of amiable society and perfect restfulness, was marvellous.' The pause was beneficial too to the survivors of his caravan, although he reports, 'when they were mustered for the march, the day before leaving, there were over one hundred people who complained of asthma, chest, spleen, liver, or lumbar pains, and declared they could not travel.'[1]

After leaving Mr. Mackay's station, Mr. Stanley had to pass through a hostile tribe, the Wasukuma, concerning his treatment of whom his accounts vary. According to one report, he submitted meekly to much

[1] *In Darkest Africa*, vol. ii. pp. 389, 391.

insult, having 'no intention of fighting anybody, but of going to the coast as quickly as possible,' and merely used his Maxim gun to 'threaten'—killing no more than eleven natives on September 20 and eight on the 21st; after which, 'though we knew the trifling mercies, such as we were able to show, seldom made any impression on tribes quivering under extraordinary excitement and rage for battle, nevertheless we abstained from needlessly augmenting this causeless madness against us, and only halted a few minutes to repel a rush.'[1] According to another and earlier report, 'the Wasukuma, from these experiences and the instant compliance with their rough humours, probably judged that they had but to rush on our column to see it collapse, and in a mood to yield, after injury and insult, to their caprices; but having charged myself with the care of the Pasha and his people, we promptly resented the attack, and the consequence was serious to the Wasukuma. They gathered in immense numbers, and for five days disputed every mile of our advance through their territory. They frequently advanced by hundreds on either flank of the column, and were most wonderfully active, but the breech-loaders restrained them from reaching the line of march.'[2] But the statements agree as to the fact that only one of Mr. Stanley's people was killed in the course of the four or five days' battling.

When Mr. Stanley arrived at Bagamoyo on December 4, there was an end, as he says, 'of that continual rising in the morning with a hundred moaning and

---

[1] *In Darkest Africa*, vol. ii. pp. 398-401.
[2] *Parliamentary Papers*, C. 5906, p. 15.

despairing invalids, wailing their helplessness, and imploring for help, of those daily scenes of disease, suffering, and unmitigable misery, and of the diurnal torture to which the long enduring caravan had been subjected during what seemed now to have been an age of hideous troubles, far beyond the range of anything we had anticipated when we so light-heartedly accepted the mission of relieving the Governor of Equatoria.'[1]

He had with him only 290 of the 570 followers of Emin Pasha, whom he had taken charge of by the Albert Nyanza on April 5. In the first three months he had lost but 15; in the next month he lost 141; in the next two months 103; in the last two months 21. Of the 'missing' 280, 'probably 80 perished from ulcers, fevers, fatigue, and debility.' 'About 200,' he said, 'have been cared for by various native chiefs, through whose territory we passed. If the head of a family suffered from a virulent ulcer in a country which furnished no carriers, and he could not possibly travel, there was no option left us but to leave him in some safe place; and as his family, wives, and harem, and children and servants, preferred to stay with him, we were forced to yield to their entreaties'—in other words, they were abandoned.

Other items in Mr. Stanley's casualty list are as follows:—

'Of the 13 Somalis engaged by Major Barttelot at Aden only one survived the journey. Three of them were killed by natives while foraging for food; nine died from fever and debility.

'Of the 60 Soudanese enlisted at Cairo only 12 returned

[1] *In Darkest Africa*, vol. ii. p. 418.

to the coast, seven having been already sent home from Yambuya. Thus 19 out of 60 leaves a loss of 41, two of whom suffered the death penalty for mutiny and murder, and one deserted.

'Of the 620 Zanzibaris only 225 were returned by us to Zanzibar; 55 were killed in the skirmishes which took place between Yambuya and the Albert Nyanza; two suffered capital punishment for selling their rifles and ammunition to our declared enemies; 202 died of starvation, ulcers, dysentery, and exhaustion; the rest deserted.' [1]

We are not told, and evidently Mr. Stanley himself neither knows nor cares, how many thousands of slaughtered natives should be added to the 311 dead Zanzibaris, Soudanese, and Somalis, to make up the huge total of mortality incident to the methods and the exploits of the Emin Relief Expedition.

[1] *Parliamentary Papers*, C. 5906, pp. 15, 16.

CHAPTER VIII

RESULTS

In summing up the main results of the Emin Relief Expedition, account must first be taken of its issues as regards the object for which it was professedly started.

That object was the relief of Emin Pasha, who had appealed to Europe in 1886 for such assistance as would enable him to carry on the civilising work to which he had devoted his life. He hoped that, besides the means of keeping in check a mutinous section of the people under him, instigated by disloyal Egyptians, and awed or tempted by the Mahdist movement, he would receive from England more lasting assistance through the opening up of a route from Wadelai to Zanzibar, or some nearer seaport, by which he could send to European markets his ivory and other produce, and could maintain frequent communication with the civilised world. This, perhaps, was more than he ought to have expected, or than it would have been reasonable for the English Government, or any private body of Englishmen, to attempt, seeing that it involved continuous obligations and risks too serious to be lightly incurred. But it was what he asked for, or declared that he would thankfully accept if it was offered to him. Failing the whole, he would have been grateful for such temporary aid as might, in his opinion, enable him to overcome his immediate difficulties. But he steadily announced his determination of remaining with his subjects so long as any were loyal to him, however trying might be the conditions. 'If the people in Great Britain think that as soon as Stanley or Thomson comes, I shall return with them,' he wrote to Dr. Felkin in April 1887, 'they greatly err.'

It was ostensibly to afford the Pasha the smaller measure of the relief he asked for that the Emin Relief Committee was organised in November 1886. It was as to 'the possibilities of conveying relief to Emin, with a view to enabling him to hold his own,' that Mr. Stanley says Sir William Mackinnon and others consulted him; and he adds: 'To them it seemed that Emin only required ammunition, and I shared their opinion.' Accordingly, the Emin Relief Committee obtained the sanction of Her Majesty's Government 'to organise and send out a private expedition to open communications with and carry relief to Emin Bey;' and that sanction was supplemented by the British Government's procuring 10,000*l.* from the Egyptian Government to be added to the 10,000*l.* or more which the Emin Relief Committee promised to raise for the work undertaken by it. The plan was considerably modified before the Expedition quitted Zanzibar; and letters from the Khedive and Nubar Pasha were entrusted to Mr. Stanley for Emin, inviting him to return with his 'officers and soldiers' to Egypt, and telling him that, if they remained in the Equatorial Province, they must do so 'at their own risk.' But Emin was not warned of this change in the project, and in a letter which Mr. Stanley forwarded to Emin from Zanzibar, he promised that he would visit Wadelai, as the accredited agent of the Egyptian Government, with an ample supply of ammunition and other stores, to be conveyed by about 1,200 Zanzibari and Central African carriers, and with an imposing body of Soudanese soldiers.

We have seen how Mr. Stanley kept his promise and fulfilled his mission. His first meeting with Emin was not in August or September 1887, as he announced, but in April 1888; not at Wadelai, but on the east side of the Albert Nyanza; and then all the 'relief' he brought up was thirty-three cases of ammunition. As Emin declined at once to abandon his people, without even going back to take farewell, and insisted on conveying to them the offer of withdrawal made by the Egyptian Government, and as Mr. Stanley could neither spare the time nor command a suitable retinue for visiting the Equatorial Province as the Khedive's ambassador, Mr. Jephson, with three Soudanese soldiers, was allowed to accompany Emin as his representative. Mr. Jephson's presence was not enough to check the mutinous inclinations of some of Emin's people. On the contrary, it quickened and strengthened the disaffection that was growing among them, and a revolt ensued. Instead of helping Emin out of his difficulties in 1888, the Relief Expedition vastly aggravated them; and when Mr. Stanley returned in January 1889 to hand over ninety-three cases of ammunition as the second and final instalment of the 'relief' brought from Zanzibar, he found Emin in desperate straits. He could not now, if he would, reinstate the Pasha as

Governor of the Equatorial Province. Nor could he, if he would, act on an earlier proposal to convey Emin and the people still loyal to him to the shores of the Victoria Nyanza, and there establish them as a new colony. Though Emin did not share his fears, Mr. Stanley was afraid that the 'rebels' would swoop down on his little camp, seize all his ammunition, as well as Emin's, make him and his whole party prisoners, and hand them over to the Mahdists. To avoid that risk, Mr. Stanley hurried out of the unsafe neighbourhood as quickly as he could, taking with him as captives Emin and the people who had by that time left the Equatorial Province and assembled by the Albert Nyanza.

The results of the Relief Expedition, so far as Emin Pasha is concerned, have been that the Equatorial Province, which he had governed worthily and with a remarkable measure of success, has been given up to barbarism and to the oppression of Mahdist fanatics; that of the 570 followers of the Pasha whom Mr. Stanley rescued only 290 reached the Zanzibar coast, and only 260 were committed to the tender mercies of the Egyptian Government in Cairo; and that Emin himself, casting off at Bagamoyo the irksome chains he had worn for eight months, has been driven into wild and hopeless effort to renew in another portion of Central Africa the work from which he was debarred in his own province. Let it be noted that the man who contributed to this ruin, and who has heaped abuse upon his victim, felt constrained to say: 'If the Pasha was able to maintain his province for five years'—Mr. Stanley should have written thirteen years—'he cannot in justice be held answerable for the wave of insanity and the epidemic of turbulence which converted his hitherto loyal soldiers into rebels. As an administrator he displayed the finest qualities; he was just, tender, loyal and merciful, and affectionate to the natives who placed themselves under his protection, and no higher and better proof of the esteem with which he was regarded by his soldiery can be desired than that he owed his life to the reputation for justice and mildness which he had won. In short, every hour saved from sleep was devoted before his final deposition'—which Mr. Stanley accomplished—'to some useful purpose conducive to increase of knowledge, improvement of humanity, and gain to civilisation.'[1]

Emin Pasha has been much blamed, and has been held up to much ridicule, for having in December 1889 declined to follow Mr. Stanley to Cairo and to London, and for having subsequently entered the service of the German East African Company. It is necessary here to say a few words in explanation, and partly in justification, of his conduct.

Let it be conceded that by long residence in the Equatorial Province, where he had been in one sense an autocrat, in another the slave of circumstances inducing methods of government adapted to the country and people he ruled, where in zealous pursuit of science he had found his principal relief from the arduous labours devolving on him as an administrator, Emin may have acquired habits and ways of thinking which would have unfitted him for kindlier restraints and more

[1] *In Darkest Africa*, vol. i. p. 8.

generous companionship than Mr. Stanley imposed upon him. He seems to have since been the object of nearly as much scorn and scolding from Major Wissman, under whom he took service at Bagamoyo, as he was from Mr. Stanley, and his recent proceedings in German East Africa appear to have afforded some excuse for this treatment. Yet the worst blunders he can be fairly charged with are trivial in comparison with the great work which he was engaged upon in the Equatorial Province, and which he bravely desired to persevere in when he was torn from it, or, as some may consider, from its wreck, by Mr. Stanley. And it must be remembered that from the moment when Mr. Stanley 'relieved' and began to 'rescue' him, he was exposed to persistent insults and outrages that could not but be intolerable to one of his high-strung temperament. For evidence of the injustice to which he was subjected we need go no further than the pages of 'In Darkest Africa.' What wonder that he grew weary of such handling after the eight months during which he was led as a captive from the Albert Nyanza to Bagamoyo, and that he then accepted Major Wissman's offer to be put in the way of making a fresh effort to spread civilisation in Africa?

It is noteworthy that the district in which Emin has of late been endeavouring to establish a new dominion is almost identical with the district to which in May 1888 Mr. Stanley had promised to transplant him with his people. One of Mr. Stanley's reasons for not acting on this proposal may have been his discovery, after the disasters he had helped to bring about in the later months of 1888, that Emin's people, even if it had been possible to collect and convey them to the Kavirondo neighbourhood of the Victoria Nyanza, were not likely to be prosperous or manageable colonists. But in now hankering after the locality that Mr. Stanley had designated for him, Emin has shown none of the inconstancy with which carping critics have credited him. If in this neighbourhood he causes annoyance to the Imperial British East Africa Company, the promoters of the Company may thank Mr. Stanley for contributing thereto.

But in other respects, and on most grounds, Sir William Mackinnon and his friends have good reason to be grateful to Mr. Stanley. As their agent, at any rate, he may be considered to have rendered efficient service both before and after he 'rescued' Emin Pasha. If his raiding among the tribes between the great Congo Forest and Lake Albert Nyanza in December 1887 was morally indefensible, and involved foolish and dishonest waste of the ammunition he had been employed to carry to Emin, it cowed the inhabitants, and frightened them into the submission they showed when he returned in April 1888 and while he resided in their midst between January and May 1889. Mazamboni and the neighbouring chiefs were the first group of vassals that he secured and made treaties with, on the westernmost confines of its lately acquired territory, for the British East Africa Company. And other vassals were secured, and other treaties were made, as he led his exploring and conquering cavalcade round the Mountains of the Moon, and down to the northern side of Lake Albert Edward Nyanza, and yet further south until he crossed the frontier of the German 'sphere of influence.' His achievements in these regions were perforce rendered exceptionally laborious by the fact that he had a great crowd of 'fugitives' from the Equatorial Province, dwindling down in numbers from the 570 with which he started, with nearly as many carriers in attendance upon them, to conduct by his tortuous path towards Zanzibar; and there was woeful suffering and death among these incumbrances. But without the pretence of an Emin Relief Expedition to lead, and of Manyuema and other warriors to protect it, he might have had no opportunity for his geographical explorations and his empire-making errand. From the statements of the Managing Director of the British East Africa Company, it would seem that in Uganda and on the way thither one of its other travelling agents, Mr. Jackson, has done more profitable and extensive work at much less cost and with much less pomp in 'concluding arrangements which will serve to protect British interests and be a benefit to the several chiefs and tribes with whom he came in contact'[1] than Mr. Stanley, attempting like work further west, can reasonably boast of. Yet it is conceivable that, without Mr. Stanley's earlier crusading and its influence, Mr. Jackson's task would have been harder and less successful. At any rate, it was Mr. Stanley who led the way as the chief of the Emin Relief Expedition appointed by Sir William Mackinnon, in exploring and exploiting the territories of the Imperial British East Africa Company.

As was shown in an earlier chapter, one of the main purposes of the Emin Relief Expedition, and one

---

[1] See a lecture by Mr. George S. Mackenzie in the *Journal of the Royal Colonial Institute* for December 1890, p. 21.

of the 'little commissions' that Mr. Stanley 'settled' at Zanzibar in February 1887, was the advancement of the scheme which took shape in the British East Africa Company, and which Sir Francis de Winton, the energetic secretary of the Emin Relief Committee, went out in 1890 to further develop as Administrator-General of the affairs of the Company. In this particular, if in no other, Mr. Stanley's occupations have had results which should be agreeable to those of his employers who are concerned in this enterprise.

The outcome of another 'little commission,' and of another purpose of the Emin Relief Expedition, does not appear to be so satisfactory.

In requiring Mr. Stanley, if he went at all to the relief of Emin Pasha, to go through the Congo Free State, the sovereign of that State evidently expected that it would derive material benefit from the further exploits of the famous traveller who had done so much to found it, and no blame attaches to King Leopold for stipulating that his officer should be thus engaged. Reference has been made to the catastrophe at Stanley Falls in 1887, when Mr. Deane, the custodian of the station, was attacked and expelled by the representatives of Tippoo-Tib. This was part of the systematic policy of Tippoo, whose tributaries and their hordes had already well-nigh exhausted the supply of ivory and slaves in the regions east of the Upper Congo. It was necessary for them to seek fresh fields of adventure, and Stanley Falls was a convenient base from which they might stretch out to the north and south as well as to the west. In seizing Stanley Falls, Tippoo secured a point of vantage for seriously hampering, if he could not crush, the bold efforts of the Congo State authorities to trade with and rule the natives by methods more humane than those patronised by the 'Bismarck of Central Africa,' as he has often been called. Belgian steamers might continue to ply up and down the Congo, exchanging cargoes of European goods for ivory and other native produce, but there was danger of Tippoo-Tib controlling all the markets, and even in time advancing from Stanley Falls to Leopoldville and beyond. While the Emin Relief Committee was arranging to send ammunition to Wadelai, King Leopold was considering the possibility of counteracting the ambitious projects of Tippoo and, apparently, of employing on that task the man who had already done so much in his service. As Mr. Stanley had been invited to 're-lieve' Emin Pasha, King Leopold may have been right in directing that if he was sent to Wadelai he should go thither by way of the Congo, especially as it probably never occurred to His Majesty that the Emin Relief Expedition would be in any way damaged by combining with it an attempt to recover Stanley Falls. Hence arose the 'little commission' on behalf of the Congo State's sovereign which Mr. Stanley 'settled' with Tippoo-Tib in February 1887.

But Mr. Stanley's contract with Tippoo-Tib, appointing him Governor of the Stanley Falls district, under King Leopold, appears to have been as unprofitable and as mischievous as his other contract with Tippoo, for the supply of carriers of the stores intended for Emin Pasha. Tippoo certainly holds office, in his own person or by proxy, as Governor of the Stanley Falls district; and it is possible that his dignity is enhanced in his own eyes, and perhaps also his authority over some of his followers has been strengthened, by his being in formal relations with King Leopold, and having a Belgian secretary to wait upon him. Yet all his tyrannies and all his extortions, all his ivory-raiding and all his slave-trading, go on just as before, or more obnoxiously than ever.

While one of the direct results of the Emin Relief Expedition has been to deprive the Equatorial Province of its Governor, and of all the civilising influences, such as they were, that Emin exerted there, and while another of its direct results has been to help in laying the foundations of what we are told promises to be a powerful and beneficent empire in East Africa under British control, one of its indirect results has been to strengthen the position of a barbaric adventurer by endowing him with nominal functions as Governor of the Stanley Falls district, and thereby seriously imperilling whatever chances there were of a powerful and beneficent empire being built up in Central Africa under Belgian direction.

This is a matter that may only be incidentally touched upon here. It is all the more worthy of consideration, however, seeing that under the arrangements arrived at by the International Conference which sat in Brussels last year, and now waiting confirmation and enforcement, it is proposed to make a stupendous effort at 'putting an end to the crimes and devastations engendered by the traffic in African slaves, protecting the aboriginal populations of Africa, and ensuring for that vast continent the benefits of peace and civilisation.' As the Congo Free State includes in its area one of the chief centres of slave-raiding and sources of the slave trade, the contemplated Brussels Treaty is to make special provisions for enabling the administrators of that State to adopt special measures with a view to restricting and ultimately suppressing this monstrous evil. Yet one of Mr. Stanley's achievements in connection with the Emin Relief Expedition has been the recognition and encouragement of the greatest and most dangerous promoter of the slave trade in Africa by his appointment as a salaried officer of the Congo Free State.

In 'In Darkest Africa' Mr. Stanley says much in denunciation of the African slave trade and its attendant evils, and something in condemnation of Tippoo-Tib and the policy he directs. But Mr. Stanley does not seem to be aware or chooses to forget that his own policy is entirely opposed to any reasonable and promising efforts that can be made to put down the slave trade and improve the condition of the people in the interior of Africa. One result of his exploits, not only in cutting a way through the great Congo Forest, but also in opening up earlier routes from the Atlantic side in the direction of Stanley Falls, has been that the paths cut and opened up have been promptly used by slave raiders for their own advantage and to the prejudice of the people living in the districts. The recommendations of the Brussels Conference as regards increasing facilities of communication between the African coast and its internal sources of wealth, by means of railroads and even of telegraph wires and electric lighting, are admirable in theory, and under slow and cautious direction may lead to the suppression of slavery, and philanthropic utilising of the vast resources, still undiscovered as well as already known, which Africa may possess. All such projects and endeavours, however, if they are to be beneficial must be worked gradually and extended step by step. Sudden and reckless spurts of enterprise like those which Mr. Stanley makes, and the Congo State authorities appear to be satisfied with, only aggravate existing evils and augment the obstacles to their removal. That is the sort of work, apart from the business properly devolving upon the Emin Relief Expedition, and so far as the Congo State is concerned, which Mr. Stanley achieved during the latest and largest of his excursions in Africa.

Is it too much to hope that the civilised world will take warning by the disasters and misdeeds of the Emin Relief Expedition, and never again allow so much mischief to be done in the name of philanthropy? If some profit to the Imperial British East Africa Company and to Mr. Stanley himself has resulted from the Expedition, the gains have been cumbrously and expensively procured, and they, like all its other and less agreeable issues, have been reached by blundering and bad faith.

'Any person who has travelled with the writer thus far,' Mr. Stanley remarked when he was half through the record of his journeyings, 'will have observed that almost every fatal accident hitherto in this Expedition has been the consequence of a breach of promise. How to adhere to a promise seems to me to be the most

P

difficult of all tasks to 999,999 men out of every million whom I meet.'[1]

For Mr. Stanley himself the task was too difficult. He has shown that he, at any rate, is not the one man among a million who can be trusted to keep a promise.

[1] *In Darkest Africa*, vol. ii. p. 21.

Third Edition. Royal 8vo. cloth extra, 14s.

FIVE YEARS WITH THE CONGO CANNIBALS.

By HERBERT WARD.

With 92 Illustrations by the Author, Victor Perard, and W. B. Davis.

'Comparisons are odious, but we are allowed our likes and dislikes; and I very much prefer "Five Years with the Congo Cannibals" to "In Darkest Africa." Mr. Ward tells his story in a simple, unaffected style; he indulges in no rhapsodies; he poses as neither prophet, martyr, nor saint. He has a quick eye; he seems fertile of resource; and pen and pencil are equally ready to answer to his call.'—Lady's Pictorial.

'The principal object of the book is to give a description of life on the Congo, the scenery of the country, and the vagrant habits of the natives who inhabit its banks. This is done most graphically, and the description is aided by a great number of most clever drawings. For this work Mr. Ward is eminently fitted. . . . A most interesting account.'—Guardian

'Mr. Ward has written a spirited account of the Congo tribes, beautifully illustrated by numerous pictures from photographs taken by himself.'—Athenæum.

'It is a handsome volume, with numerous illustrations, presenting many scenes and adventures of an exciting character.'—Illustrated London News.

'We have seen no better account of the natives along the river from the mouth to Stanley Falls; and the book is embellished with a very large number of singularly spirited and singularly faithful drawings from Mr. Ward's own pencil. It is a very pleasant book to read, and shows remarkable familiarity with, and aptitude for, travel and adventure.'—Saturday Review.

'The book is written with good temper and spirit; the drawings are capital.'—World.

'Mr. Ward has managed to bring together a great many interesting facts, which are, perhaps, none the less trustworthy, inasmuch as he has neither observed nor written in the advocacy of any special theory. . . . The volume, which is beautifully got up, is illustrated with more than eighty engravings, most of which are either reproductions of photographs or from sketches taken on the spot by the author, and are therefore exceptionally trustworthy.'—Glasgow Herald.

'The story of Mr. Ward's wanderings is full of adventurous incident, and the book contains much valuable and significant information concerning the history and character of Tippo Tib and his principal associates.'—Times.

'There is a mysterious fascination about African travel that most travellers feel, and the reader can begin to feel it too as he glances through the pages of this bright and interesting book.'—St. James's Gazette.

'Mr. Ward writes an interesting account of his experiences among the Congo savages. His book should be read by all young people who sigh for a life of adventure.'—Daily News.

'From every point of view Mr. Ward's book should be read with avidity by all who have taken an interest in the perplexing story of the Emin Relief Expedition.'—European Mail.

'Mr. Ward relates the story of his marches and voyages with much spirit. He was an industrious sketcher and note-taker, and his readers have now the benefit of his skill with pencil and pen in a volume which, in illustration and letterpress, deserves to take a high place among books of African travel.'—Scotsman.

'One of the most interesting additions to the literature of the Congo Free State. We get a very fascinating account of the life and condition of the people.'—Manchester Guardian.

London: CHATTO & WINDUS, 214 Piccadilly, W.

Post 8vo. Portrait cover, with a Map by F. S. WELLER, 1s.;
cloth, 1s. 6d.

MY LIFE WITH STANLEY'S REAR GUARD.

By HERBERT WARD.

'Mr. Ward has already told us a good deal about his "Five Years with the Congo Cannibals"; but in the little volume he now publishes there is much that is new, and nothing that is not interesting.'—MANCHESTER EXAMINER.

'The descriptive and controversial passages are brought compactly and skilfully together; in whatever else they may have been wanting, the companions and adversaries of Stanley have the art of writing pithily and brightly.'—SCOTSMAN.

'The book has many lively passages, and will be relished by those who have not the leisure or inclination to study the now considerable library of Stanley literature.'—ST. JAMES'S GAZETTE.

'A short, interesting, and very readable little book which puts the matter perhaps more clearly and better than any of its forerunners.'—SATURDAY REVIEW.

'Mr. Ward tells his story fairly and simply, and the reader will not fail to sympathise with him.'—NORTH BRITISH DAILY MAIL.

'The book may be regarded as the conclusion of the case for the officers of the Rear Column.'—MORNING POST.

'Mr. Ward tells his story modestly, temperately, and vividly withal; and, though he protests strongly against Mr. Stanley's charges as regards himself, he does not exceed the bounds of legitimate indignation. . . . It would be well if the whole controversy had been conducted in this generous spirit.'—TIMES.

'The book is not without interest, and its moderate price places within reach of the humblest reader a fairly full account of the much-discussed Rear Guard. It has also some value inasmuch as it helps to corroborate or modify the statements and views of previous writers.'—DAILY GRAPHIC.

'Mr. Ward gives a graphic picture of life at Yambuya.'—SPEAKER.

'Mr. Herbert Ward brings up the rear of the Rear Guard literature with a well-written book, small, because it is concise.'—MAGAZINE AND BOOK REVIEW.

London: CHATTO & WINDUS, 214 Piccadilly, W.

January, 1891.

A List of Books
PUBLISHED BY
CHATTO & WINDUS,
214, Piccadilly, London, W.

Sold by all Booksellers, or sent post-free for the published price by the Publishers.

ABOUT.—THE FELLAH: An Egyptian Novel. By EDMOND ABOUT. Translated by Sir RANDAL ROBERTS. Post 8vo, illustrated boards, **2s.**

ADAMS (W. DAVENPORT), WORKS BY.
A DICTIONARY OF THE DRAMA. Being a comprehensive Guide to the Plays, Playwrights, Players, and Playhouses of the United Kingdom and America. Crown 8vo, half-bound, **12s. 6d.** *[Preparing.*
QUIPS AND QUIDDITIES. Selected by W. D. ADAMS. Post 8vo, cloth limp, **2s. 6d.**

ADAMS (W. H. D.).—WITCH, WARLOCK, AND MAGICIAN: Historical Sketches of Magic and Witchcraft in England and Scotland. By W. H. DAVENPORT ADAMS. Demy 8vo, cloth extra, **12s.**

AGONY COLUMN (THE) OF "THE TIMES," from 1800 to 1870. Edited, with an Introduction, by ALICE CLAY. Post 8vo, cloth limp, **2s. 6d.**

AIDE (HAMILTON), WORKS BY. Post 8vo, illustrated boards, **2s.** each.
CARR OF CARRLYON. | CONFIDENCES.

ALEXANDER (MRS.), NOVELS BY. Post 8vo, illustrated boards, **2s.** each.
MAID, WIFE, OR WIDOW? | VALERIE'S FATE.

ALLEN (GRANT), WORKS BY. Crown 8vo, cloth extra, **6s.** each.
THE EVOLUTIONIST AT LARGE. | COLIN CLOUT'S CALENDAR.
VIGNETTES FROM NATURE.

Crown 8vo, cloth extra, **6s.** each; post 8vo, illustrated boards, **2s.** each.
STRANGE STORIES. With a Frontispiece by GEORGE DU MAURIER.
THE BECKONING HAND. With a Frontispiece by TOWNLEY GREEN.

Crown 8vo, cloth extra, **3s. 6d.** each; post 8vo, illustrated boards, **2s.** each.
PHILISTIA. | BABYLON. | IN ALL SHADES.
THE DEVIL'S DIE. | FOR MAIMIE'S SAKE. | THIS MORTAL COIL.
| THE TENTS OF SHEM. |

THE GREAT TABOO. Crown 8vo, cloth extra, **3s. 6d.**

AMERICAN LITERATURE, A LIBRARY OF, from the Earliest Settlement to the Present Time. Compiled and Edited by EDMUND CLARENCE STEDMAN and ELLEN MACKAY HUTCHINSON. Eleven Vols., royal 8vo, cloth extra. A few copies are for sale by Messrs. CHATTO & WINDUS (published in New York by C. L. WEBSTER & Co.), price **£6 12s.** the set.

ARCHITECTURAL STYLES, A HANDBOOK OF. By A. ROSENGARTEN. Translated by W. COLLETT-SANDARS. With 639 Illusts. Cr. 8vo, cl. ex., **7s. 6d.**

ART (THE) OF AMUSING: A Collection of Graceful Arts, GAMES, Tricks, Puzzles, and Charades. By FRANK BELLEW. 300 Illusts. Cr. 8vo, cl. ex., **4s. 6d.**

ARNOLD (EDWIN LESTER), WORKS BY.
THE WONDERFUL ADVENTURES OF PHRA THE PHŒNICIAN. With Introduction by Sir EDWIN ARNOLD, K.C.I.E., and 12 Illusts. by H. M. PAGET. Three Vols.
BIRD LIFE IN ENGLAND. Crown 8vo, cloth extra, 6s.

ARTEMUS WARD'S WORKS:
The Works of CHARLES FARRER BROWNE, better known as ARTEMUS WARD. With Portrait and Facsimile. Crown 8vo, cloth extra, 7s. 6d.—Also a POPULAR EDITION, post 8vo, picture boards, 2s.
THE GENIAL SHOWMAN: Life and Adventures of ARTEMUS WARD. By EDWARD P. HINGSTON. With a Frontispiece. Crown 8vo, cloth extra, 3s. 6d.

ASHTON (JOHN), WORKS BY. Crown 8vo, cloth extra, 7s. 6d. each.
HISTORY OF THE CHAP-BOOKS OF THE 18th CENTURY. With 334 Illusts.
SOCIAL LIFE IN THE REIGN OF QUEEN ANNE. With 85 Illustrations.
HUMOUR, WIT, AND SATIRE OF SEVENTEENTH CENTURY. With 82 Illusts.
ENGLISH CARICATURE AND SATIRE ON NAPOLEON THE FIRST. 115 Illusts.
MODERN STREET BALLADS. With 57 Illustrations.

BACTERIA.—A SYNOPSIS OF THE BACTERIA AND YEAST
FUNGI AND ALLIED SPECIES. By W. B. GROVE, B.A. With 87 Illustrations. Crown 8vo, cloth extra, 3s. 6d.

BARDSLEY (REV. C. W.), WORKS BY.
ENGLISH SURNAMES: Their Sources and Significations. Cr. 8vo, cloth, 7s. 6d.
CURIOSITIES OF PURITAN NOMENCLATURE. Crown 8vo, cloth extra, 6s.

BARING GOULD (S., Author of "John Herring," &c.), NOVELS BY.
Crown 8vo, cloth extra, 3s. 6d. each; post 8vo, illustrated boards, 2s. each.
RED SPIDER. | **EVE.**

BARRETT (FRANK, Author of "Lady Biddy Fane,") NOVELS BY.
FETTERED FOR LIFE. Post 8vo, illustrated boards, 2s.; cloth, 2s. 6d.
BETWEEN LIFE AND DEATH. Three Vols., crown 8vo.

BEACONSFIELD, LORD: A Biography. By T. P. O'CONNOR, M.P.
Sixth Edition, with an Introduction. Crown 8vo, cloth extra, 5s.

BEAUCHAMP.—GRANTLEY GRANGE: A Novel. By SHELSLEY
BEAUCHAMP. Post 8vo, illustrated boards, 2s.

BEAUTIFUL PICTURES BY BRITISH ARTISTS: A Gathering of
Favourites from our Picture Galleries, beautifully engraved on Steel. With Notices of the Artists by SYDNEY ARMYTAGE, M.A. Imperial 4to, cloth extra, gilt edges, 21s.

BECHSTEIN.—AS PRETTY AS SEVEN, and other German Stories.
Collected by LUDWIG BECHSTEIN. With Additional Tales by the Brothers GRIMM, and 100 Illustrations by RICHTER. Square 8vo, cloth extra, 6s. 6d.; gilt edges, 7s. 6d.

BEERBOHM.—WANDERINGS IN PATAGONIA; or, Life among the
Ostrich Hunters. By JULIUS BEERBOHM. With Illusts. Cr. 8vo, cl. extra, 3s. 6d.

BESANT (WALTER), NOVELS BY.
Cr. 8vo, cl. ex., 3s. 6d. each; post 8vo, illust. bds., 2s. each; cl. limp, 2s. 6d. each.
ALL SORTS AND CONDITIONS OF MEN. With Illustrations by FRED. BARNARD.
THE CAPTAINS' ROOM, &c. With Frontispiece by E. J. WHEELER.
ALL IN A GARDEN FAIR. With 6 Illustrations by HARRY FURNISS.
DOROTHY FORSTER. With Frontispiece by CHARLES GREEN.
UNCLE JACK, and other Stories. | **CHILDREN OF GIBEON.**
THE WORLD WENT VERY WELL THEN. With 12 Illustrations by A. FORESTIER.
HERR PAULUS: His Rise, his Greatness, and his Fall.
FOR FAITH AND FREEDOM. With Illustrations by A. FORESTIER and F. WADDY.

Crown 8vo, cloth extra, 3s. 6d. each.
TO CALL HER MINE, &c. With 9 Illustrations by A. FORESTIER.
THE BELL OF ST. PAUL'S.

THE HOLY ROSE, &c. With Frontispiece by F. BARNARD. Cr. 8vo, cloth extra, 6s.
ARMOREL OF LYONESSE: A Romance of To-day. Three Vols., crown 8vo.

FIFTY YEARS AGO. With 137 Plates and Woodcuts. Demy 8vo, cloth extra, 16s.
THE EULOGY OF RICHARD JEFFERIES. With Portrait. Cr. 8vo, cl. extra, 6s.
THE ART OF FICTION. Demy 8vo, 1s.

BESANT (WALTER) AND JAMES RICE, NOVELS BY.
Cr. 8vo, cl. ex., 3s. 6d. each; post 8vo, illust. bds., 2s. each; cl. limp, 2s. 6d. each.

READY-MONEY MORTIBOY.
MY LITTLE GIRL.
WITH HARP AND CROWN.
THIS SON OF VULCAN.
THE GOLDEN BUTTERFLY.
THE MONKS OF THELEMA.
BY CELIA'S ARBOUR.
THE CHAPLAIN OF THE FLEET.
THE SEAMY SIDE.
THE CASE OF MR. LUCRAFT, &c.
'TWAS IN TRAFALGAR'S BAY, &c.
THE TEN YEARS' TENANT, &c.

⁎ There is also a LIBRARY EDITION of the above Twelve Volumes, handsomely set in new type, on a large crown 8vo page, and bound in cloth extra, 6s. each.

BENNETT (W. C., LL.D.), WORKS BY. Post 8vo, cloth limp, 2s. each.
A BALLAD HISTORY OF ENGLAND. | SONGS FOR SAILORS.

BEWICK (THOMAS) AND HIS PUPILS. By AUSTIN DOBSON. With 95 Illustrations. Square 8vo, cloth extra, 6s.

BLACKBURN'S (HENRY) ART HANDBOOKS.
ACADEMY NOTES, separate years, from 1875-1887, 1889, and 1890, each 1s.
ACADEMY NOTES, 1891. With Illustrations. 1s. [Preparing.
ACADEMY NOTES, 1875-79. Complete in One Vol., with 600 Illusts. Cloth limp, 6s.
ACADEMY NOTES, 1880-84. Complete in One Vol., with 700 Illusts. Cloth limp, 6s.
GROSVENOR NOTES, 1877. 6d.
GROSVENOR NOTES, separate years, from 1878 to 1890, each 1s.
GROSVENOR NOTES, Vol. I., 1877-82. With 300 Illusts. Demy 8vo, cloth limp, 6s.
GROSVENOR NOTES, Vol. II., 1883-87. With 300 Illusts. Demy 8vo, cloth limp, 6s.
THE NEW GALLERY, 1888-1890. With numerous Illustrations, each 1s.
THE NEW GALLERY, 1891. With Illustrations. 1s. [Preparing.
ENGLISH PICTURES AT THE NATIONAL GALLERY. 114 Illustrations. 1s.
OLD MASTERS AT THE NATIONAL GALLERY. 128 Illustrations. 1s. 6d.
ILLUSTRATED CATALOGUE TO THE NATIONAL GALLERY. 242 Illusts. cl., 3s.
THE PARIS SALON, 1891. With Facsimile Sketches. 3s. [Preparing.
THE PARIS SOCIETY OF FINE ARTS, 1891. With Sketches. 3s. [Preparing.

BLAKE (WILLIAM): India-proof Etchings from his Works by WILLIAM BELL SCOTT. With descriptive Text. Folio, half-bound boards, 21s.

BLIND.—THE ASCENT OF MAN: A Poem. By MATHILDE BLIND. Crown 8vo, printed on hand-made paper, cloth extra, 5s.

BOURNE (H. R. FOX), WORKS BY.
ENGLISH MERCHANTS: Memoirs in Illustration of the Progress of British Commerce. With numerous Illustrations. Crown 8vo, cloth extra, 7s. 6d.
ENGLISH NEWSPAPERS: The History of Journalism. Two Vols., demy 8vo, cl., 25s.
THE OTHER SIDE OF THE EMIN PASHA RELIEF EXPEDITION. Crown 8vo, cloth extra, 6s. [Shortly.

BOWERS' (G.) HUNTING SKETCHES. Oblong 4to, hf.-bd. bds., 21s. each.
CANTERS IN CRAMPSHIRE. | LEAVES FROM A HUNTING JOURNAL.

BOYLE (FREDERICK), WORKS BY. Post 8vo, illustrated boards, 2s. each.
CHRONICLES OF NO-MAN'S LAND. | CAMP NOTES.
SAVAGE LIFE. Crown 8vo, cloth extra, 3s. 6d.; post 8vo, picture boards, 2s.

BRAND'S OBSERVATIONS ON POPULAR ANTIQUITIES; chiefly illustrating the Origin of our Vulgar Customs, Ceremonies, and Superstitions. With the Additions of Sir HENRY ELLIS, and Illustrations. Cr. 8vo, cloth extra, 7s. 6d.

BREWER (REV. DR.), WORKS BY.
THE READER'S HANDBOOK OF ALLUSIONS, REFERENCES, PLOTS, AND STORIES. Fifteenth Thousand. Crown 8vo, cloth extra, 7s. 6d.
AUTHORS AND THEIR WORKS, WITH THE DATES: Being the Appendices to "The Reader's Handbook," separately printed. Crown 8vo, cloth limp, 2s.
A DICTIONARY OF MIRACLES. Crown 8vo, cloth extra, 7s. 6d.

BREWSTER (SIR DAVID), WORKS BY. Post 8vo, cl. ex.; 4s. 6d. each.
MORE WORLDS THAN ONE: The Creed of the Philosopher and the Hope of the Christian. With Plates.
THE MARTYRS OF SCIENCE: GALILEO, TYCHO BRAHE, and KEPLER. With Portraits.
LETTERS ON NATURAL MAGIC. With numerous Illustrations.

COLLINS (CHURTON).—A MONOGRAPH ON DEAN SWIFT. By J. Churton Collins. Crown 8vo, cloth extra, 8s. [*Shortly.*

COLMAN'S HUMOROUS WORKS: "Broad Grins," "My Nightgown and Slippers," and other Humorous Works of George Colman. With Life by G. B. Buckstone, and Frontispiece by Hogarth. Crown 8vo, cloth extra, 7s. 6d.

COLQUHOUN.—EVERY INCH A SOLDIER: A Novel. By M. J. Colquhoun. Post 8vo, illustrated boards, 2s.

CONVALESCENT COOKERY: A Family Handbook. By Catherine Ryan. Crown 8vo, 1s.; cloth limp, 1s. 6d.

CONWAY (MONCURE D.), WORKS BY.
DEMONOLOGY AND DEVIL-LORE. With 65 Illustrations. Third Edition. Two Vols., demy 8vo, cloth extra, 28s.
A NECKLACE OF STORIES. 25 Illusts. by W. J. Hennessy. Sq. 8vo, cloth, 6s.
PINE AND PALM: A Novel. Two Vols., crown 8vo, cloth extra, 21s.
GEORGE WASHINGTON'S RULES OF CIVILITY Traced to their Sources and Restored. Fcap. 8vo, Japanese vellum, 2s. 6d.

COOK (DUTTON), NOVELS BY.
PAUL FOSTER'S DAUGHTER. Cr. 8vo, cl. ex., 3s. 6d.; post 8vo, illust. boards, 2s.
LEO. Post 8vo, illustrated boards, 2s.

CORNWALL.—POPULAR ROMANCES OF THE WEST OF ENGLAND; or, The Drolls, Traditions, and Superstitions of Old Cornwall. Collected by Robert Hunt, F.R.S. Two Steel-plates by Geo. Cruikshank. Cr. 8vo, cl., 7s. 6d.

CRADDOCK.—THE PROPHET OF THE GREAT SMOKY MOUNTAINS. By Charles Egbert Craddock. Post 8vo, illust. bds., 2s.; cl. limp, 2s. 6d.

CRUIKSHANK'S COMIC ALMANACK. Complete in Two Series: The First from 1835 to 1843; the Second from 1844 to 1853. A Gathering of the Best Humour of Thackeray, Hood, Mayhew, Albert Smith, A'Beckett, Robert Brough, &c. With numerous Steel Engravings and Woodcuts by Cruikshank, Hine, Landells, &c. Two Vols., crown 8vo, cloth gilt, 7s. 6d. each.
THE LIFE OF GEORGE CRUIKSHANK. By Blanchard Jerrold. With 84 Illustrations and a Bibliography. Crown 8vo, cloth extra, 7s. 6d.

CUMMING (C. F. GORDON), WORKS BY. Demy 8vo, cl. ex., 8s. 6d. each.
IN THE HEBRIDES. With Autotype Facsimile and 23 Illustrations.
IN THE HIMALAYAS AND ON THE INDIAN PLAINS. With 42 Illustrations.

VIA CORNWALL TO EGYPT. With Photogravure Frontis. Demy 8vo, cl., 7s. 6d.

CUSSANS.—A HANDBOOK OF HERALDRY; with Instructions for Tracing Pedigrees and Deciphering Ancient MSS., &c. By John E. Cussans. With 408 Woodcuts, Two Coloured and Two Plain Plates. Crown 8vo, cloth extra, 7s. 6d.

CYPLES (W.)—HEARTS of GOLD. Cr. 8vo, cl., 3s. 6d.; post 8vo, bds., 2s.

DANIEL.—MERRIE ENGLAND IN THE OLDEN TIME. By George Daniel. With Illustrations by Robert Cruikshank. Crown 8vo, cloth extra, 3s. 6d.

DAUDET.—THE EVANGELIST; or, Port Salvation. By Alphonse Daudet. Crown 8vo, cloth extra, 3s. 6d.; post 8vo, illustrated boards, 2s.

DAVENANT.—HINTS FOR PARENTS ON THE CHOICE OF A PROFESSION FOR THEIR SONS. By F. Davenant, M.A. Post 8vo, 1s.; cl., 1s. 6d.

DAVIES (DR. N. E. YORKE-), WORKS BY.
Crown 8vo, 1s. each; cloth limp, 1s. 6d. each.
ONE THOUSAND MEDICAL MAXIMS AND SURGICAL HINTS.
NURSERY HINTS: A Mother's Guide in Health and Disease.
FOODS FOR THE FAT: A Treatise on Corpulency, and a Dietary for its Cure.

AIDS TO LONG LIFE. Crown 8vo, 2s.; cloth limp, 2s. 6d.

DAVIES' (SIR JOHN) COMPLETE POETICAL WORKS, including Psalms I. to L. in Verse, and other hitherto Unpublished MSS., for the first time Collected and Edited, with Memorial-Introduction and Notes, by the Rev. A. B. Grosart, D.D. Two Vols., crown 8vo, cloth boards, 12s.

DE MAISTRE.—A JOURNEY ROUND MY ROOM. By XAVIER DE MAISTRE. Translated by HENRY ATTWELL. Post 8vo, cloth limp, 2s. 6d.

DE MILLE.—A CASTLE IN SPAIN. By JAMES DE MILLE. With a Frontispiece. Crown 8vo, cloth extra, 3s. 6d.; post 8vo, illustrated boards, 2s.

DERBY (THE).—THE BLUE RIBBON OF THE TURF: A Chronicle of the RACE FOR THE DERBY, from Diomed to Donovan. With Notes on the Winning Horses, the Men who trained them, Jockeys who rode them, and Gentlemen to whom they belonged; also Notices of the Betting and Betting Men of the period, and Brief Accounts of THE OAKS. By LOUIS HENRY CURZON. Cr. 8vo, cloth extra, 6s.

DERWENT (LEITH), NOVELS BY. Cr. 8vo, cl., 3s. 6d. ea.; post 8vo, bds., 2s. ea.
OUR LADY OF TEARS. | CIRCE'S LOVERS.

DICKENS (CHARLES), NOVELS BY. Post 8vo, illustrated boards, 2s. each.
SKETCHES BY BOZ. | NICHOLAS NICKLEBY.
THE PICKWICK PAPERS. | OLIVER TWIST.
THE SPEECHES OF CHARLES DICKENS, 1841-1870. With a New Bibliography. Edited by RICHARD HERNE SHEPHERD. Crown 8vo, cloth extra, 6s.—Also a SMALLER EDITION, in the *Mayfair Library*, post 8vo, cloth limp, 2s. 6d.
ABOUT ENGLAND WITH DICKENS. By ALFRED RIMMER. With 57 Illustrations by C. A. VANDERHOOF, ALFRED RIMMER, and others. Sq. 8vo, cloth extra, 7s. 6d.

DICTIONARIES.
A DICTIONARY OF MIRACLES: Imitative, Realistic, and Dogmatic. By the Rev. E. C. BREWER, LL.D. Crown 8vo, cloth extra, 7s. 6d.
THE READER'S HANDBOOK OF ALLUSIONS, REFERENCES, PLOTS, AND STORIES. By the Rev. E. C. BREWER, LL.D. With an ENGLISH BIBLIOGRAPHY. Fifteenth Thousand. Crown 8vo, cloth extra, 7s. 6d.
AUTHORS AND THEIR WORKS, WITH THE DATES. Cr. 8vo, cloth limp, 2s.
FAMILIAR SHORT SAYINGS OF GREAT MEN. With Historical and Explanatory Notes. By SAMUEL A. BENT, A.M. Crown 8vo, cloth extra, 7s. 6d.
SLANG DICTIONARY: Etymological, Historical, and Anecdotal. Cr. 8vo, cl., 6s. 6d.
WOMEN OF THE DAY: A Biographical Dictionary. By F. HAYS. Cr. 8vo, cl., 5s.
WORDS, FACTS, AND PHRASES: A Dictionary of Curious, Quaint, and Out-of-the-Way Matters. By ELIEZER EDWARDS. Crown 8vo, cloth extra, 7s. 6d.

DIDEROT.—THE PARADOX OF ACTING. Translated, with Annotations, from Diderot's "Le Paradoxe sur le Comédien," by WALTER HERRIES POLLOCK. With a Preface by HENRY IRVING. Crown 8vo, parchment, 4s. 6d.

DOBSON (AUSTIN), WORKS BY.
THOMAS BEWICK & HIS PUPILS. With 95 Illustrations. Square 8vo, cloth, 6s.
FOUR FRENCHWOMEN: MADEMOISELLE DE CORDAY; MADAME ROLAND; THE PRINCESS DE LAMBALLE; MADAME DE GENLIS. Fcap. 8vo, hf.-roxburghe, 2s. 6d.

DOBSON (W. T.), WORKS BY. Post 8vo, cloth limp, 2s. 6d. each.
LITERARY FRIVOLITIES, FANCIES, FOLLIES, AND FROLICS.
POETICAL INGENUITIES AND ECCENTRICITIES.

DONOVAN (DICK), DETECTIVE STORIES BY.
Post 8vo, illustrated boards, 2s. each; cloth limp, 2s. 6d. each.
THE MAN-HUNTER. | TRACKED AND TAKEN.
CAUGHT AT LAST! | WHO POISONED HETTY DUNCAN?
THE MAN FROM MANCHESTER. With 23 Illustrations. Crown 8vo, cloth, 6s.; post 8vo, illustrated boards, 2s.

DOYLE (A. CONAN, Author of "Micah Clarke"), NOVELS BY.
THE FIRM OF GIRDLESTONE. Crown 8vo, cloth extra, 6s.
STRANGE SECRETS. Told by CONAN DOYLE, PERCY FITZGERALD, FLORENCE MARRYAT, &c. Cr. 8vo, cl. ex., Eight Illusts., 6s.; post 8vo, illust. bds., 2s.

DRAMATISTS, THE OLD. With Vignette Portraits. Cr. 8vo, cl. ex., 6s. per Vol.
BEN JONSON'S WORKS. With Notes Critical and Explanatory, and a Biographical Memoir by WM. GIFFORD. Edited by Col. CUNNINGHAM. Three Vols.
CHAPMAN'S WORKS. Complete in Three Vols. Vol. I. contains the Plays complete; Vol. II., Poems and Minor Translations, with an Introductory Essay by A. C. SWINBURNE; Vol. III., Translations of the Iliad and Odyssey.
MARLOWE'S WORKS. Edited, with Notes, by Col. CUNNINGHAM. One Vol.
MASSINGER'S PLAYS. From GIFFORD's Text, Edit. by Col. CUNNINGHAM. One Vol.

DUNCAN (SARA JEANNETTE), WORKS BY.
　A SOCIAL DEPARTURE: How Orthodocia and I Went round the World by Ourselves. With 111 Illustrations by F. H. TOWNSEND. Crown 8vo, cloth, 7s. 6d.
　AN AMERICAN GIRL IN LONDON. With 82 Illustrations by F. H. TOWNSEND. Crown 8vo, cloth extra, 7s. 6d. *[Preparing.*

DYER.—THE FOLK-LORE OF PLANTS. By Rev. T. F. THISELTON DYER, M.A. Crown 8vo, cloth extra, 6s.

EARLY ENGLISH POETS. Edited, with Introductions and Annotations, by Rev. A. B. GROSART, D.D. Crown 8vo, cloth boards, 6s. per Volume.
　FLETCHER'S (GILES) COMPLETE POEMS. One Vol.
　DAVIES' (SIR JOHN) COMPLETE POETICAL WORKS. Two Vols.
　HERRICK'S (ROBERT) COMPLETE COLLECTED POEMS. Three Vols.
　SIDNEY'S (SIR PHILIP) COMPLETE POETICAL WORKS. Three Vols.

EDGCUMBE.—ZEPHYRUS: A Holiday in Brazil and on the River Plate. By E. R. PEARCE EDGCUMBE. With 41 Illustrations. Crown 8vo, cloth extra, 5s.

EDWARDES (MRS. ANNIE), NOVELS BY:
　A POINT OF HONOUR. Post 8vo, illustrated boards, 2s.
　ARCHIE LOVELL. Crown 8vo, cloth extra, 3s. 6d.; post 8vo, illust. boards, 2s.

EDWARDS (ELIEZER).—WORDS, FACTS, AND PHRASES: A Dictionary of Curious, Quaint, and Out-of-the-Way Matters. By ELIEZER EDWARDS. Crown 8vo, cloth extra, 7s. 6d.

EDWARDS (M. BETHAM-).—KITTY. Post 8vo, illustrated boards, 2s.
　FELICIA. With Frontispiece. Crown 8vo, cloth, 3s. 6d.; post 8vo, illust. bds., 2s.

EGGLESTON (EDWARD).—ROXY: A Novel. Post 8vo, illust. bds., 2s.

EMANUEL.—ON DIAMONDS AND PRECIOUS STONES: Their History, Value, and Properties; with Simple Tests for ascertaining their Reality. By HARRY EMANUEL, F.R.G.S. With Illustrations, tinted and plain. Cr. 8vo, cl. ex., 6s.

ENGLISHMAN'S HOUSE, THE: A Practical Guide to all interested in Selecting or Building a House; with Estimates of Cost, Quantities, &c. By C. J. RICHARDSON. With Coloured Frontispiece and 600 Illusts. Crown 8vo, cloth, 7s. 6d.

EWALD (ALEX. CHARLES, F.S.A.), WORKS BY.
　THE LIFE AND TIMES OF PRINCE CHARLES STUART, Count of Albany (THE YOUNG PRETENDER). With a Portrait. Crown 8vo, cloth extra, 7s. 6d.
　STORIES FROM THE STATE PAPERS. With an Autotype. Crown 8vo, cloth, 6s.

EYES, OUR: How to Preserve Them from Infancy to Old Age. By JOHN BROWNING, F.R.A.S. With 70 Illusts. Eleventh Edition. Crown 8vo, cl., 1s.

FAMILIAR SHORT SAYINGS OF GREAT MEN. By SAMUEL ARTHUR BENT, A.M. Fifth Edition, Revised and Enlarged. Crown 8vo, cloth extra, 7s. 6d.

FARADAY (MICHAEL), WORKS BY. Post 8vo, cloth extra, 4s. 6d. each.
　THE CHEMICAL HISTORY OF A CANDLE: Lectures delivered before a Juvenile Audience. Edited by WILLIAM CROOKES, F.C.S. With numerous Illustrations.
　ON THE VARIOUS FORCES OF NATURE, AND THEIR RELATIONS TO EACH OTHER: Lectures delivered before a Juvenile Audience at the Royal Institution. Edited by WILLIAM CROOKES, F.C.S. With numerous Illustrations.

FARRER (J. ANSON), WORKS BY.
　MILITARY MANNERS AND CUSTOMS. Crown 8vo, cloth extra, 6s.
　WAR: Three Essays, reprinted from "Military Manners." Cr. 8vo, 1s.; cl., 1s. 6d.

FELLOW (A) OF TRINITY: A Novel. By ALAN ST. AUBYN and WALT WHEELER. With a "Note" by OLIVER WENDELL HOLMES. Crown 8vo, cloth extra, 3s. 6d.; post 8vo, illustrated boards, 2s.

FIN-BEC.—THE CUPBOARD PAPERS: Observations on the Art of Living and Dining. By FIN-BEC. Post 8vo, cloth limp, 2s. 6d.

FIREWORKS, THE COMPLETE ART OF MAKING; or, The Pyrotechnist's Treasury. By THOMAS KENTISH. With 267 Illustrations. Cr. 8vo, cl., 5s.

FITZGERALD (PERCY), WORKS BY.
THE WORLD BEHIND THE SCENES. Crown 8vo, cloth extra, 3s. 6d.
LITTLE ESSAYS: Passages from Letters of Charles Lamb. Post 8vo, cl., 2s. 6d.
A DAY'S TOUR: Journey through France and Belgium. With Sketches. Cr. 4to, 1s.
FATAL ZERO. Crown 8vo, cloth extra, 3s. 6d.; post 8vo, illustrated boards, 2s.

Post 8vo, illustrated boards, 2s. each.
BELLA DONNA. | LADY OF BRANTOME. | THE SECOND MRS. TILLOTSON.
POLLY. | NEVER FORGOTTEN. | SEVENTY-FIVE BROOKE STREET.

THE LIFE OF JAMES BOSWELL (of Auchinleck). With an Account of his Writings, Sayings, and Doings, and Two Portraits. Two Vols., demy 8vo, cloth extra, 24s. [*Preparing*.

FLETCHER'S (GILES, B.D.) COMPLETE POEMS: Christ's Victorie in Heaven, Christ's Victorie on Earth, Christ's Triumph over Death, and Minor Poems. With Notes by Rev. A B. Grosart, D.D. Crown 8vo, cloth boards, 6s.

FLUDYER (HARRY) AT CAMBRIDGE: A Series of Family Letters. Post 8vo, picture cover, 1s.; cloth limp, 1s. 6d.

FONBLANQUE (ALBANY).—FILTHY LUCRE. Post 8vo, illust. bds., 2s.

FRANCILLON (R. E.), NOVELS BY.
Crown 8vo, cloth extra, 3s. 6d. each; post 8vo, illustrated boards, 2s. each.
ONE BY ONE. | QUEEN COPHETUA. | A REAL QUEEN. | KING OR KNAVE?
OLYMPIA. Post 8vo, illust. bds., 2s. | ESTHER'S GLOVE. Fcap. 8vo, pict. cover, 1s.
ROMANCES OF THE LAW. Crown 8vo, cloth, 6s.; post 8vo, illust. boards, 2s.

FREDERIC (HAROLD), NOVELS BY.
SETH'S BROTHER'S WIFE. Post 8vo, illustrated boards, 2s.
THE LAWTON GIRL. With Frontispiece by F. Barnard. Cr. 8vo, cloth ex., 6s.; post 8vo, illustrated boards, 2s.

FRENCH LITERATURE, A HISTORY OF. By Henry Van Laun. Three Vols., demy 8vo, cloth boards, 7s. 6d. each.

FRENZENY.—FIFTY YEARS ON THE TRAIL: Adventures of John Y. Nelson, Scout, Guide, and Interpreter. By Harrington O'Reilly. With 100 Illustrations by Paul Frenzeny. Crown 8vo, 3s. 6d.; cloth extra, 4s. 6d.

FRERE.—PANDURANG HARI; or, Memoirs of a Hindoo. With a Preface by Sir H. Bartle Frere, G.C.S.I., &c. Crown 8vo, cloth extra, 3s. 6d.

FRISWELL (HAIN).—ONE OF TWO: A Novel. Post 8vo, illust. bds., 2s.

FROST (THOMAS), WORKS BY. Crown 8vo, cloth extra, 3s. 6d. each.
CIRCUS LIFE AND CIRCUS CELEBRITIES. | LIVES OF THE CONJURERS.
THE OLD SHOWMEN AND THE OLD LONDON FAIRS.

FRY'S (HERBERT) ROYAL GUIDE TO THE LONDON CHARITIES. Showing their Name, Date of Foundation, Objects, Income, Officials, &c. Edited by John Lane. Published Annually. Crown 8vo, cloth, 1s. 6d.

GARDENING BOOKS. Post 8vo. 1s. each; cloth limp, 1s. 6d. each.
A YEAR'S WORK IN GARDEN AND GREENHOUSE: Practical Advice as to the Management of the Flower, Fruit, and Frame Garden. By George Glenny.
OUR KITCHEN GARDEN: Plants, and How we Cook Them. By Tom Jerrold.
HOUSEHOLD HORTICULTURE. By Tom and Jane Jerrold. Illustrated.
THE GARDEN THAT PAID THE RENT. By Tom Jerrold.

MY GARDEN WILD, AND WHAT I GREW THERE. By Francis G. Heath. Crown 8vo, cloth extra, gilt edges, 6s.

GARRETT.—THE CAPEL GIRLS: A Novel. By Edward Garrett. Crown 8vo, cloth extra, 3s. 6d.; post 8vo, illustrated boards, 2s.

GENTLEMAN'S MAGAZINE, THE. 1s. Monthly. In addition to the Articles upon subjects in Literature, Science, and Art, for which this Magazine has so high a reputation, "TABLE TALK" by Sylvanus Urban appears monthly.
⁎ *Bound Volumes for recent years kept in stock, 8s. 6d. each; Cases for binding, 2s.*

GENTLEMAN'S ANNUAL, THE. Published Annually in November. 1s.

GERMAN POPULAR STORIES. Collected by the Brothers GRIMM and Translated by EDGAR TAYLOR. With Introduction by JOHN RUSKIN, and 22 Steel Plates by GEORGE CRUIKSHANK. Square 8vo, cloth, 6s. 6d.; gilt edges, 7s. 6d.

GIBBON (CHARLES), NOVELS BY.
Crown 8vo, cloth extra, 3s. 6d. each; post 8vo, illustrated boards, 2s. each.
- ROBIN GRAY.
- LOVING A DREAM.
- QUEEN OF THE MEADOW.
- THE FLOWER OF THE FOREST.
- FANCY FREE.
- A HEART'S PROBLEM.
- THE GOLDEN SHAFT.
- OF HIGH DEGREE.
- IN HONOUR BOUND.

Post 8vo, illustrated boards, 2s. each.
- THE DEAD HEART.
- FOR LACK OF GOLD.
- WHAT WILL THE WORLD SAY?
- FOR THE KING.
- BLOOD-MONEY.
- IN PASTURES GREEN.
- IN LOVE AND WAR.
- BY MEAD AND STREAM.
- THE BRAES OF YARROW.
- A HARD KNOT.
- HEART'S DELIGHT.

GIBNEY (SOMERVILLE).—SENTENCED! Cr. 8vo, 1s.; cl., 1s. 6d.

GILBERT (WILLIAM), NOVELS BY. Post 8vo, illustrated boards, 2s. each.
- DR. AUSTIN'S GUESTS.
- THE WIZARD OF THE MOUNTAIN.
- JAMES DUKE, COSTERMONGER.

GILBERT (W. S.), ORIGINAL PLAYS BY. In Two Series, each complete in itself, price 2s. 6d. each.
The FIRST SERIES contains: The Wicked World—Pygmalion and Galatea—Charity—The Princess—The Palace of Truth—Trial by Jury.
The SECOND SERIES: Broken Hearts—Engaged—Sweethearts—Gretchen—Dan'l Druce—Tom Cobb—H.M.S. "Pinafore"—The Sorcerer—Pirates of Penzance.

EIGHT ORIGINAL COMIC OPERAS written by W. S. GILBERT. Containing: The Sorcerer—H.M.S. "Pinafore"—Pirates of Penzance—Iolanthe—Patience—Princess Ida—The Mikado—Trial by Jury. Demy 8vo, cloth limp, 2s. 6d.

THE "GILBERT AND SULLIVAN" BIRTHDAY BOOK: Quotations for Every Day in the Year, Selected from Plays by W. S. GILBERT set to Music by Sir A. SULLIVAN. Compiled by ALEX. WATSON. Royal 16mo, Jap. leather, 2s. 6d.

GLANVILLE.—THE LOST HEIRESS: A Tale of Love and Battle. By ERNEST GLANVILLE. 2 Illusts. by HUME NISBET. Cr. 8vo, cloth extra, 3s. 6d.

GLENNY.—A YEAR'S WORK IN GARDEN AND GREENHOUSE: Practical Advice to Amateur Gardeners as to the Management of the Flower, Fruit, and Frame Garden. By GEORGE GLENNY. Post 8vo, 1s.; cloth limp, 1s. 6d.

GODWIN.—LIVES OF THE NECROMANCERS. By WILLIAM GODWIN. Post 8vo, cloth limp, 2s.

GOLDEN TREASURY OF THOUGHT, THE: An Encyclopædia of Quotations. Edited by THEODORE TAYLOR. Crown 8vo. cloth gilt, 7s. 6d.

GOWING.—FIVE THOUSAND MILES IN A SLEDGE: A Midwinter Journey Across Siberia. By LIONEL F. GOWING. With 30 Illustrations by C. J. UREN, and a Map by E. WELLER. Large crown 8vo, cloth extra, 8s.

GRAHAM.—THE PROFESSOR'S WIFE: A Story. By LEONARD GRAHAM. Fcap. 8vo, picture cover, 1s.

GREEKS AND ROMANS, THE LIFE OF THE, described from Antique Monuments. By ERNST GUHL and W. KONER. Edited by Dr. F. HUEFFER. With 545 Illustrations. Large crown 8vo, cloth extra, 7s. 6d.

GREENWOOD (JAMES), WORKS BY. Cr. 8vo, cloth extra, 3s. 6d. each.
- THE WILDS OF LONDON.
- LOW-LIFE DEEPS.

GREVILLE (HENRY), NOVELS BY:
NIKANOR. Translated by ELIZA E. CHASE. With 8 Illusts. Cr. 8vo, cl. extra, 6s.
A NOBLE WOMAN. Translated by ALBERT D. VANDAM. Crown 8vo, cloth extra, 5s.; post 8vo, illustrated boards, 2s.

HABBERTON (JOHN, Author of "Helen's Babies"), **NOVELS BY.**
Post 8vo, illustrated boards 2s. each; cloth limp, 2s. 6d. each.
- BRUETON'S BAYOU.
- COUNTRY LUCK.

HAIR, THE: Its Treatment in Health, Weakness, and Disease. Translated from the German of Dr. J. PINCUS. Crown 8vo, 1s.; cloth limp, 1s. 6d.

HAKE (DR. THOMAS GORDON), POEMS BY. Cr. 8vo, cl. ex., 6s. each.
NEW SYMBOLS. | LEGENDS OF THE MORROW. | THE SERPENT PLAY,
MAIDEN ECSTASY. Small 4to, cloth extra, 8s.

HALL.—SKETCHES OF IRISH CHARACTER. By Mrs. S. C. HALL. With numerous Illustrations on Steel and Wood by MACLISE, GILBERT, HARVEY, and GEORGE CRUIKSHANK. Medium 8vo, cloth extra, 7s. 6d.

HALLIDAY (ANDR.).—EVERY-DAY PAPERS. Post 8vo, bds., 2s.

HANDWRITING, THE PHILOSOPHY OF. With over 100 Facsimiles and Explanatory Text. By DON FELIX DE SALAMANCA. Post 8vo, cloth limp, 2s. 6d.

HANKY-PANKY: A Collection of Very Easy Tricks, Very Difficult Tricks, White Magic, Sleight of Hand. &c. Edited by W. H. CREMER. With 200 Illustrations. Crown 8vo, cloth extra, 4s. 6d.

HARDY (LADY DUFFUS).—PAUL WYNTER'S SACRIFICE. By Lady DUFFUS HARDY. Post 8vo, illustrated boards, 2s.

HARDY (THOMAS).—UNDER THE GREENWOOD TREE. By THOMAS HARDY, Author of "Far from the Madding Crowd." Post 8vo, illust. bds., 2s.

HARWOOD.—THE TENTH EARL. By J. BERWICK HARWOOD. Post 8vo, illustrated boards, 2s.

HAWEIS (MRS. H. R.), WORKS BY. Square 8vo, cloth extra, 6s. each.
THE ART OF BEAUTY. With Coloured Frontispiece and 91 Illustrations.
THE ART OF DECORATION. With Coloured Frontispiece and 74 Illustrations.
CHAUCER FOR CHILDREN. With 8 Coloured Plates and 30 Woodcuts.
THE ART OF DRESS. With 32 Illustrations. Post 8vo, 1s.; cloth, 1s. 6d.
CHAUCER FOR SCHOOLS. Demy 8vo, cloth limp, 2s. 6d.

HAWEIS (Rev. H. R., M.A.).—AMERICAN HUMORISTS: WASHINGTON IRVING, OLIVER WENDELL HOLMES, JAMES RUSSELL LOWELL, ARTEMUS WARD, MARK TWAIN, and BRET HARTE. Third Edition. Crown 8vo, cloth extra, 6s.

HAWLEY SMART.—WITHOUT LOVE OR LICENCE: A Novel. By HAWLEY SMART. Crown 8vo, cloth extra, 3s. 6d.

HAWTHORNE.—OUR OLD HOME. By NATHANIEL HAWTHORNE. Annotated with Passages from the Author's Note-book, and Illustrated with 31 Photogravures. Two Vols., crown 8vo, buckram, gilt top, 15s.

HAWTHORNE (JULIAN), NOVELS BY.
Crown 8vo, cloth extra, 3s. 6d. each; post 8vo, illustrated boards, 2s. each.
GARTH. | ELLICE QUENTIN. | BEATRIX RANDOLPH.
FORTUNE'S FOOL. | DAVID POINDEXTER.
SEBASTIAN STROME. | DUST. | THE SPECTRE OF THE CAMERA.

Post 8vo, illustrated boards, 2s. each.
MISS CADOGNA. | LOVE—OR A NAME?
MRS. GAINSBOROUGH'S DIAMONDS. Fcap. 8vo, illustrated cover, 1s.
A DREAM AND A FORGETTING. Post 8vo, cloth limp, 1s. 6d.

HAYS.—WOMEN OF THE DAY: A Biographical Dictionary of Notable Contemporaries. By FRANCES HAYS. Crown 8vo, cloth extra, 5s.

HEATH.—MY GARDEN WILD, AND WHAT I GREW THERE. By FRANCIS GEORGE HEATH. Crown 8vo, cloth extra, gilt edges, 6s.

HELPS (SIR ARTHUR), WORKS BY. Post 8vo, cloth limp, 2s. 6d. each.
ANIMALS AND THEIR MASTERS. | SOCIAL PRESSURE.
IVAN DE BIRON: A Novel. Cr. 8vo, cl. extra, 3s. 6d.; post 8vo, illust. bds., 2s.

HENDERSON.—AGATHA PAGE: A Novel. By ISAAC HENDERSON. Crown 8vo, cloth extra, 3s. 6d.

HERRICK'S (ROBERT) HESPERIDES, NOBLE NUMBERS, AND COMPLETE COLLECTED POEMS. With Memorial-Introduction and Notes by the Rev. A. B. GROSART, D.D., Steel Portrait, Index of First Lines, Glossarial Index, &c. Three Vols., crown 8vo, cloth boards, **18s.**

HESSE-WARTEGG.—TUNIS: The Land and the People. By Chevalier ERNST VON HESSE-WARTEGG. With 22 Illustrations. Cr. 8vo, cloth extra, **3s. 6d.**

HINDLEY (CHARLES), WORKS BY.
TAVERN ANECDOTES AND SAYINGS: Including the Origin of Signs, and Reminiscences connected with Taverns, Coffee Houses, Clubs, &c. With Illustrations. Crown 8vo, cloth extra, **3s. 6d.**
THE LIFE AND ADVENTURES OF A CHEAP JACK. By ONE OF THE FRATERNITY. Edited by CHARLES HINDLEY. Crown 8vo, cloth extra, **3s. 6d.**

HOEY.—THE LOVER'S CREED. By Mrs. CASHEL HOEY. Post 8vo, illustrated boards, **2s.**

HOLLINGSHEAD (JOHN).—NIAGARA SPRAY. Crown 8vo, **1s.**

HOLMES.—THE SCIENCE OF VOICE PRODUCTION AND VOICE PRESERVATION: A Popular Manual for the Use of Speakers and Singers. By GORDON HOLMES, M.D. With Illustrations. Crown 8vo, **1s.**; cloth, **1s. 6d.**

HOLMES (OLIVER WENDELL), WORKS BY.
THE AUTOCRAT OF THE BREAKFAST-TABLE. Illustrated by J. GORDON THOMSON. Post 8vo, cloth limp, **2s. 6d.**—Another Edition, in smaller type, with an Introduction by G. A. SALA. Post 8vo, cloth limp, **2s.**
THE PROFESSOR AT THE BREAKFAST-TABLE. Post 8vo, cloth limp, **2s.**

HOOD'S (THOMAS) CHOICE WORKS, in Prose and Verse. Including the Cream of the COMIC ANNUALS. With Life of the Author, Portrait, and 200 Illustrations. Crown 8vo, cloth extra, **7s. 6d.**
HOOD'S WHIMS AND ODDITIES. With 85 Illustrations. Post 8vo, printed on laid paper and half-bound, **2s.**

HOOD (TOM).—FROM NOWHERE TO THE NORTH POLE: A Noah's Arkæological Narrative. By TOM HOOD. With 25 Illustrations by W. BRUNTON and E. C. BARNES. Square 8vo, cloth extra, gilt edges, **6s.**

HOOK'S (THEODORE) CHOICE HUMOROUS WORKS; including his Ludicrous Adventures, Bons Mots, Puns, and Hoaxes. With Life of the Author, Portraits, Facsimiles, and Illustrations. Crown 8vo, cloth extra, **7s. 6d.**

HOOPER.—THE HOUSE OF RABY: A Novel. By Mrs. GEORGE HOOPER. Post 8vo, illustrated boards, **2s.**

HOPKINS.—"'TWIXT LOVE AND DUTY:" A Novel. By TIGHE HOPKINS. Post 8vo, illustrated boards, **2s.**

HORNE. — ORION: An Epic Poem. By RICHARD HENGIST HORNE. With Photographic Portrait by SUMMERS. Tenth Edition. Cr. 8vo, cloth extra, **7s.**

HORSE (THE) AND HIS RIDER: An Anecdotic Medley. By "THORMANBY." Crown 8vo, cloth extra, **6s.**

HUNT.—ESSAYS BY LEIGH HUNT: A TALE FOR A CHIMNEY CORNER, and other Pieces. Edited, with an Introduction, by EDMUND OLLIER. Post 8vo, printed on laid paper and half-bound, **2s.**

HUNT (MRS. ALFRED), NOVELS BY.
Crown 8vo, cloth extra, **3s. 6d.** each; post 8vo, illustrated boards, **2s.** each.
THE LEADEN CASKET. | SELF-CONDEMNED. | THAT OTHER PERSON.
THORNICROFT'S MODEL. Post 8vo, illustrated boards, **2s.**

HYDROPHOBIA: An Account of M. PASTEUR'S System. Containing a Translation of all his Communications on the Subject, the Technique of his Method, and Statistics. By RENAUD SUZOR, M.B. Crown 8vo, cloth extra, **6s.**

INGELOW (JEAN).—FATED TO BE FREE. With 24 Illustrations by G. J. PINWELL. Cr. 8vo, cloth extra, **3s. 6d.**; post 8vo, illustrated boards, **2s.**

INDOOR PAUPERS. By ONE OF THEM. Crown 8vo, **1s.**; cloth, **1s. 6d.**

IRISH WIT AND HUMOUR, SONGS OF. Collected and Edited by A. Perceval Graves. Post 8vo, cloth limp, 2s. 6d.

JAMES.—A ROMANCE OF THE QUEEN'S HOUNDS. By Charles James. Post 8vo, picture cover, 1s.; cloth limp, 1s. 6d.

JANVIER.—PRACTICAL KERAMICS FOR STUDENTS. By Catherine A. Janvier. Crown 8vo, cloth extra, 6s.

JAY (HARRIETT), NOVELS BY. Post 8vo, illustrated boards, 2s. each.
THE DARK COLLEEN. | THE QUEEN OF CONNAUGHT.

JEFFERIES (RICHARD), WORKS BY. Post 8vo, cloth limp, 2s. 6d. each.
NATURE NEAR LONDON. | THE LIFE OF THE FIELDS. | THE OPEN AIR.
THE EULOGY OF RICHARD JEFFERIES. By Walter Besant. Second Edition. With a Photograph Portrait. Crown 8vo, cloth extra, 6s.

JENNINGS (H. J.), WORKS BY.
CURIOSITIES OF CRITICISM. Post 8vo, cloth limp, 2s. 6d.
LORD TENNYSON: A Biographical Sketch. With a Photograph. Cr. 8vo, cl., 6s.

JEROME.—STAGELAND: Curious Habits and Customs of its Inhabitants. By Jerome K. Jerome. With 64 Illustrations by J. Bernard Partridge. Sixteenth Thousand. Fcap. 4to, cloth extra, 3s. 6d.

JERROLD.—THE BARBER'S CHAIR; & THE HEDGEHOG LETTERS. By Douglas Jerrold. Post 8vo, printed on laid paper and half-bound, 2s.

JERROLD (TOM), WORKS BY. Post 8vo, 1s. each; cloth limp, 1s. 6d. each.
THE GARDEN THAT PAID THE RENT.
HOUSEHOLD HORTICULTURE: A Gossip about Flowers. Illustrated.
OUR KITCHEN GARDEN: The Plants we Grow, and How we Cook Them.

JESSE.—SCENES AND OCCUPATIONS OF A COUNTRY LIFE. By Edward Jesse. Post 8vo, cloth limp, 2s.

JONES (WILLIAM, F.S.A.), WORKS BY. Cr. 8vo, cl. extra, 7s. 6d. each.
FINGER-RING LORE: Historical, Legendary, and Anecdotal. With nearly 300 Illustrations. Second Edition, Revised and Enlarged.
CREDULITIES, PAST AND PRESENT. Including the Sea and Seamen, Miners, Talismans, Word and Letter Divination, Exorcising and Blessing of Animals, Birds, Eggs, Luck, &c. With an Etched Frontispiece.
CROWNS AND CORONATIONS: A History of Regalia. With 100 Illustrations.

JONSON'S (BEN) WORKS. With Notes Critical and Explanatory, and a Biographical Memoir by William Gifford. Edited by Colonel Cunningham. Three Vols., crown 8vo, cloth extra, 6s. each.

JOSEPHUS, THE COMPLETE WORKS OF. Translated by Whiston. Containing "The Antiquities of the Jews" and "The Wars of the Jews." With 52 Illustrations and Maps. Two Vols., demy 8vo, half-bound, 12s. 6d.

KEMPT.—PENCIL AND PALETTE: Chapters on Art and Artists. By Robert Kempt. Post 8vo, cloth limp, 2s. 6d.

KERSHAW.—COLONIAL FACTS AND FICTIONS: Humorous Sketches. By Mark Kershaw. Post 8vo, illustrated boards, 2s.; cloth, 2s. 6d.

KEYSER.—CUT BY THE MESS: A Novel. By Arthur Keyser. Crown 8vo, picture cover, 1s.; cloth limp, 1s. 6d.

KING (R. ASHE), NOVELS BY. Cr. 8vo, cl., 3s. 6d. ea.; post 8vo, bds., 2s. ea.
A DRAWN GAME. | "THE WEARING OF THE GREEN."
PASSION'S SLAVE. Post 8vo, illustrated boards, 2s.
BELLE BARRY. 2 vols. Crown 8vo.

KINGSLEY (HENRY), NOVELS BY.
OAKSHOTT CASTLE. Post 8vo, illustrated boards, 2s.
NUMBER SEVENTEEN. Crown 8vo, cloth extra, 3s. 6d.

KNIGHTS (THE) OF THE LION: A Romance of the Thirteenth Century. Edited, with an Introduction, by the Marquess of Lorne, K.T. Cr. 8vo, cl. ex., 6s.

KNIGHT.—THE PATIENT'S VADE MECUM: How to Get Most Benefit from Medical Advice. By WILLIAM KNIGHT, M.R.C.S., and EDWARD KNIGHT, L.R.C.P. Crown 8vo, 1s.; cloth limp, 1s. 6d.

LAMB'S (CHARLES) COMPLETE WORKS, in Prose and Verse. Edited, with Notes and Introduction, by R. H. SHEPHERD. With Two Portraits and Facsimile of a page of the "Essay on Roast Pig." Cr. 8vo, cl. ex., 7s. 6d.
THE ESSAYS OF ELIA. Post 8vo, printed on laid paper and half-bound, 2s.
LITTLE ESSAYS: Sketches and Characters by CHARLES LAMB, selected from his Letters by PERCY FITZGERALD. Post 8vo, cloth limp, 2s. 6d.

LANDOR.—CITATION AND EXAMINATION OF WILLIAM SHAKSPEARE, &c., before Sir THOMAS LUCY, touching Deer-stealing, 19th September, 1582. To which is added, A CONFERENCE OF MASTER EDMUND SPENSER with the Earl of Essex, touching the State of Ireland, 1595. By WALTER SAVAGE LANDOR. Fcap. 8vo, half-Roxburghe, 2s. 6d. [Shortly.

LANE.—THE THOUSAND AND ONE NIGHTS, commonly called in England THE ARABIAN NIGHTS' ENTERTAINMENTS. Translated from the Arabic, with Notes, by EDWARD WILLIAM LANE. Illustrated by many hundred Engravings from Designs by HARVEY. Edited by EDWARD STANLEY POOLE. With a Preface by STANLEY LANE-POOLE. Three Vols., demy 8vo, cloth extra, 7s. 6d. each.

LARWOOD (JACOB), WORKS BY.
THE STORY OF THE LONDON PARKS. With Illusts. Cr. 8vo, cl. extra, 3s. 6d.
ANECDOTES OF THE CLERGY: The Antiquities, Humours, and Eccentricities of the Cloth. Post 8vo, printed on laid paper and half-bound, 2s.

Post 8vo, cloth limp, 2s. 6d. each.
FORENSIC ANECDOTES. | THEATRICAL ANECDOTES.

LEIGH (HENRY S.), WORKS BY.
CAROLS OF COCKAYNE. Printed on hand-made paper, bound in buckram, 5s.
JEUX D'ESPRIT. Edited by HENRY S. LEIGH. Post 8vo, cloth limp, 2s. 6d.

LEYS (JOHN).—THE LINDSAYS: A Romance. Post 8vo, illust. bds., 2s.

LIFE IN LONDON; or, The History of JERRY HAWTHORN and CORINTHIAN TOM. With CRUIKSHANK's Coloured Illustrations. Crown 8vo, cloth extra, 7s. 6d. [New Edition preparing.

LINSKILL.—IN EXCHANGE FOR A SOUL. By MARY LINSKILL. Post 8vo, illustrated boards, 2s.

LINTON (E. LYNN), WORKS BY. Post 8vo, cloth limp, 2s. 6d. each.
WITCH STORIES. | OURSELVES: ESSAYS ON WOMEN.

Crown 8vo, cloth extra, 3s. 6d. each; post 8vo, illustrated boards, 2s. each.
PATRICIA KEMBALL. | UNDER WHICH LORD?
ATONEMENT OF LEAM DUNDAS. | "MY LOVE!" | IONE.
THE WORLD WELL LOST. | PASTON CAREW, Millionaire & Miser.
SOWING THE WIND.

Post 8vo, illustrated boards, 2s. each.
WITH A SILKEN THREAD. | THE REBEL OF THE FAMILY.

LONGFELLOW'S POETICAL WORKS. With numerous Illustrations on Steel and Wood. Crown 8vo, cloth extra, 7s. 6d.

LUCY.—GIDEON FLEYCE: A Novel. By HENRY W. LUCY. Crown 8vo, cloth extra, 3s. 6d.; post 8vo, illustrated boards, 2s.

LUSIAD (THE) OF CAMOENS. Translated into English Spenserian Verse by ROBERT FFRENCH DUFF. With 14 Plates. Demy 8vo, cloth boards, 18s.

MACALPINE (AVERY), NOVELS BY.
TERESA ITASCA, and other Stories. Crown 8vo, bound in canvas, 2s. 6d.
BROKEN WINGS. With Illusts. by W. J. HENNESSY. Crown 8vo, cloth extra, 6s.

MACCOLL.—MR. STRANGER'S SEALED PACKET: A Story of Adventure. By HUGH MACCOLL. Second Edition. Crown 8vo, cloth extra, 5s.

McCARTHY (JUSTIN, M.P.), WORKS BY.

A HISTORY OF OUR OWN TIMES, from the Accession of Queen Victoria to the General Election of 1880. Four Vols. demy 8vo, cloth extra, **12s.** each.—Also a POPULAR EDITION, in Four Vols., crown 8vo, cloth extra, **6s.** each.—And a JUBILEE EDITION, with an Appendix of Events to the end of 1886, in Two Vols., large crown 8vo, cloth extra, **7s. 6d.** each.

A SHORT HISTORY OF OUR OWN TIMES. One Vol., crown 8vo, cloth extra, **6s.** —Also a CHEAP POPULAR EDITION, post 8vo, cloth limp, **2s. 6d.**

A HISTORY OF THE FOUR GEORGES. Four Vols. demy 8vo, cloth extra, **12s.** each. [Vols. I. & II. *ready.*

Crown 8vo, cloth extra, **3s. 6d.** each; post 8vo, illustrated boards, **2s.** each.

DEAR LADY DISDAIN.	THE WATERDALE NEIGHBOURS.
FAIR SAXON. | LINLEY ROCHFORD.	DONNA QUIXOTE. | MAID OF ATHENS.
MISS MISANTHROPE.	THE COMET OF A SEASON.
MY ENEMY'S DAUGHTER.	CAMIOLA: A Girl with a Fortune.

"**THE RIGHT HONOURABLE.**" By JUSTIN McCARTHY, M.P., and Mrs. CAMPBELL-PRAED. Fourth Edition. Crown 8vo, cloth extra, **6s.**

McCARTHY (JUSTIN H., M.P.), WORKS BY.

THE FRENCH REVOLUTION. Four Vols., 8vo, **12s.** each. [Vols. I. & II. *ready.*
AN OUTLINE OF THE HISTORY OF IRELAND. Crown 8vo, **1s.**; cloth, **1s. 6d.**
IRELAND SINCE THE UNION: Irish History, 1798-1886. Crown 8vo, cloth, **6s.**
ENGLAND UNDER GLADSTONE, 1880-85. Crown 8vo, cloth extra, **6s.**

HAFIZ IN LONDON: Poems. Small 8vo, gold cloth, **3s. 6d.**
HARLEQUINADE: Poems. Small 4to, Japanese vellum, **8s.**

OUR SENSATION NOVEL. Crown 8vo, picture cover, **1s.**; cloth limp, **1s. 6d.**
DOLLY: A Sketch. Crown 8vo, picture cover, **1s.**; cloth limp, **1s. 6d.**
LILY LASS: A Romance. Crown 8vo, picture cover, **1s.**; cloth limp, **1s. 6d.**

MACDONALD.—WORKS OF FANCY AND IMAGINATION.
By GEORGE MACDONALD, LL.D. Ten Vols., in cloth case, **21s.**—Or the Vols. may be had separately, grolier cloth, at **2s. 6d.** each.

Vol. I. WITHIN AND WITHOUT.—THE HIDDEN LIFE.
  " II. THE DISCIPLE.—THE GOSPEL WOMEN.—BOOK OF SONNETS.—ORGAN SONGS.
  " III. VIOLIN SONGS.—SONGS OF THE DAYS AND NIGHTS.—A BOOK OF DREAMS.—ROADSIDE POEMS.—POEMS FOR CHILDREN.
  " IV. PARABLES.—BALLADS.—SCOTCH SONGS.
  " V. & VI. PHANTASTES: A Faerie Romance. | Vol. VII. THE PORTENT.
  " VIII. THE LIGHT PRINCESS.—THE GIANT'S HEART.—SHADOWS.
  " IX. CROSS PURPOSES.—THE GOLDEN KEY.—THE CARASOYN.—LITTLE DAYLIGHT.
  " X. THE CRUEL PAINTER.—THE WOW O' RIVVEN.—THE CASTLE.—THE BROKEN SWORDS.—THE GRAY WOLF.—UNCLE CORNELIUS.

MACDONELL.—QUAKER COUSINS: A Novel.
By AGNES MACDONELL. Crown 8vo, cloth extra, **3s. 6d.**; post 8vo, illustrated boards, **2s.**

MACGREGOR.—PASTIMES AND PLAYERS: Notes on Popular Games.
By ROBERT MACGREGOR. Post 8vo, cloth limp, **2s. 6d.**

MACKAY.—INTERLUDES AND UNDERTONES; or, Music at Twilight.
By CHARLES MACKAY, LL.D. Crown 8vo, cloth extra, **6s.**

MACLISE PORTRAIT GALLERY (THE) OF ILLUSTRIOUS LITERARY CHARACTERS: 85 PORTRAITS;
with Memoirs — Biographical, Critical, Bibliographical, and Anecdotal—illustrative of the Literature of the former half of the Present Century, by WILLIAM BATES, B.A. Crown 8vo, cloth extra, **7s. 6d.**

MACQUOID (MRS.), WORKS BY.
Square 8vo, cloth extra, **7s. 6d.** each.

IN THE ARDENNES. With 50 Illustrations by THOMAS R. MACQUOID.
PICTURES AND LEGENDS FROM NORMANDY AND BRITTANY. With 34 Illustrations by THOMAS R. MACQUOID.
THROUGH NORMANDY. With 92 Illustrations by T. R. MACQUOID, and a Map.
THROUGH BRITTANY. With 35 Illustrations by T. R. MACQUOID, and a Map.
ABOUT YORKSHIRE. With 67 Illustrations by T. R. MACQUOID.

Post 8vo, illustrated boards, **2s.** each.

THE EVIL EYE, and other Stories.	LOST ROSE.

MAGIC LANTERN, THE, and its Management: including full Practical Directions for producing the Limelight, making Oxygen Gas, and preparing Lantern Slides. By T. C. HEPWORTH. With 10 Illustrations. Cr. 8vo. **1s.**; cloth, **1s. 6d.**

MAGICIAN'S OWN BOOK, THE: Performances with Cups and Balls, Eggs, Hats, Handkerchiefs, &c. All from actual Experience. Edited by W. H. CREMER. With 200 Illustrations. Crown 8vo, cloth extra, **4s. 6d.**

MAGNA CHARTA: An Exact Facsimile of the Original in the British Museum, 3 feet by 2 feet, with Arms and Seals emblazoned in Gold and Colours, **5s.**

MALLOCK (W. H.), WORKS BY.
THE NEW REPUBLIC. Post 8vo, picture cover, **2s.**; cloth limp, **2s. 6d.**
THE NEW PAUL & VIRGINIA: Positivism on an Island. Post 8vo, cloth, **2s. 6d.**
POEMS. Small 4to, parchment, **8s.**
IS LIFE WORTH LIVING? Crown 8vo, cloth extra, **6s.**

MALLORY'S (SIR THOMAS) MORT D'ARTHUR: The Stories of King Arthur and of the Knights of the Round Table. (A Selection.) Edited by B. MONTGOMERIE RANKING. Post 8vo, cloth limp, **2s.**

MARK TWAIN, WORKS BY. Crown 8vo, cloth extra, **7s. 6d.** each.
THE CHOICE WORKS OF MARK TWAIN. Revised and Corrected throughout by the Author. With Life, Portrait, and numerous Illustrations.
ROUGHING IT, and INNOCENTS AT HOME. With 200 Illusts. by F. A. FRASER.
THE GILDED AGE. By MARK TWAIN and C. D. WARNER. With 212 Illustrations.
MARK TWAIN'S LIBRARY OF HUMOUR. With 197 Illustrations.
A YANKEE AT THE COURT OF KING ARTHUR. With 220 Illusts. by BEARD.

Crown 8vo, cloth extra (illustrated), **7s. 6d.** each; post 8vo, illust. boards, **2s.** each.
THE INNOCENTS ABROAD; or, New Pilgrim's Progress. With 234 Illustrations. (The Two-Shilling Edition is entitled MARK TWAIN'S PLEASURE TRIP.)
THE ADVENTURES OF TOM SAWYER. With 111 Illustrations.
THE PRINCE AND THE PAUPER. With 190 Illustrations.
A TRAMP ABROAD. With 314 Illustrations.
LIFE ON THE MISSISSIPPI. With 300 Illustrations.
ADVENTURES OF HUCKLEBERRY FINN. With 174 Illusts. by E. W. KEMBLE.

THE STOLEN WHITE ELEPHANT, &c. Cr. 8vo, cl., **6s.**; post 8vo, illust. bds., **2s.**

MARLOWE'S WORKS. Including his Translations. Edited, with Notes and Introductions, by Col. CUNNINGHAM. Crown 8vo, cloth extra, **6s.**

MARRYAT (FLORENCE), NOVELS BY. Post 8vo, illust. boards, **2s.** each.
A HARVEST OF WILD OATS. | WRITTEN IN FIRE. | FIGHTING THE AIR.
OPEN! SESAME! Crown 8vo, cloth extra, **3s. 6d.**; post 8vo, picture boards, **2s.**

MASSINGER'S PLAYS. From the Text of WILLIAM GIFFORD. Edited by Col. CUNNINGHAM. Crown 8vo, cloth extra, **6s.**

MASTERMAN.—HALF-A-DOZEN DAUGHTERS: A Novel. By J. MASTERMAN. Post 8vo, illustrated boards, **2s.**

MATTHEWS.—A SECRET OF THE SEA, &c. By BRANDER MATTHEWS. Post 8vo, illustrated boards, **2s.**; cloth limp, **2s. 6d.**

MAYHEW.—LONDON CHARACTERS AND THE HUMOROUS SIDE OF LONDON LIFE. By HENRY MAYHEW. With Illusts. Crown 8vo, cloth, **3s. 6d.**

MENKEN.—INFELICIA: Poems by ADAH ISAACS MENKEN. With Biographical Preface, Illustrations by F. E. LUMMIS and F. O. C. DARLEY, and Facsimile of a Letter from CHARLES DICKENS. Small 4to, cloth extra, **7s. 6d.**

MEXICAN MUSTANG (ON A), through Texas to the Rio Grande. By A. E. SWEET and J. ARMOY KNOX. With 265 Illusts. Cr. 8vo, cloth extra, **7s. 6d.**

MIDDLEMASS (JEAN), NOVELS BY. Post 8vo, illust. boards, **2s.** each.
TOUCH AND GO. | MR. DORILLION.

MILLER.—PHYSIOLOGY FOR THE YOUNG; or, The House of Life. Human Physiology, with its application to the Preservation of Health. By Mrs F. FENWICK MILLER. With numerous Illustrations. Post 8vo, cloth limp, **2s. 6d.**

MILTON (J. L.), WORKS BY. Post 8vo, 1s. each ; cloth, 1s. 6d. each.
THE HYGIENE OF THE SKIN. With Directions for Diet, Soaps, Baths, &c.
THE BATH IN DISEASES OF THE SKIN.
THE LAWS OF LIFE, AND THEIR RELATION TO DISEASES OF THE SKIN.
THE SUCCESSFUL TREATMENT OF LEPROSY. Demy 8vo, 1s.

MINTO (WM.)—WAS SHE GOOD OR BAD? Cr. 8vo, 1s. ; cloth, 1s. 6d.

MOLESWORTH (MRS.), NOVELS BY.
HATHERCOURT RECTORY. Post 8vo, illustrated boards, 2s.
THAT GIRL IN BLACK. Crown 8vo, picture cover, 1s. ; cloth, 1s. 6d.

MOORE (THOMAS), WORKS BY.
THE EPICUREAN; and ALCIPHRON. Post 8vo, half-bound, 2s.
PROSE AND VERSE, Humorous, Satirical, and Sentimental, by THOMAS MOORE ; with Suppressed Passages from the MEMOIRS OF LORD BYRON. Edited by R. HERNE SHEPHERD. With Portrait. Crown 8vo, cloth extra, 7s. 6d.

MUDDOCK (J. E.), STORIES BY.
STORIES WEIRD AND WONDERFUL. Post 8vo, illust. boards, 2s. ; cloth, 2s. 6d.
THE DEAD MAN'S SECRET; or, The Valley of Gold: A Narrative of Strange Adventure. With a Frontispiece by F. BARNARD. Crown 8vo, cloth extra, 5s. ; post 8vo, illustrated boards, 2s.

MURRAY (D. CHRISTIE), NOVELS BY.
Crown 8vo, cloth extra, 3s. 6d. each ; post 8vo, illustrated boards, 2s. each.
A LIFE'S ATONEMENT.	COALS OF FIRE.	A BIT OF HUMAN NATURE.
VAL STRANGE. HEARTS.	CYNIC FORTUNE.	FIRST PERSON SINGULAR.
A MODEL FATHER.	JOSEPH'S COAT.	THE WAY OF THE WORLD.

BY THE GATE OF THE SEA. Post 8vo, picture boards, 2s.
OLD BLAZER'S HERO. With Three Illustrations by A. McCORMICK. Crown 8vo, cloth extra, 6s. ; post 8vo, illustrated boards, 2s.

MURRAY (D. CHRISTIE) & HENRY HERMAN, WORKS BY.
Crown 8vo, cloth extra, 6s. each ; post 8vo, illustrated boards, 2s. each.
ONE TRAVELLER RETURNS.
PAUL JONES'S ALIAS. With 13 Illustrations by A. FORESTIER and G. NICOLET.
THE BISHOPS' BIBLE. Crown 8vo, cloth extra, 3s. 6d.

MURRAY.—A GAME OF BLUFF: A Novel. By HENRY MURRAY. Post 8vo, picture boards, 2s. ; cloth limp, 2s. 6d.

NISBET.—"BAIL UP!" A Romance of BUSHRANGERS AND BLACKS. By HUME NISBET. With Frontispiece and Vignette. Crown 8vo, cloth extra, 3s. 6d.

NOVELISTS.—HALF-HOURS WITH THE BEST NOVELISTS OF THE CENTURY. Edit. by H. T. MACKENZIE BELL. Cr. 8vo, cl., 3s. 6d. [*Preparing*.

O'CONNOR. — LORD BEACONSFIELD: A Biography. By T. P. O'CONNOR, M.P. Sixth Edition, with an Introduction. Crown 8vo, cloth extra, 5s.

O'HANLON (ALICE), NOVELS BY. Post 8vo, illustrated boards, 2s. each.
THE UNFORESEEN. | CHANCE? OR FATE?

OHNET (GEORGES), NOVELS BY.
DOCTOR RAMEAU. Translated by Mrs. CASHEL HOEY. With 9 Illustrations by E. BAYARD. Crown 8vo, cloth extra, 6s. ; post 8vo, illustrated boards, 2s.
A LAST LOVE. Translated by ALBERT D. VANDAM. Crown 8vo, cloth extra, 5s. ; post 8vo, illustrated boards, 2s.
A WEIRD GIFT. Translated by ALBERT D. VANDAM. Crown 8vo, cloth, 3s. 6d.

OLIPHANT (MRS.), NOVELS BY. Post 8vo, illustrated boards, 2s. each.
THE PRIMROSE PATH. | THE GREATEST HEIRESS IN ENGLAND.
WHITELADIES. With Illustrations by ARTHUR HOPKINS and HENRY WOODS, A.R.A. Crown 8vo, cloth extra, 3s. 6d. ; post 8vo, illustrated boards, 2s.

O'REILLY (MRS.).—PHŒBE'S FORTUNES. Post 8vo, illust. bds., 2s.

O'SHAUGHNESSY (ARTHUR), POEMS BY.
LAYS OF FRANCE. Crown 8vo, cloth extra, 10s. 6d.
MUSIC AND MOONLIGHT. Fcap. 8vo, cloth extra, 7s. 6d.
SONGS OF A WORKER. Fcap. 8vo, cloth extra, 7s. 6d.

OUIDA, NOVELS BY. Cr. 8vo, cl., 3s. 6d. each; post 8vo, illust. bds., 2s. each.

HELD IN BONDAGE.	IDALIA.	MOTHS.
STRATHMORE.	TRICOTRIN.	BIMBI.
CHANDOS.	PUCK.	PIPISTRELLO.
UNDER TWO FLAGS.	FOLLE FARINE.	IN MAREMMA.
CECIL CASTLEMAINE'S GAGE.	PASCAREL.	A VILLAGE COMMUNE.
	SIGNA.	WANDA.
TWO LITTLE WOODEN SHOES.	ARIADNE.	FRESCOES.
	IN A WINTER CITY.	PRINCESS NAPRAXINE.
A DOG OF FLANDERS.	FRIENDSHIP.	OTHMAR. | GUILDEROY.

Crown 8vo, cloth extra, 3s. 6d. each.

SYRLIN. | RUFFINO.

WISDOM, WIT, AND PATHOS, selected from the Works of OUIDA by F. SYDNEY MORRIS. Post 8vo, cloth extra, 5s.—CHEAP EDITION, illustrated boards, 2s.

PAGE (H. A.), WORKS BY.
THOREAU: His Life and Aims. With Portrait. Post 8vo, cloth limp, 2s. 6d.
ANIMAL ANECDOTES. Arranged on a New Principle. Crown 8vo, cloth extra, 5s.

PASCAL'S PROVINCIAL LETTERS. A New Translation, with Historical Introduction and Notes by T. M'CRIE, D.D. Post 8vo, cloth limp, 2s.

PAUL.—GENTLE AND SIMPLE. By MARGARET A. PAUL. With Frontispiece by HELEN PATERSON. Crown 8vo, cloth, 3s. 6d.; post 8vo, illust. boards, 2s.

PAYN (JAMES), NOVELS BY.
Crown 8vo, cloth extra, 3s. 6d. each; post 8vo, illustrated boards, 2s. each.

LOST SIR MASSINGBERD.	SOME PRIVATE VIEWS.
WALTER'S WORD.	A GRAPE FROM A THORN.
UNDER ONE ROOF.	THE TALK OF THE TOWN.
LESS BLACK THAN WE'RE PAINTED.	FROM EXILE.
	THE CANON'S WARD.
BY PROXY.	HOLIDAY TASKS.
HIGH SPIRITS.	GLOW-WORM TALES.
A CONFIDENTIAL AGENT.	THE MYSTERY OF MIRBRIDGE.

Post 8vo, illustrated boards, 2s. each.

KIT: A MEMORY.	A WOMAN'S VENGEANCE.
CARLYON'S YEAR.	THE CLYFFARDS OF CLYFFE.
A PERFECT TREASURE.	THE FAMILY SCAPEGRACE.
BENTINCK'S TUTOR.	THE FOSTER BROTHERS.
MURPHY'S MASTER.	FOUND DEAD.
THE BEST OF HUSBANDS.	GWENDOLINE'S HARVEST.
FOR CASH ONLY.	HUMOROUS STORIES.
WHAT HE COST HER.	LIKE FATHER, LIKE SON.
CECIL'S TRYST.	A MARINE RESIDENCE.
FALLEN FORTUNES.	MARRIED BENEATH HIM.
HALVES.	MIRK ABBEY.
A COUNTY FAMILY.	NOT WOOED, BUT WON.
AT HER MERCY.	TWO HUNDRED POUNDS REWARD.

IN PERIL AND PRIVATION: Stories of MARINE ADVENTURE Re-told. With 17 Illustrations. Crown 8vo, cloth extra, 3s. 6d.
NOTES FROM THE "NEWS." Crown 8vo, portrait cover, 1s.; cloth, 1s. 6d.
THE BURNT MILLION. Crown 8vo, cloth extra, 3s. 6d.
THE WORD AND THE WILL. Three Vols., crown 8vo.

PENNELL (H. CHOLMONDELEY), WORKS BY. Post 8vo, cl., 2s. 6d. each.
PUCK ON PEGASUS. With Illustrations.
PEGASUS RE-SADDLED. With Ten full-page Illustrations by G. DU MAURIER.
THE MUSES OF MAYFAIR. Vers de Société, Selected by H. C. PENNELL.

PHELPS (E. STUART), WORKS BY. Post 8vo, 1s. each; cloth, 1s. 6d. each.
BEYOND THE GATES. By the Author of "The Gates Ajar." | AN OLD MAID'S PARADISE.
| BURGLARS IN PARADISE.

JACK THE FISHERMAN. Illustrated by C. W. REED. Cr. 8vo, 1s.; cloth, 1s. 6d.

PIRKIS (C. L.), NOVELS BY.
TROOPING WITH CROWS. Fcap. 8vo, picture cover, 1s.
LADY LOVELACE. Post 8vo, illustrated boards, 2s.

PLANCHE (J. R.), WORKS BY.
THE PURSUIVANT OF ARMS; or, Heraldry Founded upon Facts. With Coloured Frontispiece, Five Plates, and 209 Illusts. Crown 8vo, cloth, 7s. 6d.
SONGS AND POEMS, 1819-1879. Introduction by Mrs. MACKARNESS. Cr. 8vo, cl., 6s.

PLUTARCH'S LIVES OF ILLUSTRIOUS MEN. Translated from the Greek, with Notes Critical and Historical, and a Life of Plutarch, by JOHN and WILLIAM LANGHORNE. With Portraits. Two Vols., demy 8vo, half-bound, 10s. 6d.

POE'S (EDGAR ALLAN) CHOICE WORKS, in Prose and Poetry. Introduction by CHAS. BAUDELAIRE, Portrait, and Facsimiles. Cr. 8vo, cloth, 7s. 6d.
THE MYSTERY OF MARIE ROGET, &c. Post 8vo, illustrated boards, 2s.

POPE'S POETICAL WORKS. Post 8vo, cloth limp, 2s.

PRICE (E. C.), NOVELS BY.
Crown 8vo, cloth extra, 3s. 6d. each; post 8vo, illustrated boards, 2s. each.
VALENTINA. | THE FOREIGNERS. | MRS. LANCASTER'S RIVAL.
GERALD. Post 8vo, illustrated boards, 2s.

PRINCESS OLGA.—RADNA; or, The Great Conspiracy of 1881. By the Princess OLGA. Crown 8vo, cloth extra, 6s.

PROCTOR (RICHARD A., B.A.), WORKS BY.
FLOWERS OF THE SKY. With 55 Illusts. Small crown 8vo, cloth extra, 3s. 6d.
EASY STAR LESSONS. With Star Maps for Every Night in the Year, Drawings of the Constellations, &c. Crown 8vo, cloth extra, 6s.
FAMILIAR SCIENCE STUDIES. Crown 8vo, cloth extra, 6s.
SATURN AND ITS SYSTEM. With 13 Steel Plates. Demy 8vo, cloth ex., 10s. 6d.
MYSTERIES OF TIME AND SPACE. With Illustrations. Cr. 8vo, cloth extra, 6s.
THE UNIVERSE OF SUNS. With numerous Illustrations. Cr. 8vo, cloth ex., 6s.
WAGES AND WANTS OF SCIENCE WORKERS. Crown 8vo, 1s. 6d.

RAMBOSSON.—POPULAR ASTRONOMY. By J. RAMBOSSON, Laureate of the Institute of France. With numerous Illusts. Crown 8vo, cloth extra, 7s. 6d.

RANDOLPH.—AUNT ABIGAIL DYKES: A Novel. By Lt.-Colonel GEORGE RANDOLPH, U.S.A. Crown 8vo, cloth extra, 7s. 6d.

READE (CHARLES), NOVELS BY.
Crown 8vo, cloth extra, illustrated, 3s. 6d. each; post 8vo, illust. bds., 2s. each.
PEG WOFFINGTON. Illustrated by S. L. FILDES, R.A.—Also a POCKET EDITION, set in New Type, in Elzevir style, fcap. 8vo, half-leather, 2s. 6d.
CHRISTIE JOHNSTONE. Illustrated by WILLIAM SMALL.—Also a POCKET EDITION, set in New Type, in Elzevir style, fcap. 8vo, half-leather, 2s. 6d.
IT IS NEVER TOO LATE TO MEND. Illustrated by G. J. PINWELL.
THE COURSE OF TRUE LOVE NEVER DID RUN SMOOTH. Illustrated by HELEN PATERSON.
THE AUTOBIOGRAPHY OF A THIEF, &c. Illustrated by MATT STRETCH.
LOVE ME LITTLE, LOVE ME LONG. Illustrated by M. ELLEN EDWARDS.
THE DOUBLE MARRIAGE. Illusts. by Sir JOHN GILBERT, R.A., and C. KEENE.
THE CLOISTER AND THE HEARTH. Illustrated by CHARLES KEENE.
HARD CASH. Illustrated by F. W. LAWSON.
GRIFFITH GAUNT. Illustrated by S. L. FILDES, R.A., and WILLIAM SMALL.
FOUL PLAY. Illustrated by GEORGE DU MAURIER.
PUT YOURSELF IN HIS PLACE. Illustrated by ROBERT BARNES.
A TERRIBLE TEMPTATION. Illustrated by EDWARD HUGHES and A. W. COOPER.
THE WANDERING HEIR. Illustrated by HELEN PATERSON, S. L. FILDES, R.A., C. GREEN, and HENRY WOODS, A.R.A.
A SIMPLETON. Illustrated by KATE CRAUFURD.
A WOMAN-HATER. Illustrated by THOMAS COULDERY.
SINGLEHEART AND DOUBLEFACE. Illustrated by P. MACNAB.
GOOD STORIES OF MEN AND OTHER ANIMALS. Illustrated by E. A. ABBEY, PERCY MACQUOID, R.W.S., and JOSEPH NASH.
THE JILT, and other Stories. Illustrated by JOSEPH NASH.
READIANA. With a Steel-plate Portrait of CHARLES READE.

BIBLE CHARACTERS: Studies of David, Paul, &c. Fcap. 8vo, leatherette, 1s.

SELECTIONS FROM THE WORKS OF CHARLES READE. With an Introduction by Mrs. ALEX. IRELAND, and a Steel-Plate Portrait. Crown 8vo, buckram, gilt top, 6s.
[Preparing.

RIDDELL (MRS. J. H.), NOVELS BY.
Crown 8vo, cloth extra, 3s. 6d. each; post 8vo, illustrated boards, 2s. each.
HER MOTHER'S DARLING. | WEIRD STORIES.
THE PRINCE OF WALES'S GARDEN PARTY.

Post 8vo, illustrated boards, 2s. each.
UNINHABITED HOUSE. | FAIRY WATER. | MYSTERY IN PALACE GARDENS.

RIMMER (ALFRED), WORKS BY. Square 8vo, cloth gilt, 7s. 6d. each.
OUR OLD COUNTRY TOWNS. With 55 Illustrations.
RAMBLES ROUND ETON AND HARROW. With 50 Illustrations.
ABOUT ENGLAND WITH DICKENS. With 58 Illusts. by C. A. VANDERHOOF, &c.

ROBINSON CRUSOE. By DANIEL DEFOE. (MAJOR'S EDITION.) With 37 Illustrations by GEORGE CRUIKSHANK. Post 8vo, half-bound, 2s.

ROBINSON (F. W.), NOVELS BY.
Crown 8vo, cloth extra, 3s. 6d. each; post 8vo, illustrated boards, 2s. each.
WOMEN ARE STRANGE. | THE HANDS OF JUSTICE.

ROBINSON (PHIL), WORKS BY. Crown 8vo, cloth extra, 7s. 6d. each.
THE POETS' BIRDS. | THE POETS' BEASTS.
THE POETS AND NATURE: REPTILES, FISHES, INSECTS. [Preparing.

ROCHEFOUCAULD'S MAXIMS AND MORAL REFLECTIONS. With Notes, and an Introductory Essay by SAINTE-BEUVE. Post 8vo, cloth limp, 2s.

ROLL OF BATTLE ABBEY, THE: A List of the Principal Warriors who came from Normandy with William the Conqueror, and Settled in this Country, A.D. 1066-7. With Arms emblazoned in Gold and Colours. Handsomely printed, 5s.

ROWLEY (HON. HUGH), WORKS BY. Post 8vo, cloth, 2s. 6d. each.
PUNIANA: RIDDLES AND JOKES. With numerous Illustrations.
MORE PUNIANA. Profusely Illustrated.

RUNCIMAN (JAMES), STORIES BY.
Post 8vo, illustrated boards, 2s. each; cloth limp, 2s. 6d. each.
SKIPPERS AND SHELLBACKS. | GRACE BALMAIGN'S SWEETHEART.
SCHOOLS AND SCHOLARS.

RUSSELL (W. CLARK), BOOKS AND NOVELS BY:
Crown 8vo, cloth extra, 6s. each; post 8vo, illustrated boards, 2s. each.
ROUND THE GALLEY-FIRE. | MYSTERY OF THE "OCEAN STAR."
IN THE MIDDLE WATCH. | THE ROMANCE OF JENNY HARLOWE.
A VOYAGE TO THE CAPE. | A BOOK FOR THE HAMMOCK.
ON THE FO'K'SLE HEAD. Post 8vo, illustrated boards, 2s.
AN OCEAN TRAGEDY. Cr. 8vo, cloth extra, 3s. 6d.; post 8vo, illust. bds., 2s.
MY SHIPMATE LOUISE. Three Vols., crown 8vo.

SALA.—GASLIGHT AND DAYLIGHT. By GEORGE AUGUSTUS SALA. Post 8vo, illustrated boards, 2s.

SANSON.—SEVEN GENERATIONS OF EXECUTIONERS: Memoirs of the Sanson Family (1688 to 1847). Crown 8vo, cloth extra, 3s. 6d.

SAUNDERS (JOHN), NOVELS BY.
Crown 8vo, cloth extra, 3s. 6d. each; post 8vo, illustrated boards, 2s. each.
GUY WATERMAN. | THE LION IN THE PATH. | THE TWO DREAMERS.
BOUND TO THE WHEEL. Crown 8vo, cloth extra, 3s. 6d.

SAUNDERS (KATHARINE), NOVELS BY.
Crown 8vo, cloth extra, 3s. 6d. each; post 8vo, illustrated boards, 2s. each.
MARGARET AND ELIZABETH. | HEART SALVAGE.
THE HIGH MILLS. | SEBASTIAN.

JOAN MERRYWEATHER. Post 8vo, illustrated boards, 2s.
GIDEON'S ROCK. Crown 8vo, cloth extra, 3s. 6d.

SCIENCE-GOSSIP: An Illustrated Medium of Interchange for Students and Lovers of Nature. Edited by Dr. J. E. TAYLOR, F.L.S., &c. Devoted to Geology, Botany, Physiology, Chemistry, Zoology, Microscopy, Telescopy, Physiography, Photography, &c. Price 4d. Monthly; or 5s. per year, post-free. Vols. I. to XIX. may be had, 7s. 6d. each; Vols. XX. to date, 5s. each. Cases for Binding, 1s. 6d.

SECRET OUT, THE: One Thousand Tricks with Cards; with Entertaining Experiments in Drawing-room or "White Magic." By W. H. CREMER. With 300 Illustrations. Crown 8vo, cloth extra, **4s. 6d.**

SEGUIN (L. G.), WORKS BY.
THE COUNTRY OF THE PASSION PLAY (OBERAMMERGAU) and the Highlands of Bavaria. With Map and 37 Illustrations. Crown 8vo, cloth extra, **3s. 6d.**
WALKS IN ALGIERS. With 2 Maps and 16 Illusts. Crown 8vo, cloth extra, **6s.**

SENIOR (WM.).—BY STREAM AND SEA. Post 8vo, cloth, **2s. 6d.**

SHAKESPEARE, THE FIRST FOLIO.—MR. WILLIAM SHAKESPEARE'S COMEDIES, HISTORIES, AND TRAGEDIES. Published according to the true Originall Copies. London, Printed by ISAAC IAGGARD and ED. BLOUNT. 1623.—A reduced Photographic Reproduction. Small 8vo, half-Roxburghe, **7s. 6d.**
SHAKESPEARE FOR CHILDREN: LAMB'S TALES FROM SHAKESPEARE. With Illustrations, coloured and plain, by J. MOYR SMITH. Crown 4to, cloth, **6s.**

SHARP.—CHILDREN OF TO-MORROW: A Novel. By WILLIAM SHARP. Crown 8vo, cloth extra, **6s.**

SHELLEY.—THE COMPLETE WORKS IN VERSE AND PROSE OF PERCY BYSSHE SHELLEY. Edited, Prefaced, and Annotated by R. HERNE SHEPHERD. Five Vols., crown 8vo, cloth boards, **3s. 6d.** each.
POETICAL WORKS, in Three Vols.:
Vol. I. Introduction by the Editor; Posthumous Fragments of Margaret Nicholson; Shelley's Correspondence with Stockdale; The Wandering Jew; Queen Mab, with the Notes; Alastor, and other Poems; Rosalind and Helen; Prometheus Unbound; Adonais, &c.
Vol. II. Laon and Cythna; The Cenci; Julian and Maddalo; Swellfoot the Tyrant; The Witch of Atlas; Epipsychidion; Hellas.
Vol. III. Posthumous Poems; The Masque of Anarchy; and other Pieces.
PROSE WORKS, in Two Vols.:
Vol. I. The Two Romances of Zastrozzi and St. Irvyne; the Dublin and Marlow Pamphlets; A Refutation of Deism; Letters to Leigh Hunt, and some Minor Writings and Fragments.
Vol. II. The Essays; Letters from Abroad; Translations and Fragments, Edited by Mrs. SHELLEY With a Bibliography of Shelley, and an Index of the Prose Works.

SHERARD.—ROGUES: A Novel. By R. H. SHERARD. Crown 8vo, picture cover, **1s.**; cloth, **1s. 6d.**

SHERIDAN (GENERAL). — PERSONAL MEMOIRS OF GENERAL P. H. SHERIDAN. With Portraits and Facsimiles. Two Vols., demy 8vo, cloth, **24s.**

SHERIDAN'S (RICHARD BRINSLEY) COMPLETE WORKS. With Life and Anecdotes. Including his Dramatic Writings, his Works in Prose and Poetry, Translations, Speeches, Jokes, &c. With 10 Illusts. Cr. 8vo, cl., **7s. 6d.**
THE RIVALS, THE SCHOOL FOR SCANDAL, and other Plays. Post 8vo, printed on laid paper and half-bound, **2s.**
SHERIDAN'S COMEDIES: THE RIVALS and THE SCHOOL FOR SCANDAL. Edited, with an Introduction and Notes to each Play, and a Biographical Sketch, by BRANDER MATTHEWS. With Illustrations. Demy 8vo, half-parchment, **12s. 6d.**

SIDNEY'S (SIR PHILIP) COMPLETE POETICAL WORKS, including all those in "Arcadia." With Portrait, Memorial-Introduction, Notes, &c., by the Rev. A. B. GROSART, D.D. Three Vols., crown 8vo, cloth boards, **18s.**

SIGNBOARDS: Their History. With Anecdotes of Famous Taverns and Remarkable Characters. By JACOB LARWOOD and JOHN CAMDEN HOTTEN. With Coloured Frontispiece and 94 Illustrations. Crown 8vo, cloth extra, **7s. 6d.**

SIMS (GEORGE R.), WORKS BY.
Post 8vo, illustrated boards, **2s.** each; cloth limp, **2s. 6d.** each.
ROGUES AND VAGABONDS. | MARY JANE MARRIED.
THE RING O' BELLS. | TALES OF TO-DAY.
MARY JANE'S MEMOIRS. | DRAMAS OF LIFE. With 60 Illustrations.

Crown 8vo, picture cover, **1s.** each; cloth, **1s. 6d.** each.
THE DAGONET RECITER AND READER: being Readings and Recitations in Prose and Verse, selected from his own Works by GEORGE R. SIMS.
HOW THE POOR LIVE; and HORRIBLE LONDON.
THE CASE OF GEORGE CANDLEMAS.

SISTER DORA: A Biography. By MARGARET LONSDALE. With Four Illustrations. Demy 8vo, picture cover, **4d.**; cloth, **6d.**

SKETCHLEY.—A MATCH IN THE DARK. By ARTHUR SKETCHLEY.
Post 8vo, illustrated boards, 2s.

SLANG DICTIONARY (THE): Etymological, Historical, and Anecdotal. Crown 8vo, cloth extra, 6s. 6d.

SMITH (J. MOYR), WORKS BY.
THE PRINCE OF ARGOLIS. With 130 Illusts. Post 8vo, cloth extra, 3s. 6d.
TALES OF OLD THULE. With numerous Illustrations. Crown 8vo, cloth gilt, 6s.
THE WOOING OF THE WATER WITCH. Illustrated. Post 8vo, cloth, 6s.

SOCIETY IN LONDON. By A FOREIGN RESIDENT. Crown 8vo, 1s.; cloth, 1s. 6d.

SOCIETY IN PARIS: The Upper Ten Thousand. A Series of Letters from Count PAUL VASILI to a Young French Diplomat. Crown 8vo, cloth, 6s.

SOMERSET. — SONGS OF ADIEU. By Lord HENRY SOMERSET.
Small 4to, Japanese vellum, 6s.

SPALDING.—ELIZABETHAN DEMONOLOGY: An Essay on the Belief in the Existence of Devils. By T. A. SPALDING, LL.B. Crown 8vo, cloth extra, 5s.

SPEIGHT (T. W.), NOVELS BY.
Post 8vo, illustrated boards, 2s. each.
THE MYSTERIES OF HERON DYKE. | HOODWINKED, and THE SANDY-
BY DEVIOUS WAYS, and A BARREN | CROFT MYSTERY.
TITLE. | THE GOLDEN HOOP.

Post 8vo, cloth limp, 1s. 6d. each.
WIFE OR NO WIFE? | A BARREN TITLE.

THE SANDYCROFT MYSTERY. Crown 8vo, picture cover, 1s.

SPENSER FOR CHILDREN. By M. H. TOWRY. With Illustrations by WALTER J. MORGAN. Crown 4to, cloth gilt, 6s.

STARRY HEAVENS (THE): A POETICAL BIRTHDAY BOOK. Royal 16mo, cloth extra, 2s. 6d.

STAUNTON.—THE LAWS AND PRACTICE OF CHESS. With an Analysis of the Openings. By HOWARD STAUNTON. Edited by ROBERT B. WORMALD. Crown 8vo, cloth extra, 5s.

STEDMAN (E. C.), WORKS BY.
VICTORIAN POETS. Thirteenth Edition. Crown 8vo, cloth extra, 9s.
THE POETS OF AMERICA. Crown 8vo, cloth extra, 9s.

STERNDALE. — THE AFGHAN KNIFE: A Novel. By ROBERT ARMITAGE STERNDALE. Cr. 8vo, cloth extra, 3s. 6d.; post 8vo, illust. boards, 2s.

STEVENSON (R. LOUIS), WORKS BY. Post 8vo, cl. limp, 2s. 6d. each.
TRAVELS WITH A DONKEY. Eighth Edit. With a Frontis. by WALTER CRANE.
AN INLAND VOYAGE. Fourth Edition. With a Frontispiece by WALTER CRANE.

Crown 8vo, buckram, gilt top, 6s. each.
FAMILIAR STUDIES OF MEN AND BOOKS. Fifth Edition.
THE SILVERADO SQUATTERS. With a Frontispiece. Third Edition.
THE MERRY MEN. Second Edition. | UNDERWOODS: Poems. Fifth Edition.
MEMORIES AND PORTRAITS. Third Edition.
VIRGINIBUS PUERISQUE, and other Papers. Fifth Edition. | BALLADS.

Crown 8vo, buckram, gilt top, 6s. each; post 8vo, illustrated boards, 2s. each.
NEW ARABIAN NIGHTS. Eleventh Edition. | PRINCE OTTO. Sixth Edition.

FATHER DAMIEN: An Open Letter to the Rev. Dr. Hyde. Second Edition. Crown 8vo, hand-made and brown paper, 1s.

STODDARD. — SUMMER CRUISING IN THE SOUTH SEAS. By C. WARREN STODDARD. Illustrated by WALLIS MACKAY. Cr. 8vo, cl. extra, 3s. 6d.

STORIES FROM FOREIGN NOVELISTS. With Notices by HELEN and ALICE ZIMMERN. Crown 8vo, cloth extra, 3s. 6d.; post 8vo, illustrated boards, 2s.

STRANGE MANUSCRIPT (A) FOUND IN A COPPER CYLINDER.
With 19 Illustrations by GILBERT GAUL. Third Edition. Crown 8vo, cloth extra, 5s.

STRUTT'S SPORTS AND PASTIMES OF THE PEOPLE OF ENGLAND; including the Rural and Domestic Recreations, May Games, Mummeries, Shows, &c., from the Earliest Period to the Present Time. Edited by WILLIAM HONE. With 140 Illustrations. Crown 8vo, cloth extra, 7s. 6d.

SUBURBAN HOMES (THE) OF LONDON: A Residential Guide. With a Map, and Notes on Rental, Rates, and Accommodation. Crown 8vo, cloth, 7s. 6d.

SWIFT'S (DEAN) CHOICE WORKS, in Prose and Verse. With Memoir, Portrait, and Facsimiles of the Maps in "Gulliver's Travels." Cr. 8vo, cl., 7s. 6d.
GULLIVER'S TRAVELS, and A TALE OF A TUB. Post 8vo, printed on laid paper and half-bound, 2s.
A MONOGRAPH ON SWIFT. By J. CHURTON COLLINS. Cr. 8vo, cloth, 8s. [Shortly.

SWINBURNE (ALGERNON C.), WORKS BY.

SELECTIONS FROM POETICAL WORKS OF A. C. SWINBURNE. Fcap. 8vo, 6s.
ATALANTA IN CALYDON. Cr. 8vo, 6s.
CHASTELARD: A Tragedy. Cr. 8vo, 7s.
NOTES ON POEMS AND REVIEWS. Demy 8vo, 1s.
POEMS AND BALLADS. FIRST SERIES. Crown 8vo or fcap. 8vo, 9s.
POEMS AND BALLADS. SECOND SERIES. Crown 8vo or fcap. 8vo, 9s.
POEMS AND BALLADS. THIRD SERIES. Crown 8vo, 7s.
SONGS BEFORE SUNRISE. Crown 8vo, 10s. 6d.
BOTHWELL: A Tragedy. Crown 8vo, 12s. 6d.
SONGS OF TWO NATIONS. Cr. 8vo, 6s.

GEORGE CHAPMAN. (See Vol. II. of G. CHAPMAN's Works.) Crown 8vo, 6s.
ESSAYS AND STUDIES. Cr. 8vo, 12s.
ERECHTHEUS: A Tragedy. Cr. 8vo, 6s.
SONGS OF THE SPRINGTIDES. Crown 8vo, 6s.
STUDIES IN SONG. Crown 8vo, 7s.
MARY STUART: A Tragedy. Cr. 8vo 8s.
TRISTRAM OF LYONESSE. Cr. 8vo. 9s.
A CENTURY OF ROUNDELS. Sm. 4to, 8s.
A MIDSUMMER HOLIDAY. Cr. 8vo, 7s.
MARINO FALIERO: A Tragedy. Crown 8vo, 6s.
A STUDY OF VICTOR HUGO. Cr. 8vo, 6s.
MISCELLANIES. Crown 8vo, 12s.
LOCRINE: A Tragedy. Cr. 8vo, 6s.
A STUDY OF BEN JONSON. Cr. 8vo, 7s.

SYMONDS.—WINE, WOMEN, AND SONG: Mediæval Latin Students' Songs. With Essay and Trans. by J. ADDINGTON SYMONDS. Fcap. 8vo, parchment, 6s.

SYNTAX'S (DR.) THREE TOURS: In Search of the Picturesque, in Search of Consolation, and in Search of a Wife. With ROWLANDSON'S Coloured Illustrations, and Life of the Author by J. C. HOTTEN. Crown 8vo, cloth extra, 7s. 6d.

TAINE'S HISTORY OF ENGLISH LITERATURE. Translated by HENRY VAN LAUN. Four Vols., medium 8vo, cloth beards, 30s.—POPULAR EDITION. Two Vols., large crown 8vo, cloth extra, 15s.

TAYLOR'S (BAYARD) DIVERSIONS OF THE ECHO CLUB: Burlesques of Modern Writers. Post 8vo, cloth limp, 2s.

TAYLOR (DR. J. E., F.L.S.), WORKS BY. Cr. 8vo, cl. ex., 7s. 6d. each.
THE SAGACITY AND MORALITY OF PLANTS: A Sketch of the Life and Conduct of the Vegetable Kingdom. With a Coloured Frontispiece and 100 Illustrations.
OUR COMMON BRITISH FOSSILS, and Where to Find Them. 331 Illustrations.

THE PLAYTIME NATURALIST. With 366 Illustrations. Crown 8vo, cloth, 5s.

TAYLOR'S (TOM) HISTORICAL DRAMAS. Containing "Clancarty," "Jeanne Darc," "'Twixt Axe and Crown," "The Fool's Revenge," "Arkwright's Wife," "Anne Boleyn," "Plot and Passion." Crown 8vo, cloth extra, 7s. 6d.
*** The Plays may also be had separately, at 1s. each.

TENNYSON (LORD): A Biographical Sketch. By H. J. JENNINGS. With a Photograph-Portrait. Crown 8vo, cloth extra, 6s.

THACKERAYANA: Notes and Anecdotes. Illustrated by Hundreds of Sketches by WILLIAM MAKEPEACE THACKERAY, depicting Humorous Incidents in his School-life, and Favourite Characters in the Books of his Every-day Reading. With a Coloured Frontispiece. Crown 8vo, cloth extra, 7s. 6d.

THAMES.—A NEW PICTORIAL HISTORY OF THE THAMES. By A. S. KRAUSSE. With 340 Illustrations. Post 8vo, 1s.; cloth, 1s. 6d.

THOMAS (BERTHA), NOVELS BY. Cr. 8vo, cl., **3s. 6d.** ea.; post 8vo, **2s.** ea.
CRESSIDA. | THE VIOLIN-PLAYER. | PROUD MAISIE.

THOMAS (MOY).—A FIGHT FOR LIFE: A Novel. By W. Moy Thomas. Post 8vo, illustrated boards, **2s.**

THOMSON'S SEASONS, and CASTLE OF INDOLENCE. Introduction by Allan Cunningham, and Illustrations on Steel and Wood. Cr. 8vo, cl., **7s. 6d.**

THORNBURY (WALTER), WORKS BY. Cr. 8vo, cl. extra, **7s. 6d.** each.
THE LIFE AND CORRESPONDENCE OF J. M. W. TURNER. Founded upon Letters and Papers furnished by his Friends. With Illustrations in Colours.
HAUNTED LONDON. Edit. by E. Walford, M.A. Illusts. by F. W. Fairholt, F.S.A.

Post 8vo, illustrated boards, **2s.** each.
OLD STORIES RE-TOLD. | TALES FOR THE MARINES.

TIMBS (JOHN), WORKS BY. Crown 8vo, cloth extra, **7s. 6d.** each.
THE HISTORY OF CLUBS AND CLUB LIFE IN LONDON: Anecdotes of its Famous Coffee-houses, Hostelries, and Taverns. With 42 Illustrations.
ENGLISH ECCENTRICS AND ECCENTRICITIES: Stories of Wealth and Fashion, Delusions, Impostures, and Fanatic Missions, Sporting Scenes, Eccentric Artists, Theatrical Folk, Men of Letters, &c. With 48 Illustrations.

TROLLOPE (ANTHONY), NOVELS BY.
Crown 8vo, cloth extra, **3s. 6d.** each; post 8vo, illustrated boards, **2s.** each
THE WAY WE LIVE NOW. | MARION FAY.
KEPT IN THE DARK. | MR. SCARBOROUGH'S FAMILY.
FRAU FROHMANN. | THE LAND-LEAGUERS.

Post 8vo, illustrated boards, **2s.** each.
GOLDEN LION OF GRANPERE. | JOHN CALDIGATE. | AMERICAN SENATOR.

TROLLOPE (FRANCES E.), NOVELS BY.
Crown 8vo, cloth extra, **3s. 6d.** each; post 8vo, illustrated boards, **2s.** each.
LIKE SHIPS UPON THE SEA. | MABEL'S PROGRESS. | ANNE FURNESS.

TROLLOPE (T. A.).—DIAMOND CUT DIAMOND. Post 8vo, illust. bds., **2s.**

TROWBRIDGE.—FARNELL'S FOLLY: A Novel. By J. T. Trowbridge. Post 8vo, illustrated boards, **2s.**

TYTLER (C. C. FRASER-).—MISTRESS JUDITH: A Novel. By C. C. Fraser-Tytler. Crown 8vo, cloth extra, **3s. 6d.**; post 8vo, illust. boards, **2s.**

TYTLER (SARAH), NOVELS BY.
Crown 8vo, cloth extra, **3s. 6d.** each; post 8vo, illustrated boards, **2s.** each.
WHAT SHE CAME THROUGH. | SAINT MUNGO'S CITY.
THE BRIDE'S PASS. | LADY BELL. | BURIED DIAMONDS.
NOBLESSE OBLIGE. | THE BLACKHALL GHOSTS.

Post 8vo, illustrated boards, **2s.** each.
BEAUTY AND THE BEAST. | DISAPPEARED.
CITOYENNE JACQUELINE. | THE HUGUENOT FAMILY.

VILLARI.—A DOUBLE BOND. By Linda Villari. Fcap. 8vo, picture cover, **1s.**

WALT WHITMAN, POEMS BY. Edited, with Introduction, by William M. Rossetti. With Portrait. Cr. 8vo, hand-made paper and buckram, **6s.**

WALTON AND COTTON'S COMPLETE ANGLER; or, The Contemplative Man's Recreation, by Izaak Walton; and Instructions how to Angle for a Trout or Grayling in a clear Stream, by Charles Cotton. With Memoirs and Notes by Sir Harris Nicolas, and 61 Illustrations. Crown 8vo, cloth antique, **7s. 6d.**

WARD (HERBERT), WORKS BY.
FIVE YEARS WITH THE CONGO CANNIBALS. With 92 Illustrations by the Author, Victor Perard, and W. B. Davis. Royal 8vo, cloth extra, **14s.**
MY LIFE WITH STANLEY'S REAR GUARD. With a Map by F. S. Weller, F.R.G.S. Post 8vo, **1s.**; cloth, **1s. 6d.**

WARNER.—A ROUNDABOUT JOURNEY. By Charles Dudley Warner. Crown 8vo, cloth extra, **6s.**

WALFORD (EDWARD, M.A.), WORKS BY.
WALFORD'S COUNTY FAMILIES OF THE UNITED KINGDOM (1891). Containing Notices of the Descent, Birth, Marriage, Education, &c., of more than 12,000 distinguished Heads of Families, their Heirs Apparent or Presumptive, the Offices they hold, their Addresses, Clubs, &c. Royal 8vo, cloth gilt, 50s.
WALFORD'S SHILLING PEERAGE (1891). Containing a List of the House of Lords, Scotch and Irish Peers, &c. 32mo, cloth, 1s.
WALFORD'S SHILLING BARONETAGE (1891). Containing a List of the Baronets of the United Kingdom, Biographical Notices, Addresses, &c. 32mo, cloth, 1s.
WALFORD'S SHILLING KNIGHTAGE (1891). Containing a List of the Knights of the United Kingdom, Biographical Notices, Addresses, &c. 32mo, cloth, 1s.
WALFORD'S SHILLING HOUSE OF COMMONS (1891). Containing a List of all Members of Parliament, their Addresses, Clubs, &c. 32mo, cloth, 1s.
WALFORD'S COMPLETE PEERAGE, BARONETAGE, KNIGHTAGE, AND HOUSE OF COMMONS (1891). Royal 32mo, cloth extra, gilt edges. 5s.
WALFORD'S WINDSOR PEERAGE, BARONETAGE, AND KNIGHTAGE (1891). Crown 8vo, cloth extra, 12s. 6d.
TALES OF OUR GREAT FAMILIES. Crown 8vo, cloth extra, 3s. 6d.
WILLIAM PITT: A Biography. Post 8vo, cloth extra, 5s.
HAUNTED LONDON. By WALTER THORNBURY. Edited by EDWARD WALFORD. With Illustrations by F. W. FAIRHOLT, F.S.A. Crown 8vo, cloth extra, 7s. 6d.

WASHINGTON'S (GEORGE) RULES OF CIVILITY traced to their Sources and Restored by MONCURE D. CONWAY. Fcap. 8vo, Japanese vellum, 2s. 6d.

WEATHER, HOW TO FORETELL THE, WITH POCKET SPECTROSCOPE. By F. W. CORY. With 10 Illustrations. Cr. 8vo, 1s.; cloth, 1s. 6d.

WESTROPP.—HANDBOOK OF POTTERY AND PORCELAIN. By HODDER M. WESTROPP. With Illusts. and List of Marks. Cr. 8vo, cloth, 4s. 6d.

WHIST.—HOW TO PLAY SOLO WHIST. By ABRAHAM S. WILKS and CHARLES F. PARDON. Crown 8vo, cloth extra, 3s. 6d.

WHISTLER'S (MR.) TEN O'CLOCK. Cr. 8vo, hand-made paper, 1s.

WHITE.—THE NATURAL HISTORY OF SELBORNE. By GILBERT WHITE, M.A. Post 8vo, printed on laid paper and half-bound, 2s.

WILLIAMS (W. MATTIEU, F.R.A.S.), WORKS BY.
SCIENCE IN SHORT CHAPTERS. Crown 8vo, cloth extra, 7s. 6d.
A SIMPLE TREATISE ON HEAT. With Illusts. Cr. 8vo, cloth limp, 2s. 6d.
THE CHEMISTRY OF COOKERY. Crown 8vo, cloth extra, 6s.
THE CHEMISTRY OF IRON AND STEEL MAKING. Crown 8vo, cloth extra, 9s.

WILSON (DR. ANDREW, F.R.S.E.), WORKS BY.
CHAPTERS ON EVOLUTION. With 259 Illustrations. Cr. 8vo, cloth extra, 7s. 6d.
LEAVES FROM A NATURALIST'S NOTE-BOOK. Post 8vo, cloth limp, 2s. 6d.
LEISURE-TIME STUDIES. With Illustrations. Crown 8vo, cloth extra, 6s.
STUDIES IN LIFE AND SENSE. With numerous Illusts. Cr. 8vo, cl. ex., 6s.
COMMON ACCIDENTS: HOW TO TREAT THEM. Illusts. Cr. 8vo, 1s.; cl., 1s. 6d.
GLIMPSES OF LIFE AND NATURE. Crown 8vo, cloth extra, 3s. 6d. [Shortly.

WINTER (J. S.), STORIES BY. Post 8vo, illustrated boards, 2s. each.
CAVALRY LIFE. | REGIMENTAL LEGENDS.

WOOD.—SABINA: A Novel. By Lady WOOD. Post 8vo, boards, 2s.

WOOD (H. F.), DETECTIVE STORIES BY.
Crown 8vo, cloth extra, 6s. each; post 8vo, illustrated boards, 2s. each.
PASSENGER FROM SCOTLAND YARD. | ENGLISHMAN OF THE RUE CAIN.

WOOLLEY.—RACHEL ARMSTRONG; or, Love and Theology. By CELIA PARKER WOOLLEY. Post 8vo, illustrated boards, 2s.; cloth, 2s. 6d.

WRIGHT (THOMAS), WORKS BY. Crown 8vo, cloth extra, 7s. 6d. each.
CARICATURE HISTORY OF THE GEORGES. With 400 Pictures, Caricatures, Squibs, Broadsides, Window Pictures, &c.
HISTORY OF CARICATURE AND OF THE GROTESQUE IN ART, LITERATURE, SCULPTURE, AND PAINTING. Illustrated by F. W. FAIRHOLT, F.S.A.

YATES (EDMUND), NOVELS BY. Post 8vo, illustrated boards, 2s. each.
LAND AT LAST. | THE FORLORN HOPE. | CASTAWAY.

LISTS OF BOOKS CLASSIFIED IN SERIES.

₊ *For full cataloguing, see alphabetical arrangement, pp. 1-25.*

THE MAYFAIR LIBRARY. Post 8vo, cloth limp, 2s. 6d. per Volume.

A Journey Round My Room. By XAVIER DE MAISTRE.
Quips and Quiddities. By W. D. ADAMS.
The Agony Column of "The Times."
Melancholy Anatomised: Abridgment of "Burton's Anatomy of Melancholy."
The Speeches of Charles Dickens.
Literary Frivolities, Fancies, Follies, and Frolics. By W. T. DOBSON.
Poetical Ingenuities. By W. T. DOBSON.
The Cupboard Papers. By FIN-BEC.
W. S. Gilbert's Plays. FIRST SERIES.
W. S. Gilbert's Plays. SECOND SERIES.
Songs of Irish Wit and Humour.
Animals and Masters. By Sir A. HELPS.
Social Pressure. By Sir A. HELPS.
Curiosities of Criticism. H. J. JENNINGS.
Holmes's Autocrat of Breakfast-Table.
Pencil and Palette. By R. KEMPT.
Little Essays: from LAMB's Letters.
Forensic Anecdotes. By JACOB LARWOOD.
Theatrical Anecdotes. JACOB LARWOOD.
Jeux d'Esprit. Edited by HENRY S. LEIGH.
Witch Stories. By E. LYNN LINTON.
Ourselves. By E. LYNN LINTON.
Pastimes & Players. By R. MACGREGOR.
New Paul and Virginia. W.H.MALLOCK.
New Republic. By W. H. MALLOCK.
Puck on Pegasus. By H. C. PENNELL.
Pegasus Re-Saddled. By H.C. PENNELL.
Muses of Mayfair. Ed. H. C. PENNELL.
Thoreau: His Life & Aims. By H. A. PAGE.
Punlana. By Hon. HUGH ROWLEY.
More Puniana. By Hon. HUGH ROWLEY.
The Philosophy of Handwriting.
By Stream and Sea. By WM. SENIOR.
Leaves from a Naturalist's Note-Book.
By Dr. ANDREW WILSON.

THE GOLDEN LIBRARY. Post 8vo, cloth limp, 2s. per Volume.

Bayard Taylor's Diversions of the Echo Club.
Bennett's Ballad History of England.
Bennett's Songs for Sailors.
Godwin's Lives of the Necromancers.
Pope's Poetical Works.
Holmes's Autocrat of Breakfast Table.
Holmes's Professor at Breakfast Table.
Jesse's Scenes of Country Life.
Mallory's Mort d'Arthur: Selections.
Pascal's Provincial Letters.
Rochefoucauld's Maxims & Reflections.

THE WANDERER'S LIBRARY. Crown 8vo, cloth extra, 3s. 6d. each.

Wanderings in Patagonia. By JULIUS BEERBOHM. Illustrated.
Camp Notes. By FREDERICK BOYLE.
Savage Life. By FREDERICK BOYLE.
Merrie England in the Olden Time. By G. DANIEL. Illustrated by CRUIKSHANK.
Circus Life. By THOMAS FROST.
Lives of the Conjurers. THOMAS FROST.
The Old Showmen and the Old London Fairs. By THOMAS FROST.
Low-Life Deeps. By JAMES GREENWOOD.
Wilds of London. JAMES GREENWOOD.
Tunis. Chev. HESSE-WARTEGG. 22 Illusts.
Life and Adventures of a Cheap Jack.
World Behind the Scenes. P. FITZGERALD.
Tavern Anecdotes and Sayings.
The Genial Showman. By E.P. HINGSTON.
Story of London Parks. JACOB LARWOOD.
London Characters. By HENRY MAYHEW.
Seven Generations of Executioners.
Summer Cruising in the South Seas.
By C. WARREN STODDARD. Illustrated.

POPULAR SHILLING BOOKS.

Harry Fludyer at Home.
Jeff Briggs's Love Story. BRET HARTE.
Twins of Table Mountain. BRET HARTE.
A Day's Tour. By PERCY FITZGERALD.
Esther's Glove. By R. E. FRANCILLON.
Sentenced! By SOMERVILLE GIBNEY.
The Professor's Wife. By L. GRAHAM.
Mrs. Gainsborough's Diamonds. By JULIAN HAWTHORNE.
Niagara Spray. By J. HOLLINGSHEAD.
A Romance of the Queen's Hounds. By CHARLES JAMES.
The Garden that Paid the Rent. By TOM JERROLD.
Cut by the Mess. By ARTHUR KEYSER.
Our Sensation Novel. Edited by JUSTIN H. McCARTHY, M.P.
Dolly. By JUSTIN H. McCARTHY, M.P.
Lily Lass. JUSTIN H. McCARTHY, M.P.
Was She Good or Bad? By W. MINTO.
That Girl in Black. Mrs. MOLESWORTH.
Notes from the "News." By JAS. PAYN.
Beyond the Gates. By E. S. PHELPS.
Old Maid's Paradise. By E. S. PHELPS.
Burglars in Paradise. By E. S. PHELPS.
Jack the Fisherman. By E. S. PHELPS.
Trooping with Crows. By C. L. PIRKIS.
Bible Characters. By CHARLES READE.
Rogues. By R. H. SHERARD.
The Dagonet Reciter. By G. R. SIMS.
How the Poor Live. By G. R. SIMS.
Case of George Candlemas. G. R. SIMS.
Sandycroft Mystery. T. W. SPEIGHT.
Hoodwinked. By T. W. SPEIGHT.
Father Damien. By R. L. STEVENSON.
A Double Bond. By LINDA VILLARI.
My Life with Stanley's Rear Guard. By HERBERT WARD.

CHATTO & WINDUS, 214, PICCADILLY.

MY LIBRARY.

Choice Works, printed on laid paper, bound half-Roxburghe, 2s. 6d. each.

Four Frenchwomen. By AUSTIN DOBSON.
Citation and Examination of William Shakspeare. By W. S. LANDOR.

Christie Johnstone. By CHARLES READE. With a Photogravure Frontispiece.
Peg Woffington. By CHARLES READE.

THE POCKET LIBRARY.

Post 8vo, printed on laid paper and hf.-bd., 2s. each.

The Essays of Elia. By CHARLES LAMB.
Robinson Crusoe. Edited by JOHN MAJOR. With 37 Illusts. by GEORGE CRUIKSHANK.
Whims and Oddities. By THOMAS HOOD. With 85 Illustrations.
The Barber's Chair, and The Hedgehog Letters. By DOUGLAS JERROLD.
Gastronomy as a Fine Art. By BRILLAT-SAVARIN. Trans. R. E. ANDERSON, M.A.

The Epicurean, &c. By THOMAS MOORE.
Leigh Hunt's Essays. Ed. E. OLLIER.
The Natural History of Selborne. By GILBERT WHITE.
Gulliver's Travels, and The Tale of a Tub. By Dean SWIFT.
The Rivals, School for Scandal, and other Plays by RICHARD BRINSLEY SHERIDAN.
Anecdotes of the Clergy. J. LARWOOD.

THE PICCADILLY NOVELS.

LIBRARY EDITIONS OF NOVELS BY THE BEST AUTHORS, many Illustrated, crown 8vo, cloth extra, 3s. 6d. each.

By GRANT ALLEN.
Philistia.
Babylon.
In all Shades.
The Tents of Shem.
For Maimie's Sake.
The Devil's Die.
This Mortal Coil.
The Great Taboo.

By ALAN ST. AUBYN.
A Fellow of Trinity.

By Rev. S. BARING GOULD.
Red Spider. | Eve.

By W. BESANT & J. RICE.
My Little Girl.
Case of Mr. Lucraft.
This Son of Vulcan.
Golden Butterfly.
Ready-Money Mortiboy.
With Harp and Crown.
'Twas in Trafalgar's Bay.
The Chaplain of the Fleet.
By Celia's Arbour.
Monks of Thelema.
The Seamy Side.
Ten Years' Tenant.

By WALTER BESANT.
All Sorts and Conditions of Men.
The Captains' Room.
All in a Garden Fair.
The World Went Very Well Then.
For Faith and Freedom.
Dorothy Forster. | Herr Paulus.
Uncle Jack. | Bell of St. Paul's.
Children of Gibeon. | To Call Her Mine.

By ROBERT BUCHANAN.
The Shadow of the Sword.
A Child of Nature.
The Martyrdom of Madeline.
God and the Man. | The New Abelard.
Love Me for Ever. | Foxglove Manor.
Annan Water. | Master of the Mine.
Matt. | Heir of Linne.

By HALL CAINE.
The Shadow of a Crime.
A Son of Hagar. | The Deemster.

MORT. & FRANCES COLLINS.
Sweet Anne Page. | Transmigration.
From Midnight to Midnight.
Blacksmith and Scholar.
Village Comedy. | You Play Me False.

By Mrs. H. LOVETT CAMERON.
Juliet's Guardian. | Deceivers Ever.

By WILKIE COLLINS.
Armadale.
After Dark.
No Name.
Antonina. | Basil.
Hide and Seek.
The Dead Secret.
Queen of Hearts.
My Miscellanies.
Woman in White.
The Moonstone.
Man and Wife.
Poor Miss Finch.
Miss or Mrs?
New Magdalen.
The Frozen Deep.
The Two Destinies.
Law and the Lady.
Haunted Hotel.
The Fallen Leaves.
Jezebel's Daughter.
The Black Robe.
Heart and Science.
"I Say No."
Little Novels.
The Evil Genius.
The Legacy of Cain.
A Rogue's Life.
Blind Love.

By DUTTON COOK.
Paul Foster's Daughter.

By WILLIAM CYPLES.
Hearts of Gold.

By ALPHONSE DAUDET.
The Evangelist; or, Port Salvation.

By JAMES DE MILLE.
A Castle in Spain.

By J. LEITH DERWENT.
Our Lady of Tears. | Circe's Lovers.

By M. BETHAM-EDWARDS.
Felicia.

By Mrs. ANNIE EDWARDES.
Archie Lovell.

By PERCY FITZGERALD.
Fatal Zero.

By R. E. FRANCILLON.
Queen Cophetua. | A Real Queen.
One by One. | King or Knave?

Pref. by Sir BARTLE FRERE.
Pandurang Hari.

By EDWARD GARRETT.
The Capel Girls.

BOOKS PUBLISHED BY

THE PICCADILLY (3/6) NOVELS—*continued.*

By CHARLES GIBBON.
Robin Gray.
In Honour Bound.
A Heart's Problem.
Queen of the Meadow.
The Flower of the Forest.
The Golden Shaft.
Of High Degree.
Loving a Dream.

By JULIAN HAWTHORNE.
Garth.
Ellice Quentin.
Sebastian Strome.
David Poindexter's Disappearance.
The Spectre of the Camera.
Dust.
Fortune's Fool.
Beatrix Randolph.

By Sir A. HELPS.
Ivan de Biron.

By ISAAC HENDERSON.
Agatha Page.

By Mrs. ALFRED HUNT.
The Leaden Casket. | Self-Condemned.
That other Person.

By JEAN INGELOW.
Fated to be Free.

By R. ASHE KING.
A Drawn Game.
"The Wearing of the Green."

By HENRY KINGSLEY.
Number Seventeen.

By E. LYNN LINTON.
Patricia Kemball.
Under which Lord?
"My Love!"
The Atonement of Leam Dundas.
The World Well Lost.
Ione.
Paston Carew.
Sowing the Wind.

By HENRY W. LUCY.
Gideon Fleyce.

By JUSTIN McCARTHY.
A Fair Saxon.
Linley Rochford.
Miss Misanthrope.
The Waterdale Neighbours.
My Enemy's Daughter.
Dear Lady Disdain.
The Comet of a Season.
Donna Quixote.
Maid of Athens.
Camiola.

By AGNES MACDONELL.
Quaker Cousins.

By FLORENCE MARRYAT.
Open! Sesame!

By D. CHRISTIE MURRAY.
Life's Atonement.
Joseph's Coat.
A Model Father.
A Bit of Human Nature.
First Person Singular.
Cynic Fortune.
The Way of the World.
Coals of Fire.
Val Strange.
Hearts.

By MURRAY & HERMAN.
The Bishops' Bible.

By GEORGES OHNET.
A Weird Gift.

THE PICCADILLY (3/6) NOVELS—*continued.*

By Mrs. OLIPHANT.
Whiteladies.

By OUIDA.
Held in Bondage.
Strathmore.
Chandos.
Under Two Flags.
Idalia.
CecilCastlemaine's Gage.
Tricotrin. | Puck.
Folle Farine.
A Dog of Flanders.
Pascarel. | Signa.
Princess Naprax- ine.
Two Little Wooden Shoes.
In a Winter City.
Ariadne.
Friendship.
Moths. | Ruffino.
Pipistrello.
A Village Commune
Bimbi. | Wanda.
Frescoes.
In Maremma.
Othmar. | Syrlin.
Guilderoy.

By MARGARET A. PAUL.
Gentle and Simple.

By JAMES PAYN.
Lost Sir Massingberd.
Less Black than We're Painted.
A Confidential Agent.
A Grape from a Thorn.
Some Private Views.
In Peril and Privation.
The Mystery of Mirbridge.
Walter's Word.
By Proxy.
High Spirits.
Under One Roof.
From Exile.
The Canon's Ward.
Glow-worm Tales.
Talk of the Town.
Holiday Tasks.
The Burnt Million.

By E. C. PRICE.
Valentina. | The Foreigners.
Mrs. Lancaster's Rival.

By CHARLES READE.
It is Never Too Late to Mend.
The Double Marriage.
Love Me Little, Love Me Long.
The Cloister and the Hearth.
The Course of True Love.
The Autobiography of a Thief.
Put Yourself in his Place.
A Terrible Temptation.
Singleheart and Doubleface.
Good Stories of Men and other Animals.
Hard Cash.
Peg Woffington.
ChristieJohnstone.
Griffith Gaunt.
Foul Play.
Wandering Heir.
A Woman-Hater.
A Simpleton.
Readiana.
The Jilt.

By Mrs. J. H. RIDDELL.
Her Mother's Darling.
Prince of Wales's Garden Party.
Weird Stories.

By F. W. ROBINSON.
Women are Strange.
The Hands of Justice.

By W. CLARK RUSSELL.
An Ocean Tragedy.

By JOHN SAUNDERS.
Guy Waterman. | Two Dreamers.
Bound to the Wheel.
The Lion in the Path.

THE PICCADILLY (3/6) NOVELS—*continued*.

By KATHARINE SAUNDERS.
Margaret and Elizabeth.
Gideon's Rock. | Heart Salvage.
The High Mills. | Sebastian.

By HAWLEY SMART.
Without Love or Licence.

By R. A. STERNDALE.
The Afghan Knife.

By BERTHA THOMAS.
Proud Maisie. | Cressida.
The Violin-player.

By FRANCES E. TROLLOPE.
Like Ships upon the Sea.
Anne Furness. | Mabel's Progress.

THE PICCADILLY (3/6) NOVELS—*continued*.

By ANTHONY TROLLOPE.
Frau Frohmann. | Kept in the Dark.
Marion Fay. | Land-Leaguers.
The Way We Live Now.
Mr. Scarborough's Family.

By IVAN TURGENIEFF, &c.
Stories from Foreign Novelists.

By C. C. FRASER-TYTLER.
Mistress Judith.

By SARAH TYTLER.
The Bride's Pass. | Lady Bell.
Noblesse Oblige. | Buried Diamonds.
What She Came Through.
Saint Mungo's City.
The Blackhall Ghosts.

CHEAP EDITIONS OF POPULAR NOVELS.
Post 8vo, illustrated boards, 2s. each.

By ARTEMUS WARD.
Artemus Ward Complete.

By EDMOND ABOUT.
The Fellah.

By HAMILTON AIDE.
Carr of Carrlyon. | Confidences.

By Mrs. ALEXANDER.
Maid, Wife, or Widow? | Valerie's Fate.

By GRANT ALLEN.
Strange Stories. | The Devil's Die.
Philistia. | This Mortal Coil.
Babylon. | In all Shades.
The Beckoning Hand.
For Maimie's Sake. | Tents of Shem.

By ALAN ST. AUBYN.
A Fellow of Trinity.

By Rev. S. BARING GOULD.
Red Spider. | Eve.

By FRANK BARRETT.
Fettered for Life.

By SHELSLEY BEAUCHAMP.
Grantley Grange.

By W. BESANT & J. RICE.
This Son of Vulcan. | By Celia's Arbour.
My Little Girl. | Monks of Thelema.
Case of Mr. Lucraft. | The Seamy Side.
Golden Butterfly. | Ten Years' Tenant.
Ready-Money Mortiboy.
With Harp and Crown.
'Twas in Trafalgar's Bay.
The Chaplain of the Fleet.

By WALTER BESANT.
Dorothy Forster. | Uncle Jack.
Children of Gibeon. | Herr Paulus.
All Sorts and Conditions of Men.
The Captains' Room.
All in a Garden Fair.
The World Went Very Well Then.
For Faith and Freedom.

By FREDERICK BOYLE.
Camp Notes. | Savage Life.
Chronicles of No-man's Land.

By BRET HARTE.
Flip. | Californian Stories
Maruja. | Gabriel Conroy.
An Heiress of Red Dog.
The Luck of Roaring Camp.
A Phyllis of the Sierras.

By HAROLD BRYDGES.
Uncle Sam at Home.

By ROBERT BUCHANAN.
The Shadow of the | The Martyrdom of
 Sword. | Madeline.
A Child of Nature. | Annan Water.
God and the Man. | The New Abelard.
Love Me for Ever. | Matt.
Foxglove Manor. | The Heir of Linne.
The Master of the Mine.

By HALL CAINE.
The Shadow of a Crime.
A Son of Hagar. | The Deemster.

By Commander CAMERON.
The Cruise of the "Black Prince."

By Mrs. LOVETT CAMERON.
Deceivers Ever. | Juliet's Guardian.

By AUSTIN CLARE.
For the Love of a Lass.

By Mrs. ARCHER CLIVE.
Paul Ferroll.
Why Paul Ferroll Killed his Wife.

By MACLAREN COBBAN.
The Cure of Souls.

By C. ALLSTON COLLINS.
The Bar Sinister.

MORT. & FRANCES COLLINS.
Sweet Anne Page. | Transmigration.
From Midnight to Midnight.
A Fight with Fortune.
Sweet and Twenty. | Village Comedy.
Frances. | You Play me False.
Blacksmith and Scholar.

BOOKS PUBLISHED BY

Two-Shilling Novels—continued.

By WILKIE COLLINS.
Armadale. | A Rogue's Life.
After Dark. | My Miscellanies.
No Name. | Woman in White.
Antonina. | Basil. | The Moonstone.
Hide and Seek. | Man and Wife.
The Dead Secret. | Poor Miss Finch.
Queen of Hearts. | The Fallen Leaves.
Miss or Mrs? | Jezebel's Daughter
New Magdalen. | The Black Robe.
The Frozen Deep. | Heart and Science.
Law and the Lady. | "I Say No."
The Two Destinies. | The Evil Genius.
Haunted Hotel. | Little Novels.
Legacy of Cain.

By M. J. COLQUHOUN.
Every Inch a Soldier.

By DUTTON COOK.
Leo. | Paul Foster's Daughter.

By C. EGBERT CRADDOCK.
Prophet of the Great Smoky Mountains.

By WILLIAM CYPLES.
Hearts of Gold.

By ALPHONSE DAUDET.
The Evangelist; or, Port Salvation.

By JAMES DE MILLE.
A Castle in Spain.

By J. LEITH DERWENT.
Our Lady of Tears. | Circe's Lovers.

By CHARLES DICKENS.
Sketches by Boz. | Oliver Twist.
Pickwick Papers. | Nicholas Nickleby.

By DICK DONOVAN.
The Man-Hunter. | Caught at Last!
Tracked and Taken.
Who Poisoned Hetty Duncan?
The Man from Manchester.

By CONAN DOYLE, &c.
Strange Secrets.

By Mrs. ANNIE EDWARDES.
A Point of Honour. | Archie Lovell.

By M. BETHAM-EDWARDS.
Felicia. | Kitty.

By EDWARD EGGLESTON.
Roxy.

By PERCY FITZGERALD.
Bella Donna. | Polly.
Never Forgotten. | Fatal Zero.
The Second Mrs. Tillotson.
Seventy-five Brooke Street.
The Lady of Brantome.

ALBANY DE FONBLANQUE.
Filthy Lucre.

By R. E. FRANCILLON.
Olympia. | Queen Cophetua.
One by One. | King or Knave?
A Real Queen. | Romances of Law.

By HAROLD FREDERICK.
Seth's Brother's Wife.
The Lawton Girl.

Two-Shilling Novels—continued.

By HAIN FRISWELL.
One of Two.

By EDWARD GARRETT.
The Capel Girls.

By CHARLES GIBBON.
Robin Gray. | In Honour Bound.
Fancy Free. | Flower of Forest.
For Lack of Gold. | Braes of Yarrow.
What will the | The Golden Shaft.
World Say? | Of High Degree.
In Love and War. | Mead and Stream.
For the King. | Loving a Dream.
In Pastures Green. | A Hard Knot.
Queen of Meadow. | Heart's Delight.
A Heart's Problem. | Blood-Money.
The Dead Heart.

By WILLIAM GILBERT.
Dr. Austin's Guests. | James Duke.
The Wizard of the Mountain.

By HENRY GREVILLE.
A Noble Woman.

By JOHN HABBERTON.
Brueton's Bayou. | Country Luck.

By ANDREW HALLIDAY.
Every-Day Papers.

By Lady DUFFUS HARDY.
Paul Wynter's Sacrifice.

By THOMAS HARDY.
Under the Greenwood Tree.

By J. BERWICK HARWOOD.
The Tenth Earl.

By JULIAN HAWTHORNE.
Garth. | Sebastian Strome.
Ellice Quentin. | Dust.
Fortune's Fool. | Beatrix Randolph.
Miss Cadogna. | Love—or a Name?
David Poindexter's Disappearance.
The Spectre of the Camera.

By Sir ARTHUR HELPS.
Ivan de Biron.

By Mrs. CASHEL HOEY.
The Lover's Creed.

By Mrs. GEORGE HOOPER.
The House of Raby.

By TIGHE HOPKINS.
'Twixt Love and Duty.

By Mrs. ALFRED HUNT.
Thornicroft's Model. | Self-Condemned.
That Other Person. | Leaden Casket.

By JEAN INGELOW.
Fated to be Free.

By HARRIETT JAY.
The Dark Colleen.
The Queen of Connaught.

By MARK KERSHAW.
Colonial Facts and Fictions.

By R. ASHE KING.
A Drawn Game. | Passion's Slave.
"The Wearing of the Green."

TWO-SHILLING NOVELS—*continued.*

By HENRY KINGSLEY.
Oakshott Castle.

By JOHN LEYS.
The Lindsays.

By MARY LINSKILL.
In Exchange for a Soul.

By E. LYNN LINTON.
Patricia Kemball. | Paston Carew.
World Well Lost. | "My Love!"
Under which Lord? | Ione.
The Atonement of Leam Dundas.
With a Silken Thread.
The Rebel of the Family.
Sowing the Wind.

By HENRY W. LUCY.
Gideon Fleyce.

By JUSTIN McCARTHY.
A Fair Saxon. | Donna Quixote.
Linley Rochford. | Maid of Athens.
Miss Misanthrope. | Camiola.
Dear Lady Disdain.
The Waterdale Neighbours.
My Enemy's Daughter.
The Comet of a Season.

By AGNES MACDONELL.
Quaker Cousins.

KATHARINE S. MACQUOID.
The Evil Eye. | Lost Rose.

By W. H. MALLOCK.
The New Republic.

By FLORENCE MARRYAT.
Open! Sesame! | Fighting the Air.
A Harvest of Wild Oats.
Written in Fire.

By J. MASTERMAN.
Half-a-dozen Daughters.

By BRANDER MATTHEWS.
A Secret of the Sea.

By JEAN MIDDLEMASS.
Touch and Go. | Mr. Dorillion.

By Mrs. MOLESWORTH.
Hathercourt Rectory.

By J. E. MUDDOCK.
Stories Weird and Wonderful.
The Dead Man's Secret.

By D. CHRISTIE MURRAY.
A Model Father. | Old Blazer's Hero.
Joseph's Coat. | Hearts.
Coals of Fire. | Way of the World.
Val Strange. | Cynic Fortune.
A Life's Atonement.
By the Gate of the Sea.
A Bit of Human Nature.
First Person Singular.

By MURRAY and HERMAN.
One Traveller Returns.
Paul Jones's Alias.

By HENRY MURRAY.
A Game of Bluff.

By ALICE O'HANLON.
The Unforeseen. | Chance? or Fate?

TWO-SHILLING NOVELS—*continued.*

By GEORGES OHNET.
Doctor Rameau. | A Last Love.

By Mrs. OLIPHANT.
Whiteladies. | The Primrose Path.
The Greatest Heiress in England.

By Mrs. ROBERT O'REILLY.
Phœbe's Fortunes.

By OUIDA.
Held in Bondage. | Two Little Wooden
Strathmore. | Shoes.
Chandos. | Ariadne.
Under Two Flags. | Friendship.
Idalia. | Moths.
CecilCastlemaine's | Pipistrello.
  Gage. | A Village Com-
Tricotrin. | mune.
Puck. | Bimbi.
Folle Farine. | Wanda.
A Dog of Flanders. | Frescoes.
Pascarel. | In Maremma.
Signa. | Othmar.
Princess Naprax- | Guilderoy.
  ine. | Ouida's Wisdom,
In a Winter City. | Wit, and Pathos.

MARGARET AGNES PAUL.
Gentle and Simple.

By JAMES PAYN.
Bentinck's Tutor. | £200 Reward.
Murphy's Master. | Marine Residence.
A County Family. | Mirk Abbey.
At Her Mercy. | By Proxy.
Cecil's Tryst. | Under One Roof.
Clyffards of Clyffe. | High Spirits.
Foster Brothers. | Carlyon's Year.
Found Dead. | From Exile.
Best of Husbands. | For Cash Only.
Walter's Word. | Kit.
Halves. | The Canon's Ward
Fallen Fortunes. | Talk of the Town.
Humorous Stories. | Holiday Tasks.
Lost Sir Massingberd.
A Perfect Treasure.
A Woman's Vengeance.
The Family Scapegrace.
What He Cost Her.
Gwendoline's Harvest.
Like Father, Like Son.
Married Beneath Him.
Not Wooed, but Won.
Less Black than We're Painted.
A Confidential Agent.
Some Private Views.
A Grape from a Thorn.
Glow-worm Tales.
The Mystery of Mirbridge.

By C. L. PIRKIS.
Lady Lovelace.

By EDGAR A. POE.
The Mystery of Marie Roget.

By E. C. PRICE.
Valentina. | The Foreigners.
Mrs. Lancaster's Rival.
Gerald.

TWO-SHILLING NOVELS—*continued.*

By CHARLES READE.
It is Never Too Late to Mend.
Christie Johnstone.
Put Yourself in His Place.
The Double Marriage.
Love Me Little, Love Me Long.
The Cloister and the Hearth.
The Course of True Love.
Autobiography of a Thief.
A Terrible Temptation.
The Wandering Heir.
Singleheart and Doubleface.
Good Stories of Men and other Animals.
Hard Cash. | A Simpleton.
Peg Woffington. | Readiana.
Griffith Gaunt. | A Woman-Hater.
Foul Play. | The Jilt.

By Mrs. J. H. RIDDELL.
Weird Stories. | Fairy Water.
Her Mother's Darling.
Prince of Wales's Garden Party.
The Uninhabited House.
The Mystery in Palace Gardens.

By F. W. ROBINSON.
Women are Strange.
The Hands of Justice.

By JAMES RUNCIMAN.
Skippers and Shellbacks.
Grace Balmaign's Sweetheart.
Schools and Scholars.

By W. CLARK RUSSELL.
Round the Galley Fire.
On the Fo'k'sle Head.
In the Middle Watch.
A Voyage to the Cape.
A Book for the Hammock.
The Mystery of the "Ocean Star."
The Romance of Jenny Harlowe.
An Ocean Tragedy.

GEORGE AUGUSTUS SALA.
Gaslight and Daylight.

By JOHN SAUNDERS.
Guy Waterman. | Two Dreamers.
The Lion in the Path.

By KATHARINE SAUNDERS.
Joan Merryweather. | Heart Salvage.
The High Mills. | Sebastian.
Margaret and Elizabeth.

By GEORGE R. SIMS.
Rogues and Vagabonds.
The Ring o' Bells.
Mary Jane Married.
Mary Jane's Memoirs.
Tales of To-day. | Dramas of Life.

By ARTHUR SKETCHLEY.
A Match in the Dark.

By T. W. SPEIGHT.
The Mysteries of Heron Dyke.
The Golden Hoop. | By Devious Ways.
Hoodwinked, &c.

By R. A. STERNDALE.
The Afghan Knife.

TWO-SHILLING NOVELS—*continued.*

By R. LOUIS STEVENSON.
New Arabian Nights. | Prince Otto.

BY BERTHA THOMAS.
Cressida. | Proud Maisie.
The Violin-player.

By W. MOY THOMAS.
A Fight for Life.

By WALTER THORNBURY.
Tales for the Marines.
Old Stories Re-told.

T. ADOLPHUS TROLLOPE.
Diamond Cut Diamond.

By F. ELEANOR TROLLOPE.
Like Ships upon the Sea.
Anne Furness. | Mabel's Progress.

By ANTHONY TROLLOPE.
Frau Frohmann. | Kept in the Dark.
Marion Fay. | John Caldigate.
The Way We Live Now.
The American Senator.
Mr. Scarborough's Family.
The Land-Leaguers.
The Golden Lion of Granpere.

By J. T. TROWBRIDGE.
Farnell's Folly.

By IVAN TURGENIEFF, &c.
Stories from Foreign Novelists.

By MARK TWAIN.
Tom Sawyer. | A Tramp Abroad.
The Stolen White Elephant.
A Pleasure Trip on the Continent.
Huckleberry Finn.
Life on the Mississippi.
The Prince and the Pauper.

By C. C. FRASER-TYTLER.
Mistress Judith.

By SARAH TYTLER.
The Bride's Pass. | Noblesse Oblige.
Buried Diamonds. | Disappeared.
Saint Mungo's City. | Huguenot Family.
Lady Bell. | Blackhall Ghosts.
What She Came Through.
Beauty and the Beast.
Citoyenne Jaqueline.

By J. S. WINTER.
Cavalry Life. | Regimental Legends.

By H. F. WOOD.
The Passenger from Scotland Yard.
The Englishman of the Rue Cain.

By Lady WOOD.
Sabina.

CELIA PARKER WOOLLEY.
Rachel Armstrong; or, Love & Theology

By EDMUND YATES.
The Forlorn Hope. | Land at Last.
Castaway.

www.ingramcontent.com/pod-product-compliance
Lightning Source LLC
Chambersburg PA
CBHW031743230426
43669CB00007B/457